Published by
The Junior League of Mobile, Incorporated

1981

Copies of **"ONE OF A KIND"** may be obtained from:

Mobile Junior League Publications
P.O. Box 7091
Mobile, Alabama 36607

Order Blanks included following the index.

ISBN #0-9603054-2-4
Library of Congress Catalog Card Number 80-85463
Copyright © 1981

First Printing	April 1981	10,000 Copies
Second Printing	July 1981	20,000 Copies
Third Printing	July 1987	5,000 Copies
Fourth Printing	November 1989	10,000 Copies
Fifth Printing*	November 1993	20,000 Copies

(*_Southern Living_® **Hall of Fame** edition)

Cover and Design: Barney and Patrick Advertising, Inc.

Illustrations by Kathy Whitinger

The purpose of The Junior League is exclusively educational and charitable, and is to promote voluntarism, to develop the potential of its members for voluntary participation in community affairs, and to demonstrate the effectiveness of trained volunteers.

Introduction

From a beginning as an Indian habitat in the 1500's through six flags, Mobile has truly developed into a "one of a kind" place. Founded in 1702, Mobile is the only city in America established under the direct auspices of the fabulous Louis XIV, and in its first hundred years was occupied by three major European powers. Its individuality comes naturally, for as one flag was lowered to be replaced by the next, each country left some of its distinctive character to be adopted and adapted into the new culture. As in the past, Mobile's rivers and harbor remain the foundation of the city's economy, while the heritage of the French, English and Spanish regimes is reflected in the city's architecture, culinary arts and customs.

Mardi Gras, an annual festival that Mobile celebrates, marks the days before the Lenten season. Its American origin began in Mobile in 1813, when a group of revelers climaxed their evening of feasting and festivities with a bell-ringing parade. Out of this group grew the oldest surviving Mystic Society in America. Since that time many mystic societies have formed and the days prior to Lent are as lively as they are memorable.

Along the Eastern shore of Mobile Bay, the almost annual cry of "Jubilee!" signals a strange phenomenon. For unknown reasons, flounder, shrimp and crabs passively swim into the shallow waters in an apparent attempt to escape their natural habitat. In a scene seldom encountered anywhere else in the world, visitors and natives alike rush to the water's edge. Calling to their neighbors, they carry nets, pails or gigs, — anything with which to snare a bounty of seafood. Natives of the area know the signs to watch for — in the moon, the tides and the wind — but even so, true Jubilees are notoriously unpredictable, making each a one of a kind experience.

Today Mobile still retains much of its early charm, but Alabama's oldest city is not one that merely re-creates a leisurely past. Although life does proceed at a somewhat slower pace than in most cities, historic old Mobile is a major, modern city which recognizes the importance of both yesterday and tomorrow.

Ecor Rouge, the Red Cliff, stands 130 feet above Mobile Bay, making it the highest point of land along the coastline from Maine to Mexico. Long ago the Indians made pottery there, and from twenty miles away one can see the rich clay banks glittering in the sun. The city itself is bound on one side by the fresh waters of the Mobile River and on another by Mobile Bay, while only a few miles to the south is the magnificent Gulf of Mexico. A myriad of streams, rivers and bayous, bordered by marshes and fields of timber, entwines these bodies of water, and miraculously fashions Mobile into an uncommon paradise.

This, then, is Mobile — charming and inimitable, contemporary yet timeless. Hopefully you will find some evidence of this uniqueness in "One Of A Kind."

Laurel Wilson

COMMITTEE

Chairman	Mrs. H. Wade Faulkner
Editor	Mrs. Thomas O. Gaillard, Jr.
Business Manager	Mrs. Victor H. Lott, Jr.
Editorial Assistant	Mrs. John N. Horner
Menus	Mrs. Floyd Fraser
Secretary	Mrs. David Hannan
Typing	Mrs. Sidney V. Knight
Sustainer	Mrs. John Wilson

SECTION CHAIRMEN

Mrs. N. Q. Adams	Mrs. Larry Harless
Mrs. William L. Bell	Mrs. J. B. Horst
Mrs. Ernest Brown	Mrs. Winston C. Patterson
Mrs. Barry Bruckmann	Mrs. H. Eldon Scott, III
Mrs. Owen E. Duke	Mrs. Thomas E. Twitty, Jr.
Mrs. David Freeman, III	Mrs. Miller Widemire

The Committee wishes to express their thanks to the members of The Junior League of Mobile, Incorporated, and the many friends of The League who worked toward the development of **"ONE OF A KIND."** All of these efforts are sincerely appreciated, and we realize that without these contributions, **"ONE OF A KIND"** would never have become a reality.

Foreword

Few American cities can boast of a history and heritage of over two and a half centuries, as can Mobile. Since the year 1711 when Jean Baptiste Le Moyne, Sieur de Bienville, moved the then nine year old settlement known as Mobile from its site at Twenty-seven Mile Bluff on the Mobile River to its present location on the western shores of Mobile Bay, the people of Mobile have been known nationwide for their civic pride, their hospitality, and their burning desire to improve the industrial, business, and social structure of the city. As a result of this public effort, one finds that Mobile possesses just about everything required to make the Complete City: gracious old homes, azalea gardens, sporting events, industrial and financial institutions, harbors and rivers, and last but certainly not least, oil and gas wells in the vicinity of the city; just to name a few of its ready assets.

As one views the historical as well as the current events for which Mobile is famous, it is small wonder that the culinary art has played a significant part in the reputation of Alabama's very excellent seaport.

So whether you are intent on a quick lunch or an elegant meal, the following pages will provide the answer to your problem. They present the combined knowledge, skill and experience of the young ladies of The Junior League of Mobile who know how to make a good life better. Of course, the suggestions herein are designed to leave you neither slim nor hungry.

Thomas H. Moorer
Admiral, U.S. Navy (Ret.)

"RECIPE JUBILEE" AND "ONE OF A KIND" ARE PUBLISHED BY MOBILE JUNIOR LEAGUE PUBLICATIONS. WHEN YOU WISH TO COMPLETE YOUR SET, PLEASE WRITE TO

Mobile Junior League Publications
P.O. Box 7091
Mobile, Alabama 36607

TABLE OF CONTENTS

MENUS

An asterisk (*) beside a recipe title suggests the usage of your own favorite recipe for this particular dish. All other recipes included in these menus are printed in "One Of A Kind."

DINNER FOR EIGHT
Crabmeat Belmont
Tournedos with Mushrooms
and Béarnaise Sauce
Grated Potatoes au Gratin
Baked Spinach Stuffed Tomatoes
Strawberry Macaroon Mold

BEFORE THE THEATRE
Caviar Hors D'Oeuvres
Broccoli Soup
Red Snapper Amoroso
Spinach Casserole
Tiny Baked Cherry Tomatoes
Raspberry Mousse

COCKTAIL BUFFET
Smoked Turkey
Food Processor Mayonnaise
Homemade Rolls
Cocktail Shrimp Remoulade
Soufflé au Caviar
Cream Cheese-Oyster Roll
Brandied Chicken Liver Paté
Stuardi's Spinach Dip
Tray of Assorted Candies

COCKTAIL PARTY
Summer Salmon Mold
with Horseradish Sauce
Party Venison
Homemade Rolls
Henry's Favorite (Chicken Wings)
Shrimp and Crabmeat Party Spread
Crunchy Fried Mushrooms
Piroshki
Dill Dip with Fresh Vegetables
Assorted Sweets on a Tray

GOURMET SUPPER CLUB

Paté Maison
Mixed Green Salad*
Roquefort and Oil Dressing
Veal Marsala
Parslied New Potatoes or Rice*
French Peas
Crusty French Bread
Grecian Pears

CHRISTENING PARTY

Punch
Judy Posey's Caviar Pie
Chicken Crepes Mornay
Asparagus Congealed Salad
Pavlova

AFTER MARDI GRAS BALL BREAKFAST

Yellow Bird
Tyropites
Curried Chicken Almond Canapés
Sausage and Rice Casserole
Surprise Scramble
Anytime Jam Muffins
Lemon-Cream Roll

MORNING COFFEE

Golden Punch
Chicken Salad Drums
Pumpkin Bread
Raisin-Nut Muffins
Orchard Apple Squares
Cinnamon Crisps
Cheese Beignets
Whole Fresh Strawberries*
Hot Tea*
Coffee*

GARDEN PARTY

Spiced Lemonade
Barbados Rum Punch
Radish Sandwiches
Asparagus Roll
Spinach Pie
Cheese Mold with Caviar
Sherry Cheese Paté
Fresh Fruit*
Dip for Fruit

SUPER BOWL PARTY

Joe's Bloody Mary
Italian Bread Sticks
Crabmeat Paté
Oyster Beef Appetizers
Greek Salad Sandwich
Cold Rice Salad
Cheesecake Triangle Cookies

FOURTH OF JULY

Miss Ann's Artichoke Spread
Spareribs on the Grill
Green Pepper Casserole
Corn Pudding
Cheesed Potatoes in Foil
Sauerkraut Salad
Deli Bread
Mile High Strawberry Pie

SENIOR BOWL
TAILGATE PICNIC

Missionary's Downfall
Bloody Marys
Blackbelt Cheese Straws
Minestrone Soup
in Individual Containers
Broccoli Quiche
Fried Almond Chicken Bites
Ham Rolls
Olive Crab Stuffed Eggs
Triple Chocolate Cookies
Raspberry and Almond Squares

WHARF PARTY

Fried Crab Appetizer
Marinated Shrimp
Marinated Pork Tenders on the Grill
Gazpacho Salad
Baked Corn and Tomatoes
French Bread
Grandmother Lyons' Fudge Cake
and Icing
Draft Beer*

TENNIS PARTY

Mason-Dixon Rye Dip
Spinach Balls
Flank Steak with
Marinade for Flank Steak
Marinated Shrimp,
Mushrooms and Artichokes
Twice Baked Potatoes
Sarah's Good Bread
Mint Stick Brownies

EASTER DINNER

Tomato Curry Soup
Gourmet Leg of Lamb
Armenian Rice
Eggplant Mediterranée
Crisp Buttered Zucchini
Spinach Salad
Celery Seed Dressing
Homemade Rolls
Pat Forman's Caramel Praline Soufflé

THANKSGIVING DINNER

Sugar Smoked Turkey or
Spiced Wild Duck
Cornbread and Oyster Stuffing
for the Turkey
Peachy Yams
Barbra's Broccoli
Carrot or Squash Soufflé
Cranberry Salad Mold
Pop Overs
The Best Pecan Pie
Brandied Apricot Dessert

CHRISTMAS DINNER

Daddy's Christmas Punch
Pheasant in Red Wine or
Venison Wellington
Nancy Sneed's Broccoli Vinaigrette
Tomatoes Stuffed with Mushrooms
Spinach Timbale
White Wine Apricot Mold
Charlotte Russe
Steamed Pears with Raspberry Sauce

NEW YEAR'S EVE SUPPER

Marinated Mushrooms
Seafood Pie
Zucchini Parmesan
Vegetable Salad Supreme
Herb Biscuits
Cold Lemon Soufflé

LOW CALORIE LUNCHEON

Perrier with a Wedge of Lime*
Low Calorie Gazpacho
Low Calorie Chicken
"Diet" Congealed Pear Salad
Fresh Fruit*

SWEET SIXTEEN

Sunshine Punch
Shrimp Dip
Pizza Burgers
Delores' Cole Slaw
Rocky Road Cake
Edith's Vanilla Ice Cream

LADIES DAY AT THE HUNTING CAMP

Beer*
Chipped Beef Dip
Potted Cheese
Venison Hindquarter
Dove Kabobs
Pecan Island Ducks
Wild Rice and Sausage Casserole
My Grandmother's Succotash
Fresh Green Beans*
Gram's Cucumbers with Sliced Tomatoes and Onions
Greek Spice Cake   Margaret's Chocolate Pie

SEWING CLUB

Spud's Sangria
Mushroom Pie
Cheese Soufflé
Avocado and Grapefruit Salad
Pots de Créme

LADIES CARD PARTY

Frappé Bloody Marys
Crab Imperial
Lynda's Tomatoes with Artichokes
Spoon Rolls
Divine Dessert

12

APPETIZERS
& BEVERAGES

WHARF SCENE, POINT CLEAR, ALABAMA
Wharf Parties are very much a part of the local scene as
families migrate to the eastern shore of Mobile Bay for
the summer months.

Caviar Hors D'Oeuvres

Serves 6

1	can artichoke bottoms
1	carton sour cream
1	jar black caviar
	Slivers of lemon peel

Quarter artichoke bottoms; put a dab of sour cream on each, and approximately 1/2 teaspoon caviar on top of sour cream. Top with a piece of lemon peel and enjoy. Serve on glass, lucite, or crystal. Simple but elegant.

Mrs. McGowin I. Patrick

Cheese Mold with Caviar

Yield: A 2-cup mold

1	can artichoke hearts or 1 jar marinated artichoke hearts, drained
1/2	envelope plain gelatin
1/4	cup water
1	(4 ounce) package Rondelé Spiced French Onion cheese
1	(3 ounce) package cream cheese
1/2	cup sour cream
1/2	cup mayonnaise
1	jar of caviar

Cut artichoke hearts in half and squeeze to remove excess liquid. Soften the gelatin in the 1/4 cup water. Place the two cheeses, sour cream and mayonnaise in the bowl of a food processor with the metal blade. Blend the ingredients thoroughly. Heat the softened gelatin over low heat until dissolved. Add to the mixture in food processor and mix slightly. Add artichoke hearts and process until chopped fairly small. Do not purée. Pour into an oiled 2 cup mold. Chill. Unmold and spoon caviar over the top or surround mold with ring of caviar. Serve on crackers. This recipe may be doubled, tripled, and so on to fit any size mold.

Mrs. David A. Richards

Soufflé Au Caviar

Serves 20

2	tablespoons gelatin
1/2	pint whipping cream
1	(8 ounce) package Philadelphia cream cheese
2	egg whites
4	egg yolks
4	tablespoons whipping cream
1/2	teaspoon M.S.G. (Accent)
1/2	teaspoon grated lemon peel
4	tablespoons lemon juice
1/2	teaspoon salt
6	shallots, run through a garlic press
1	(4 ounce) jar caviar

Put gelatin in a small Pyrex bowl and add just enough cold water to dissolve. Place this bowl in a saucepan of hot water until the gelatin melts. Set aside. Beat the 1/2 pint whipping cream stiff. Press the cream cheese through a sieve. Beat the egg whites stiff. Place egg yolks in a saucepan with 4 tablespoons cream. Beat over low fire until creamy. Now add the melted gelatin and slowly add the sieved cream cheese. Add the lemon peel, juice, M.S.G., salt, and shallots. When all of this is thick, add all the whipping cream and the stiffly beaten egg whites. This is all done away from the fire. Put in a one quart soufflé dish, cover, and refrigerate for at least 2 hours, preferably overnight. Just before serving, unmold on a large plate. Put caviar over the top, and have masses of chopped chives around the base. Also offer chopped onion and lemon wedges. Note: You may use inexpensive caviar, but put it in a sieve first and rinse lightly. There are a few steps to this treat, but they are well worth it. Serve with crackers as an appetizer. A second jar of caviar may be added as the first one runs low.

Mrs. Merlin Stickleber

Overseason gelatin mixtures slightly since chilling subdues flavors.

Judy Posey's Caviar Pie

Yield: Two 5" bowls

5   hard cooked eggs,
diced or finely
chopped
1   onion, finely chopped
Sour cream
Black caviar
Lemon peel, finely
grated
Melba toast

In 2 glass bowls, approximately 5" in diameter, layer eggs, onion and a 1/4-1/2" layer of sour cream, sealing the sour cream all the way to the edges of the bowls. Cover with black caviar. Sprinkle with finely grated lemon peel. Serve with Melba toast. Divine. Note: don't put eggs or caviar on silver as it will cause the silver to turn black.

Mrs. McGowin I. Patrick

Blackbelt Cheese Straws

Serves 12

1   (10 ounce) stick of
Kraft Sharp Cracker
Barrel Cheese
1/2 cup butter or
margarine
1   cup flour
1/2 teaspoon red pepper
1/4 teaspoon salt

Have ingredients at room temperature. Grate cheese. Mix with butter until thoroughly blended. Add other ingredients and mix with the hands. (If you have a food processor, you can put flour, butter, pepper and salt in bottom container. Grate cheese in and mix until blended.) Put the dough in a cookie press and make desired shapes. Cook in 325° oven 15 to 20 minutes. They should be golden brown and crisp. Sprinkle with salt. Variations: Dough may be mixed a day ahead, rolled into a "log" and refrigerated. The next day, slice, top with pecan half and bake. You may add toasted sesame seeds or form into small balls with an olive in the center and bake.

Mrs. Rose White

17

Cheese Beignets

Yield: 4 Dozen

2 cups water
2 sticks (1 cup) unsalted butter, cut in pieces
2 cups sifted flour
8 eggs
1/2 teaspoon salt
Pinch Cayenne pepper
2 teaspoons dry mustard
4 tablespoons Dijon-style mustard or more to taste
1 cup freshly grated Parmesan cheese
1 cup coarsely grated imported Swiss cheese
Vegetable oil for frying
Additional Parmesan cheese for garnish

In a heavy saucepan, bring the water and butter to a rolling boil, at which point the butter should be melted. Add the flour all at once. Lower the heat and cook, stirring constantly with a wooden spoon, for a minute or two, until the mixture comes away from the sides of the pan. Place the paste in the bowl of an electric mixer, and beat vigorously for a minute or so to cool slightly. Beat in the eggs one at a time, on medium speed, incorporating each thoroughly before adding the next. Beat in the salt, Cayenne, mustards, and cheese.

Heat the oil to 350 degrees and fry the beignets by teaspoonfuls until golden brown, about 4 to 5 minutes. Turn with a spoon to ensure even browning. Drain on paper towels and serve sprinkled with more Parmesan cheese. Yield about 4 dozen with about 1 inch puffs. These may be mixed up and chilled, then fried as you are ready to serve. The beignets may be fried ahead of time and reheated at serving time in a preheated 375 degree oven. Chopped ham may be incorporated into the paste before frying. You may wish to use chopped artichokes, or your own ideas.

Mrs. Miller Widemire

Cream Cheese Ball

Yield: 2 cups

2   (8 ounce) packages cream cheese
2   teaspoons garlic salt
1/2 teaspoon Tabasco
1   tablespoon horseradish
1   tablespoon chives
    Paprika
    Salt and pepper

Let cream cheese soften enough to mix with other ingredients. Form into ball and sprinkle with paprika. Chill until serving with crackers.

Mrs. Robert McGinley

Cream Cheese-Oyster Roll

Yield: 30-36 servings

1   (3 ounce) can smoked oysters
1   (8 ounce) package cream cheese (room temperature)
2   tablespoons mayonnaise
1/2 teaspoon garlic powder
    Salt and pepper to taste
    Milk (as needed for consistency)
1/2 cup pecans, chopped fine
    Dehydrated or frozen chopped chives
    Assorted crackers

Drain oysters; chop fine and set aside. Combine and mix cheese, mayonnaise and garlic powder. Add salt and pepper to taste. Add milk if needed for consistency. Spread cheese mixture evenly about 1/8 inch thick in an 8 x 10 inch rectangle on a sheet of aluminum foil. Put in freezer until very firm. Combine chopped oysters and nuts; mix well. Sprinkle evenly over cheese and roll up jelly roll fashion, peeling foil away as you roll up. Sprinkle chives evenly over a sheet of waxed paper and coat roll. Wrap in waxed paper. Refrigerate overnight or until firm. Serve with assorted crackers.

Mrs. Floyd Fraser

Almond-Bacon-Cheese Spread

Yield: About 2 cups

1/2 cup roasted, unblanched almonds
2 strips bacon, fried crisp
1 cup American cheese, shredded and packed
1 tablespoon green onions or chives, chopped
1/2 cup mayonnaise
1/4 teaspoon salt

Chop the almonds fine. Crumble the bacon, and blend all the ingredients together thoroughly. A wonderful spread for open-face party sandwiches. Can also be served with crackers.

Mrs. Don S. Boughton

Potted Cheese

Yield: 2½ cups

1 pound Cheddar cheese, grated
3 tablespoons onion, chopped
3 tablespoons parsley, chopped
1 teaspoon Dijon mustard
2 tablespoons soft butter
2 tablespoons Sherry
  Dash Tabasco
  Dash Worcestershire sauce
  Salt to taste

Allow cheese to be at room temperature. Mix all together. (Using your fingers is faster.) Serve on warm crackers. Note: This is easily prepared in a food processor.

Mrs. John Megginson

Green Chilies and Cheese

Serves 8

2   (2½ ounce) cans chopped green chilies
3   eggs
3   tablespoons milk
10 ounces sharp cheese, grated
    Club crackers

Place chilies in a 9" round pie dish. Cover with grated cheese. Mix eggs and milk and pour over cheese. Bake at 350° for 45 minutes. Serve with club crackers along with drinks.

Mrs. H. Taylor Morrissette

Sherry Cheese Paté

Serves 12

2   (3 ounce) packages cream cheese
1   cup (4 ounces) sharp Cheddar cheese, shredded
4   tablespoons dry Sherry
1/2 teaspoon curry powder
1/4 teaspoon salt
1   (8 ounce) jar of chutney or Chut-nut
2   green onions with tops, finely chopped

Mix cheeses, wine and seasonings thoroughly. Spread about one inch thick on a serving plate. Chill. Spread chutney on top of chilled cheese. Sprinkle with the onions. Serve with wheat wafers or sesame crackers.

Mrs. William L. Bell

Festive Appetizer Quiche

1 (9 inch) pie shell, partially baked
6 ounces (1½ cups) Swiss cheese, shredded
1 (4½ ounces) can shrimp, well drained, chopped. (You may use 1 cup fresh shrimp.)
3 eggs
1½ cups light cream or Half and Half
1 tablespoon chives, chopped
3/4 teaspoon salt
1/2 teaspoon dry mustard
Dash of nutmeg
1/4 cup Parmesan cheese

Yield: 12 slices

Sprinkle Swiss cheese, then shrimp, over bottom of pastry shell. Beat together the eggs, cream, chives, salt, dry mustard and nutmeg. Pour into pastry shell. Sprinkle with the Parmesan cheese. Bake at 375 degrees for 30-35 minutes. Let stand about 20 minutes before serving. Cut into thin slices. May be served either warm or chilled.

Mrs. Ramsey Stuart

Tyropites

Yield: 40 pastries

8 ounces cream cheese, at room temperature
1/2 cup Feta cheese, crumbled
2/3 cup Gruyère cheese, grated
3 tablespoons parsley, minced
1 egg
2 sticks butter, melted and cooled
10 sheets of Phyllo dough

Cream the softened cream cheese and add the crumbled Feta. Cream these 2 cheeses until the mixture is light. Blend in the Gruyère, parsley and BEAT in the egg.

Brush 1 sheet of the Phyllo with butter and cut it into 3" strips. Put a heaping teaspoon of the filling in 1 corner of each cut strip and fold the Phyllo over the filling, enclosing cheese mixture and forming a triangle. Continue to fold the filled pastries, keeping the triangle shape and put them on a large buttered baking sheet. Make pastries with remaining Phyllo and filling in the same manner. Brush all the triangles with melted butter and bake in a pre-heated oven (375°) for 20 minutes or until they are puffed and golden. NOTE: Let frozen Phyllo thaw overnight in refrigerator. When using dough, place damp towel beneath and on top of Phyllo. Take off one sheet at a time; re-cover remainder while you work. These freeze well, after baking.

Mrs. Larry Harless

Chipped Beef Dip

Yield: 2 cups

1	(8 ounce) package cream cheese
2	tablespoons milk
1/2	cup sour cream
1	package or small jar dried chipped beef, snipped fine
2	tablespoons green pepper, chopped
2	tablespoons onion, chopped
1	to 2 tablespoons horseradish (optional)
1/4	cup nuts, chopped

Blend together cream cheese, milk and sour cream until smooth. Stir in all remaining ingredients except chopped nuts. Pour into shallow baking dish. Top with chopped nuts. Bake at 350° for 15 minutes, or until mixture starts to bubble slightly and brown around edges. Serve with crisp crackers.

Mrs. Edward J. Neville

Dill Dip

Yield: 1½ cups

2/3	cup sour cream
2/3	cup Hellman's mayonnaise
1	tablespoon parsley, chopped
1	tablespoon green onion, chopped
1	teaspoon dill weed
1	teaspoon beau monde
1	teaspoon Worcestershire sauce
2	teaspoons lemon juice

Mix together well and refrigerate. Great with fresh vegetables.

Mrs. James Fibbe

Curry Dip

Yield: 1½ cups

1	cup mayonnaise
1	tablespoon curry powder
3	tablespoons catsup
2	tablespoons onion, grated
1	tablespoon Worcestershire sauce
1/2	teaspoon bottled pepper sauce
	Salt

Make 3 days ahead. Combine all ingredients well. Serve in a purple cabbage hollowed out with carrot sticks, celery sticks, zucchini, cucumber, broccoli, etc., for dipping.

Mrs. Harrison Southworth

Mason-Dixon Rye Dip

Yield: 1½ cups

2/3	cup sour cream
2/3	cup mayonnaise
1	teaspoon dill seed
1	teaspoon beau monde
1	tablespoon dry minced onion
1	tablespoon parsley flakes
1	large round loaf rye bread, unsliced

Combine all ingredients for dip 24 hours before serving and refrigerate. At serving time, cut top off of rye bread and scoop out the inside, forming a crust "bowl." Break scooped out bread into bite-size pieces. Pour dip into crust bowl and use broken bread for dipping. If unsliced bread is unavailable, may be served with party rye bread slices.

Mrs. C. Vearn Partridge, Jr.

Mary Winslow's Baked Clam Dip

Yield: 2½ cups

2 (8 ounce) packages
cream cheese
2 tablespoons
dehydrated onions
2 cans minced clams,
save juice of one can,
drain the other

Blend all ingredients in a blender. Pour into a 9 inch pie plate and bake at 325° for 50-60 minutes. Serve warm, leave in the pie plate and surround the plate with large size Fritos for dipping.

Mrs. Winston C. Patterson

Crab and Shrimp Dip

Yield: 5-6 cups

1/2 pound fresh lump or
regular crabmeat
2 pounds shrimp,
boiled, peeled and
chopped
1 package (8 ounce)
cream cheese
1 carton sour cream
Add: garlic salt,
onion salt,
horseradish and
lemon juice, to taste
1 tablespoon vinegar

Mix all together and chill. Serve with crackers.

Mrs. Paul Brock

Shrimp Dip

Serves 6

1   pound fresh shrimp,
     boiled and peeled
     OR
1   large can shrimp
2   (3 ounce) packages
     cream cheese
1   cup mayonnaise
1/4 small onion, finely
     minced
2   dashes
     Worcestershire sauce
     Chili sauce to color
     Dash Tabasco
     (optional)
     Crackers or chips

Crumble drained shrimp into a bowl. Mix cream cheese and mayonnaise until creamy. Add onion and Worcestershire and chili sauce. Mix well, chill, and serve. Serve on crackers, perhaps Melba Rounds, since this is probably too thick for a chip. But, if this mixture seems light enough, go ahead and use chips.

Mrs. Charles H. Dodson, Jr.

Stuardi's Spinach Dip

Yield: About 4 cups

2   packages frozen
     spinach, defrosted
     and drained (DO NOT
     COOK)
2   cups mayonnaise
1   small onion, grated
     Juice of 1 small
     lemon
1   tablespoon
     Worcestershire
     Few drops Tabasco
1   tablespoon garlic salt

Blend all ingredients in blender or food processor. Refrigerate until ready to serve. Serve with any assortment of fresh vegetables. Let your imagination run wild. Men love this!

Mrs. Edward Fields

Low-Calorie Vegetable Dip

Yield: Approximately 1 cup

1/2   cup cottage cheese
1/4   cup Kraft low-calorie
     Italian dressing
2   tablespoons low
     calorie mayonnaise
1   teaspoon parsley
1   teaspoon dehydrated
     onion flakes

Place all ingredients in a blender, blend well and chill. Serve with raw vegetables. Less than 16 calories per tablespoon.

Mrs. Russell Terry

Dip for Fresh Fruit

Sour cream
Brown sugar
Poppy seeds

This is a marvelous dip for fresh fruit of all kinds. Use proportions to your taste. I recommend 1 or 2 parts sugar to 3 parts sour cream (depending on tartness of fruit) and a large dash of poppy seed. Delicious for strawberries!

Mrs. Richard O'Neill

Mini-Eggs Benedict

Yield: 2 Dozen

24   bread rounds, toasted
     on both sides
24   thin slices of ham to
     fit the toast rounds
24   center slices of hard
     cooked eggs (about 6
     eggs)
     Hollandaise sauce
     Chopped parsley

Assemble as follows: On a cookie sheet, place toast rounds and top with ham. Place a slice of egg on each and then carefully spoon on some Hollandaise sauce. Sprinkle with parsley and broil until hot and bubbly. Watch carefully so the sauce doesn't burn. Broiling should only take a minute or two. Serve at once.

Mrs. Miller Widemire

Olive Crab Stuffed Eggs

Serves 8

8   hard boiled eggs
1/3 cup green olives,
     chopped
1/3 cup sweet pickle
     relish
1/4 teaspoon mustard
1/2 cup celery, finely
     chopped
1/2 pound fresh
     crabmeat (or less)
1/4 cup mayonnaise

Slice eggs lengthwise and remove yolks. Mix all together except egg whites. Stuff egg whites and chill. For a first course, serve on a bed of lettuce and garnish.

Mrs. Smith Downing

Fried Almond Chicken Bites

Yield: 2 dozen

1   egg white, lightly
     beaten
3   tablespoons dry
     Sherry
1/4 teaspoon sugar
1   tablespoon soy sauce
2   tablespoons
     cornstarch, divided
3/4 pound chicken
     breasts, boned and
     skinned
3/4 cup almonds,
     blanched and finely
     chopped

In a bowl combine lightly beaten egg white, Sherry, sugar, soy sauce and 1 tablespoon cornstarch. Cut chicken into 1½ inch pieces. Let marinate in Sherry mixture for 30 minutes. In a dish combine the almonds and other tablespoon of cornstarch. Coat the chicken with almond mixture and fry in deep fat at 375° for 3 minutes or until browned. Drain on paper towels and sprinkle with salt. Serve warm or at room temperature.

Mrs. Stewart Thames, Jr.

29

Curried Chicken Almond Canapes

1 cup cooked chicken, minced
1 cup mayonnaise
3/4 cup Monterey Jack cheese, shredded (3 ounces)
1/3 cup almonds, ground
1/4 cup parsley leaves, minced
2 green onions, minced
2 teaspoons fresh lemon juice
1½ teaspoons curry powder
Dash of hot pepper sauce
Salt and freshly ground black pepper
1 box plain Melba rounds
OR
60-72 1½" rounds of thinly sliced bread
60-72 almond slices

Yield: 5-6 dozen
Combine all ingredients except bread and almond slices in large bowl and blend well. Cover and refrigerate. Just before you are ready to serve, preheat oven to 500° F. Mound chicken mixture on each round. Top each with an almond slice. Place on baking sheet and bake until lightly colored and sizzling, about 5-8 minutes. Serve hot.

Mrs. Victor H. Lott, Jr.

Chicken Salad Drums

Yield: 2 dozen

1/4 pound cooked chicken breast, minced
1 rib celery, minced
1 tablespoon red onion, finely minced
1/4 teaspoon curry powder
Salt and freshly ground pepper to taste
2-4 tablespoons homemade mayonnaise
12 thin slices good whole wheat bread
3/4 cup sliced almonds, toasted and finely chopped
Additional mayonnaise

Combine chicken, celery, onion, curry, salt, pepper and mayonnaise. Blend well and correct seasonings. Cut bread into small rounds and make sandwiches. Spread the sides of each sandwich all around with additional mayonnaise and roll in the nuts. Chill and serve.

Mrs. Miller Widemire

Henry's Favorite

Serves 8-10

2 dozen chicken wings
2 sticks butter, melted
1 clove garlic, minced
2 cups Progresso Italian bread crumbs
3/4 cup Romano or Parmesan cheese, grated
1/4 cup parsley, chopped
2 teaspoons salt
1 teaspoon Accent
1/2 teaspoon black pepper

Mix butter and garlic. Dip each chicken wing into garlic butter, then into crumb mixture. Place in shallow pan (15 inch jelly roll pan). Pour any remaining butter over all. Bake at 350° until tender (30-40 minutes). Baste frequently with pan drippings. (Note: this can be made with bigger pieces of chicken as an entrée. Two fryers should serve 4 to 6).

Mrs. Wade Faulkner

Brandied Chicken Liver Paté

Yield: 2½ cups

3 small onions, chopped
2 tablespoons butter
1 pound chicken livers
2/3 cup dry Sherry
3 tablespoons Brandy or more to taste
Salt and pepper to taste

Sauté onions in butter until golden (use a wooden spoon). Add the chicken livers and Sherry. Cover and simmer for 30 minutes. Discard pan juices. Purée mixture in a blender. Add the Brandy, salt and pepper. (Do not add Brandy, salt and pepper until after cooking). Refrigerate and serve with crackers or Melba toast.

Serves 8 as a first course appetizer or 30 or more as a canapé. When serving as appetizer, line salad plate with lettuce. Use ice cream scoop for 1 serving. Add crackers and quartered hard boiled eggs as garnish.

Mrs. Larry Harless

Paté Maison

Yield: 2 cups

1	pound chicken livers
2	sticks (1 cup) butter
1	cup mushrooms, chopped
1/4	cup green onions or shallots, chopped
1	clove garlic, finely chopped
1	bouquet garni
1½	teaspoons salt
	Black pepper, freshly ground
	Dash cayenne pepper
1/4	teaspoon allspice
1/8	teaspoon thyme

Wash, dry and chop the livers. Melt the butter in a heavy skillet and sauté the mushrooms for 5 to 8 minutes. Remove from the skillet. Sauté the onions and garlic for 5-8 minutes. Add the livers and the bouquet garni and cook over medium heat for about 10 minutes. The liver should be just pink inside. Remove the bouquet garni and place the livers, onions, garlic, mushrooms and seasonings in a food processor or blender and process until the mixture is smooth. Place in a crock or mold and refrigerate. Serve at room temperature and garnish with parsley.

Mrs. Barry Bruckmann

Crabmeat Paté

Serves 10-12

1	pound lump crabmeat
2	tablespoons chili sauce
1/2	cup celery, chopped
1	cup green onions, chopped
1	teaspoons parsley, chopped
1/2	teaspoon hot sauce
1/2	cup mayonnaise

Mix all together and form into a mound or ball. Serve with crackers. Garnish as desired.

Mrs. Charles H. Ritchey

Piroshki

1   box pie crust mix or your favorite pie crust dough
1   onion, minced
     Several scallions, finely chopped
     Butter
1   small package ground beef
1   cup cooked rice
2   tablespoons sour cream
     Thyme to taste
     Marjoram to taste
     Salt
     Pepper
     Oil for frying

Prepare pie crust dough and refrigerate ahead of time. Sauté the onion and scallions in small amount of butter. When limp, add the ground beef and brown. Add the cooked rice, spices and sour cream and mix thoroughly. Set aside. Roll out the pie dough to about 1/8 inch thickness. Take a water glass or jar lid and cut out circles of dough. Fill with a spoonful of meat mixture, fold in half and pinch to close. Then fry, turning to cook both sides in about 1/2 inch hot oil. Note: These can also be deep fat fried or baked, but are better pan fried.

Mrs. Henry R. Seawell, III

Ham Rolls

Yield: 2 dozen

1   (3 ounce) package cream cheese, softened
6   stuffed olives, chopped
2   tablespoons whipping cream
1   teaspoon prepared horseradish
1/4   teaspoon salt
1/4   teaspoon paprika
     Dash white pepper
6   slices boiled ham

Combine all ingredients except ham; mix well, spread cream cheese mixture on one side of each ham slice; roll up and secure with a wooden pick. Cover rolls and chill. Slice rolls into 1 inch pieces; serve with toothpicks.

Mrs. Harrison Southworth

Oyster Beef Appetizers

Serves 6-8

1/4 cup oyster sauce
(found in most
Oriental markets)
2 tablespoons salad oil
2 tablespoons soy sauce
1 clove garlic, mashed
2 green onions,
chopped
1/4 teaspoon sugar
1 pound beef sirloin,
cut into bite-size
strips or cubes
1/2 pound fresh
mushrooms, cleaned
1 can (6½ ounces)
whole water
chestnuts, drained
3 green onions, cut into
1-inch pieces

Combine the oyster sauce, salad oil, soy sauce, garlic, chopped onion and sugar in a bowl. Marinate the beef and mushrooms in this mixture for 1 to 2 hours in the refrigerator. Then string meat, mushrooms, water chestnuts and pieces of green onion on small skewers. Broil or grill about 5 inches from source of heat for 5 minutes, turning once.

Mrs. Edwin Weigel

Crabmeat Appetizer

Serves 6-8

8 ounces cream cheese
1 tablespoon milk
1/2 pound crabmeat
2 teaspoons onion,
grated
1/2 teaspoon horseradish
1/4 teaspoon salt
Dash white pepper
Slivered almonds
Crackers

Mix all ingredients together except almonds. Sprinkle almonds on top before baking at 375° for 20-25 minutes. Serve with your favorite crackers.

Mrs. Gus Thames

Fried Crab Appetizer

**Whole baby crabs —
silver dollar size
Beaten eggs
Cracker crumbs or
pancake mix or
cornmeal**

Wash crabs, lifting shell and cleaning under it. (Just like for soft shells.) It's easier if crabs are refrigerated or iced first. Drain on paper towels. Dip in egg and then in crumbs or meal. Fry in hot deep fat fryer until brown and crisp. Drain; salt and pepper to taste. Serve with hot cocktail sauce for dipping. When sorting your catch after pulling the shrimp net, watch carefully for these tiny crabs. Save them and fry up a real treat. (You eat the whole thing!)

Mrs. Thomas O. Gaillard, Jr.

Crabmeat Belmont

Serves 4-6

1	**pod garlic**
2	**tablespoons butter**
2	**tablespoons flour**
1	**cup whipping cream**
1/2	**teaspoon salt**
	Dash red pepper
1/8	**teaspoon pepper**
	Paprika
1	**cup catsup**
1½	**tablespoons Worcestershire Sauce**
1	**pound lump crabmeat Buttered cracker crumbs**

Rub individual baking dishes with garlic. Melt butter, add flour. Gradually add cream and cook, stirring constantly. Add salt, pepper, paprika, catsup and Worcestershire. Stir in crabmeat. Pour into individual baking dishes and top with crumbs. Bake at 400° for 15 minutes or until bubbly. Serve as a first course or appetizer.

Mrs. Burgess Thomasson

Crabmeat Ursuline

1 pound white lump crabmeat
1/2 bell pepper, chopped fine
1 cup celery, chopped fine
1 cup onion, chopped fine
1 medium can mushrooms, chopped small
1/2 cup fresh parsley, chopped
1 tablespoon Worcestershire sauce
4 dashes Tabasco
1 teaspoon Nature's Seasoning
1/2 teaspoon seafood seasoning
1/2 teaspoon garlic powder
1 tablespoon celery seed
1/4 cup white wine
1 can cream of mushroom soup
1 can cream of celery soup
1 stick butter
Salt to taste

Serves 25 or 6-8 as an entrée

Sauté bell pepper, onion, celery and parsley in butter until onion is clear. Add all other ingredients except wine and cook over low heat about 10 minutes. Just before serving, add wine. May be served from a chafing dish in tiny patty shells as an appetizer, or in large patty shells as a main dish. Serves 25 as an appetizer; 6 to 8 as an entrée.

Mrs. John N. Horner

Aunt Sue's Shrimp Bavarian

Serves 10-12

2-3 pounds shrimp, cleaned and peeled
2 sticks butter (1 cup)
  Parsley
  Lemon juice
1 cup mayonnaise
1/2 cup sour cream
3 tablespoons catsup
1 teaspoon Worcestershire sauce
  Horseradish to taste
3/4 jigger Cognac or Brandy

Cook shrimp in butter, parsley and lemon juice for 3-7 minutes, depending on size of shrimp. Mix together the remaining ingredients. Remove shrimp with slotted spoon and put into individual ramekins. Spoon sauce over shrimp and serve immediately. A delightful first course.

Mrs. James A. Yance

Shrimp and Crabmeat Party Spread

Yield: 4 cups

1 (8 ounce) package cream cheese, softened
1 tablespoon lemon juice
1½ tablespoons mayonnaise
1½ pounds shrimp, boiled, peeled and chopped coarsely
1 can (6½ ounces) white crab meat or 1/2 pound fresh crabmeat
1/2 cup green onion tops salt and pepper to taste
  Worcestershire sauce
  Tabasco sauce

Cream together cream cheese, lemon juice and mayonnaise. Add the shrimp and crabmeat. Season with salt, pepper, Tabasco and Worcestershire sauce. Refrigerate for 8 hours before serving to allow seasonings to flavor the seafood.

Mrs. Robert A. Cloninger

Marinated Shrimp

1   cup white wine vinegar
1   teaspoon prepared horseradish
2   tablespoons prepared mustard
2   tablespoons tomato purée
    Chili powder to taste (about 1/2 teaspoon)
    Salt to taste
1   cup salad oil
    Dash of orégano
1   pound shrimp, cooked and peeled
2   tomatoes, sliced very thin
1   large Spanish or Bermuda onion, sliced in very thin rings

Combine all ingredients except the shrimp, tomato slices and onion rings, and stir until thoroughly blended. Taste for seasonings, adding more chili powder and salt if desired. Pour mixture over shrimp; cover and refrigerate about 5 hours. Soak onion rings in cold water so they will be crisp at serving time. When shrimp are well marinated and chilled, arrange on tomato slices and top with onion rings; pour the dressing over all. Serve as a first course.

Mrs. William L. Bell

Deviled Oysters

Serves 4

1   pint oysters
1/4   cup Dijon mustard
1   egg, beaten
1   tablespoon oil
    Bread crumbs, fresh
    Melted butter
    Lemon wedges
    Salt and freshly
     ground pepper

Heat oysters in their own liquid until the edges curl; drain. Add mustard to the drained oysters and heat for 2 minutes. Dip the oysters into egg and oil, beaten together, then roll in bread crumbs. Place in a greased layer cake pan, dribble with melted butter and broil for 2 to 3 minutes on each side. Sprinkle with a little salt and pepper. Serve as a first course with lemon wedges.

Mrs. Wade Faulkner

Marinated Shrimp

Serves 25

5   pounds cooked,
    cleaned shrimp
    Juice of 1 lemon
1   pint Wesson Oil
8   average onions, sliced
3/4   cup vinegar
1   bottle capers with
    juice
1½   tablespoons celery
    seed
1   tablespoon
    Worcestershire sauce
8-10 drops Tabasco sauce
    Lots of salt

Mix all ingredients together. Let stand overnight.

Mrs. C. R. Butler, Jr.

Cocktail Shrimp Remoulade

Serves 4-6

1 pound shrimp (cooked and peeled)
4 shakes Tabasco sauce or 4 shakes cayenne pepper
1/2 cup parsley, chopped well
1 clove garlic, minced, or 1/4 teaspoon garlic powder
1/2 cup onion, chopped
4 teaspoons prepared mustard
1/3 cup tarragon vinegar
4 teaspoons lemon juice
2 teaspoons fresh ground horseradish
1/2 cup olive oil or corn oil
1 teaspoon salt
2 teaspoons paprika
1/2 cup celery, diced

Combine all ingredients and marinate shrimp in the refrigerator overnight. Serve with toothpicks.

Mrs. J. Mac Bell

Marinated Shrimp, Mushrooms, and Artichokes

Serves 50-75

15 pounds of shrimp
   Crab boil
10 pounds of fresh
   mushrooms
6 cans of artichoke
   hearts
4 onions, sliced
6 cups of oil
3 cups white vinegar
12 tablespoons capers
9 teaspoons celery seed
6 teaspoons salt
6 to 8 drops Tabasco,
   more or less
30 bay leaves

Cook shrimp in crab boil and water. Peel and devein shrimp. Clean mushrooms. Drain artichokes; if large, slice in half. Slice onions. Mix oil, vinegar, capers, celery seed, salt and Tabasco. In a very large bowl or pan, alternate shrimp, artichokes, onions, bay leaves and mushrooms. Pour marinade over and refrigerate 24 hours before serving. Stir to be sure everything mixes well. Use toothpicks to serve. Recipe may be cut in half or to one-third. Variations: add cherry tomatoes, green pepper strips and cauliflower.

Mrs. Owen E. Duke

Miss Ann's Artichoke Spread

Yield: About 3½ cups

1 (14 ounce) can
   artichoke hearts,
   drained and chopped
6 slices bacon, fried
   crisp and crumbled
1 small onion, very
   finely chopped
1 cup mayonnaise
1 tablespoon
   Worcestershire sauce
   Few drops Tabasco
1 tablespoon lemon
   juice
   Crackers

Mix all ingredients together. This may be made in a food processor. Refrigerate until ready to serve. Serve with crackers. (I use Escort.) There are few things this good and easy, too.

Mrs. Edward Fields

Artichoke Squares

Yield: 60 squares

1 (6 ounce) jar marinated artichoke hearts
1 (14 ounce) can plain artichoke hearts
1 small onion, finely chopped
1 clove garlic, minced
4 eggs
1/4 cup fine bread crumbs
2 teaspoons parsley, minced
1/4 teaspoon salt
1/8 teaspoon orégano
1/4 teaspoon Tabasco
1/2 pound sharp Cheddar cheese, shredded

Drain marinade from jar of artichokes into skillet. Drain juice from can of plain artichokes and discard juice. Chop all artichokes into small pieces and set aside. Add onion and garlic to skillet and sauté until clear. Beat eggs. Add crumbs and seasonings. Stir in cheese, parsley, artichokes and onion mixture. Turn into a greased 10" x 6" baking pan. Bake at 325° for 30 minutes. Allow to cool in pan. Cut into 1-inch squares. Serve hot or cold. This freezes well.

Mrs. Owen E. Duke

Spinach Balls

Yield: 60-70 balls

2 (10 ounce) packages frozen spinach, cooked, drained very well
2 cups packaged stuffing mix
1 cup Parmesan cheese, grated
6 eggs, beaten
3/4 cup butter, softened
Salt
Pepper

Combine all ingredients, mixing well. Roll into balls the size of walnuts. Freeze. Before serving, place on cookie sheet still frozen. Bake at 350° for 10 minutes.

Mrs. Raymond J. Artabasy

43

Asparagus Rolls (Food Processor)

Yield: 50-60 rolls

2 (4-ounce) packages ham or 8 ounces baked ham
3/4 cup pecans
1 stick butter (1/2 cup)
1 (8-ounce) package cream cheese
Dash garlic salt
1 to 2 tablespoons mayonnaise
1 tablespoon parsley, chopped
1 loaf sandwich bread, crusts removed
1 can asparagus spears, drained and dried

Chop ham and pecans in processor; remove. Blend butter, cream cheese, garlic salt, mayonnaise and parsley in processor. Combine all ingredients. Press bread slices with rolling pin, spread with ham mixture. Place 1 asparagus spear on each piece of bread and roll up. Place in rectangular dish, seam side down, and chill until ready to serve. To serve: Slice each roll into 3 or 4 pieces, place on a tray and serve. Variations: Leave rolls whole. Sauté in butter. Serve with a fork. Or — cut rolls into pieces and bake at 350 degrees until golden brown.

Mrs. Wade Faulkner

Crunchy Fried Mushrooms

Serves 4-6

2 eggs
1 cup milk
1 cup flour
1 teaspoon pepper
2 teaspoons salt
1 cup seasoned breadcrumbs
1/4 cup Parmesan cheese
1/2 to 1 teaspoon dill
1 pound fresh mushrooms (not large ones), cleaned

Combine eggs and milk in one bowl. Mix flour, pepper, salt, breadcrumbs, cheese and dill in another bowl. Cut stems off of mushrooms. Place the mushrooms in the egg and milk for a minute, coating well. Then coat a few mushrooms at a time in the crumb mixture. Let sit for several minutes to let coating set before frying. Fry in deep fat until golden brown. Drain. Serve as an appetizer with Ranch Dressing, Tartar sauce, or catsup and horseradish as a dip. The mushrooms may also be served as a vegetable to accompany red meat.

Mrs. Winston C. Patterson

Red Bean Balls

Yield: 2 dozen

2   cups cooked red beans, well mashed by hand
2   tablespoons onion, chopped
1/2 teaspoon orégano
1   can (small) green chilies, finely chopped
4   tablespoons Parmesan cheese, grated
   Salt to taste
1/3 pound Monterey Jack cheese, cut in cubes (small)
1   whole egg, beaten lightly with 1 tablespoon water
   Bread crumbs
   Oil for frying

Combine the first 6 ingredients, mix well and form into balls, placing a cheese cube in the center of each. Be sure cheese is well covered by bean mixture. Roll in crumbs, beaten egg, again in crumbs and fry in deep oil until brown. Serve hot with picks, or with chili sauce to dip in. Makes about 24 balls. Especially good if made with left over red beans which already have seasoning in them.

Mrs. Charles H. Ritchey

Rich Mushroom Roll

Serves 6

Oil
1½ pounds mushrooms, chopped (save 6 pretty mushrooms)
6 eggs, separated
1/4 pound butter, melted
2 tablespoons butter
Salt and pepper
3 tablespoons lemon juice, separated
Fresh parsley, chopped
Hollandaise sauce

Oil a 10½ X 15 inch jelly roll pan, line it with wax paper and oil the paper. Clean the mushrooms and chop all but 6 in a food processor. Squeeze in a cloth to remove the moisture. Beat the egg yolks until fluffy, stir in the chopped mushrooms, 1/4 pound butter, 1/2 teaspoon salt, 1/4 teaspoon pepper and 2 tablespoons of the lemon juice. Beat the egg whites until soft peaks form. Fold the whites into mushroom mixture and pour into pan. Smooth the top with a spatula. Bake in a 350 degree oven for 15 minutes. Let cool slightly. Turn out onto a sheet of wax paper (carefully) and peel off old wax paper. Roll up from the long side using paper to turn it over. Put on a platter with the last turn. Sauté 6 mushrooms in 2 tablespoons butter and 1 tablespoon lemon juice for 2 minutes over high heat. Remove and place along the top of roll evenly. Sprinkle chopped parsley over top. Serve by cutting between mushrooms and pass Hollandaise sauce.

Mrs. Thomas Gaillard, Jr.

Radish Sandwiches

Yield: 2 Dozen

8 radishes, trimmed
6 ounces cream cheese
2 tablespoons unsalted
   butter
1 tablespoon parsley,
   no stems
1 teaspoon snipped
   chives, fresh or freeze
   dried
   Fresh lemon juice
   Salt and freshly
   ground black pepper
6 to 9 slices
   pumpernickel bread
Garnish:
4 to 6 radishes,
   trimmed
   Coarse salt

For filling, grate the radishes in a food processor or on a hand grater. Place in a colander and squeeze out all excess liquid. Cream the cream cheese and butter until well blended and fluffy in the food processor; add grated radishes, parsley, chives, lemon juice, salt and pepper to taste. Flavor this filling assertively. Cut bread into small rounds, spread with filling, and garnish with thinly sliced radishes. Put a pinch of coarse salt on top of each. Chill and serve.

Mrs. Miller Widemire

Yellow Bird

Serves 4

6 ounces Rum
8 ounces orange juice
2 ounces Galliano
   liqueur
4 ounces Sprite or 7-Up
   Crème de Banana
   liqueur

Combine Rum, orange juice, Galliano and Sprite and blend with ice in a shaker. Serve over ice. Float a VERY LITTLE splash of Crème de Banana on top of each glass. Garnish with cherry and orange slice. Excellent for pre-brunch, and an early morning eye opener for those of us who can't drink tomato juice. Also, liquor can be decreased and proportions changed to be less potent. A very sweet drink.

Mrs. Howard Schramm, Jr.

Spinach Pie

Yield: 15-20 squares

8   eggs, beaten
1   (16 ounce) jar Feta cheese, drained and crumbled
2   cups cottage cheese
1   small onion, finely chopped
2   (10 ounce) packages frozen spinach, thawed and pressed
14   sheets of Phyllo pastry
    Melted butter

Combine eggs, Feta cheese and cottage cheese; add the onion and spinach. Stir well. Layer 7 sheets of pastry, brushing each layer with melted butter, in a greased 13x9x2 inch pan. Spread with the spinach mixture. Add remaining pastry sheets, brushing each with butter. Bake at 350 degrees for 1 hour. Cut into squares. May be served hot or cold. Phyllo tips: Frozen Phyllo should not be thawed at room temperature (outside sheets are sticky and the center is still frozen). Thaw in refrigerator for 8 to 24 hours. Lay thawed sheets on a dampened tea towel (towel moistened in warm water and wrung out), cover with another dampened towel. Remove one at a time keeping the stack covered. Unused sheets thawed in the refrigerator may be refrozen for later use.

Mrs. Stewart Thames, Jr.

Sunshine Punch

Yield: 41 6-ounce servings

1   (12 ounce) can frozen orange juice, undiluted
3   (6 ounce) cans lemonade (follow can directions)
1   can apricot nectar
1   (46 ounce) can pineapple juice
1/2   gallon orange sherbet
2   quarts ginger ale

Mix first four ingredients together and chill. Place ice cubes in bottom of punchbowl along with sherbet, which has been mashed. Add chilled juice mixture and pour ginger ale over all. Stir well.

Mrs. H. Eldon Scott, III

Spud's Sangria

Serves 4-6

2 lemons
1 orange
1/3 cup sugar
1 (750 milliliter) bottle dry red wine
3 ounces soda
1 tray of ice

Into a tall pitcher put strained juices of lemons and orange. Add the rest of the ingredients. Stir well and let sit for 5-10 minutes before serving. Garnish glasses with orange or lemon peel or slices.

Mrs. Howard Schramm, Jr.

Sangria

Serves 4

1 cup Burgundy
2 cups orange juice
1 cup water
1/2 cup sugar
2 tablespoons lemon juice

Mix all ingredients together. Serve well chilled.

Mrs. Robert Zarzour

Bloody Marys

Yield: 36 (6-ounce) drinks

4 (46 ounce) cans of V-8 juice
1 quart Vodka
1 teaspoon celery salt
6 ounces Worcestershire
Tabasco
Pepper
Juice of 2 lemons
Celery stalks

Mix all ingredients together and add Tabasco and pepper to taste. Best made ahead and kept chilled. This recipe makes drinks of moderate strength, for which most guests will thank you at a morning party. Serve with ice and garnish with small celery stalk.

Jimmy Hirs

Cranberry Punch

Serves 10

2 quarts ginger ale, one frozen into ice cubes
1 pint cranberry juice
1 quart Tom Collins mix
1 quart pineapple juice
1 small can frozen lemonade concentrate, thawed

Freeze one quart ginger ale in ice cube trays. Mix together the juices and Tom Collins mix and chill. Just before serving, combine the chilled mixture with the remaining ginger ale and the ginger ale ice cubes. (Increase the proportions "times 4" to serve 40-45.)

Mrs. J. B. Horst

To keep punch cool without diluting it, freeze berries, grapes, or melon balls on a baking sheet and when frozen, add to punch.

Spicy Cranberry Punch

Serves 20 (5 ounce servings)

3/4 cup brown sugar, firmly packed
1 cup water
1/4 teaspoon salt
1/4 teaspoon nutmeg
1/2 teaspoon allspice
1/2 teaspoon cinnamon
3/4 teaspoon ground cloves
1½ quart bottle cranberry juice
46 ounce can unsweetened pineapple juice
Butter (optional)

Combine the brown sugar, water, salt, spices, and cranberry juice in a 5 quart pan. Bring mixture to a boil. Add pineapple juice to the hot mixture and heat again to boiling. Pour into a warmed 4 quart punch bowl. Dot with butter if desired.

Mrs. Frederick S. Crown, Jr.

Cranberry Wassail

Serves 8 (5 ounce servings)

2½ cups boiling water
6 tea bags
1/4 teaspoon cinnamon
1/4 teaspoon nutmeg
1/4 teaspoon allspice
3/4 cup sugar
1/2 cup orange juice
1/3 cup lemon juice
1½ cups water
1 pint cranberry cocktail

Pour boiling water over tea and spices and let steep for 5 minutes. *Strain* and add sugar. Stir to dissolve. Add juices, additional water and cranberry cocktail. Good served hot or cold. Makes 40 ounces.

Mrs. Harris Sommer

Spiced Lemonade

Yield: 1 generous quart

3/4 cup sugar
4¾ cups water, divided
12 whole cloves
7 cinnamon sticks, divided
Juice of 6 lemons
Lemon slices

Combine sugar and 3/4 cup water. Boil about 5 minutes. Add cloves and 1 cinnamon stick. Cook for 5 minutes over medium heat. Strain. Add lemon juice and remaining 4 cups of water. Chill. Serve over ice. Garnish each glass with a lemon slice and a cinnamon stick.

Mrs. Thomas Torbert

Admiral's Choice Punch

Serves: 8-10

1/2 gallon French vanilla ice cream
2 trays strong coffee ice cubes (crushed)
1/2 bottle Rum

Put ice cream, coffee ice cubes and Rum in punch bowl before dinner. Stir after dinner and serve in coffee cups, punch cups or mugs. Serves as after dinner coffee, dessert and drink.

Mrs. Walter Cleverdon

Spiced Tea

Yield: 18 cups

8	cups boiling water
5	tablespoons tea leaves
2	cups sugar
1	teaspoon whole cloves
8	cups water
	Juice of 1 lemon
	Juice of 6 oranges
	Fresh mint leaves

Add boiling water to tea leaves; let stand for 5 minutes and strain. Make a syrup by boiling sugar, cloves, and water together. Add this and fruit juice to tea. Fresh mint leaves may be added to tea leaves and boiling water.

Mrs. William Goodloe

Daddy's Christmas Punch

Yield: 30 servings

1	gallon apple cider
1	pint cranberry juice
1/2	dozen lemons, sliced
4	oranges, sliced
	Allspice
1/2	quart dark Rum
1	quart light Rum

Bring the first five ingredients to a boil. Add Rum and serve warm.

Mrs. Ramsey McKinney

Milk Punch For A Bunch

Serves 18-20

6	tablespoons sugar
4	cups half and half cream
10	cups milk
2	teaspoons vanilla
2	cups Bourbon
	Nutmeg

Dissolve sugar in half and half. Combine with other ingredients and chill thoroughly. Serve from a punch bowl, if desired, and sprinkle nutmeg over each serving. Makes 1 gallon. Note: This averages about 1 ounce Bourbon per serving. Adjust "spirits" as desired.

Mrs. John Wilson

Paw-Paw's Egg Nog

1	egg for each cup of egg nog
1½	tablespoons sugar for each egg
	Whiskey, desired strength; 1/2 - 1 ounce per egg suggested
	Whipped cream, according to thickness desired (about 1 pint to 2 dozen eggs)
	Nutmeg

Separate eggs; whip whites very, very stiff. Beat yolks until thick and light in color. Add sugar slowly and mix thoroughly. Add whiskey slowly, beating well after each addition. Fold in whipped cream. Fold in egg whites with very large spoon. Garnish with nutmeg, if desired.

Mrs. Joe Gunter

To chill many bottles of wine or champagne, fill washing machine with cracked ice.

Mint Julep

Yield: 1 drink

1	small stem of mint, plus several more leaves
1/2-1	teaspoon superfine sugar
	Crushed ice
1½-2	ounces good Bourbon

Put several fresh mint leaves in bottom of cup (preferably silver) and mash with a spoon. Fill cup half full with crushed ice. Sprinkle sugar to cover top of ice. Add more crushed ice to fill cup. Garnish with stem of mint sticking out of cup. Place cup in freezer. To serve, pour Bourbon over ice.

Farra M. Alford

Barbados Rum Drink

Yield: 1 drink

1   jigger dark Rum
1/2 jigger Myers Rum
1/2 jigger lime juice
2   dashes Peychaud's
      bitters
1   tablespoon
      Grenadine
      Nutmeg

Combine well and pour over ice. Sprinkle with nutmeg. Delicious, but quite potent!

Marion S. Adams, Jr.

Rum Slush

Yield: 25 servings

1   large can
      unsweetened
      pineapple juice
1   (6 ounce) can frozen
      lemonade
      concentrate (regular
      or pink)
2   cups Rum
      Ginger Ale
      Cherry
      Mint

Mix ingredients. Pour into plastic container and freeze. When ready to serve, take out portions desired (for individual serving or pitcher full) and add ginger ale, stirring to a slushy consistency. Add a cherry and perhaps a sprig of mint. Yummy and so cooling.

Mrs. James L. Tate

Missionary's Downfall

Serves 4

In a blender put:
1   small can frozen
      limeade
1   limeade can of Vodka
1   handful of fresh mint
      leaves

Fill blender with ice. Turn on, "blend" until mint leaves are chopped fine. Serve in glasses garnished with sprig of fresh mint.

Mrs. Charles L. Rutherford, Jr.

The Wright Punch

Yield: 12 quarts

1	(12 ounce) can frozen orange juice	
1	(12 ounce) can frozen pink lemonade	
1	(46 ounce) can pineapple juice	
2	teaspoons almond extract	
3½	cups sugar	
5	cups water	
2	(3 ounce) boxes strawberry Jello	
1	gallon water	
2	(2 liter) bottles ginger ale	

Mix the first six ingredients in a kettle. Bring to a boil. Remove from the heat and add the Jello. Stir until dissolved. Then add the gallon of water. Mix well and pour into 4 half gallon containers. Freeze until ready to serve. Thaw for 2 to 3 hours at room temperature. To each half gallon container of punch in the punch bowl add 1 quart of ginger ale. Since the punch does not thaw completely, no ice is needed. Each half gallon container of punch and quart of ginger ale will serve 15 to 18. The total recipe will serve 60-70.

Mrs. John Wilson

Punch

Serves 8-10

1	large can pineapple juice plus 2 cups more
1/2	cup sugar
1/2	jar Maraschino cherries, optional
1	large can frozen orange juice
2	juice cans water
1/3	cup lemon juice
1	bottle ginger ale or Champagne, chilled

Combine ingredients except for ginger ale or Champagne and chill. Serve over ice, adding the chilled ginger ale or Champagne at the last minute.

Mrs. Harris Sommer

Frappé Bloody Marys

Serves 20

2 large cans V-8 juice
5 lemons, juiced
1 quart Vodka
Worcestershire sauce, to taste
Tabasco, to taste

Place all ingredients in plastic gallon jug, not glass, shaking well together. A dash or 2 of the last 2 ingredients is good, but a matter of preference. Important: Place in freezer for any number of days, but at least until frozen. Three hours ahead of time, for serving, remove from freezer. Shake jug briskly every now and then, which will make the ice crystals appear. Looks attractive served from a tomato shaped bowl or any punch bowl. When served in punch cups, it will serve about 20 with 2 cups each. Shake while de-freezing and serve while many ice crystals are still there, so it contains its own ice.

Mrs. Neal A. Collins

Joe's Bloody Mary

Yield: 1 serving

Vodka
Worcestershire sauce
Tony's Creole
Seasoning
Fresh lime
Mott's Beefamato

Put one jigger of Vodka in a glass. Add one good squirt of Worcestershire sauce, a couple of shakes of Tony's, and a squeeze of lime juice. Fill the glass with ice. Now pour in Beefamato to the top, stir. Float two shakes of Tony's on top. Take the lime and run around rim of glass, then add to glass. Divine.

Mrs. Joe B. Stuart

A GUIDE TO WINE

Wine is generally believed to be one of the oldest beverages known to man. It is guessed that as early as the Stone Age, some 5,000 years ago, ancient man cultivated grapes for food and quickly discovered that the juice of fermented grapes was pleasant to drink. We read of the widespread use of wine in Greek and Roman times, in numerous Biblical passages, and in classical literature of all ages.

The Viking explorers ages ago referred to America as Vinland. Yet it is only in the last few years that wine drinking has become not only fashionable but popular with people from all walks of life.

At last Americans have come of age! The development in recent years of better production and marketing techniques of quality wines made right here in our own country is largely responsible for this awakening of Americans to the joys of wine. Educating the public about this often complex beverage is an awesome yet rewarding task. It is our purpose here to share enough information so that both novices and experienced wine drinkers will use wine to enhance the many wonderful foods in **ONE OF A KIND.**

WHAT IS WINE?

Very simply defined, wine is the fermented juice of grapes. While many fruits and even some vegetables can produce a fermented drink, only grapes make wine! Wine as we know it wasn't invented by a genius, but is simply a natural process. As grapes ripen on the vine, there is natural yeast that forms on the skin. This yeast, aided by the process of picking and pressing to break the skin, attacks the natural sugar in the grape juice and changes it to alcohol. This process is known as fermentation.

It must be remembered, therefore, that wine is a living, changing thing. In general, fine wines improve with age if stored properly. The exception to this is pasteurized wine which includes many of the mass-produced jug wines.

FOUR BASIC TYPES OF WINE

Over the years, man has continually improved the wine-making technique. At the same time, he has complicated matters by making additions to the fermented juice. The result of these additions is a classification of wine into four basic types. While a brief explanation of each is in order, we will devote ourselves to discussing the properties of table wines, as this is the wine most commonly enjoyed with meals.

The four basic wine groups are:
1. Fortified Wine — Wine to which brandy has been added in order to stop fermentation and at the same time increase alcohol content. Port, Sherry, and Madeira are popular fortified wines and range from 14% to 21% in alcohol.
2. Sparkling Wine — Wine with carbon dioxide bubbles. This is the champagne family of wines and averages about 12% alcohol.
3. Aromatic Wine — Wine to which herbs, roots, flowers or spices have been added. Vermouth and other aperitifs are included in this group of wines which average up to 21% alcohol.
4. Table Wine — Has no additions to the basic fermented grape juice and ranges from 9-14% alcohol. This is the type of wine that usually accompanies a meal, thus the name "table wine." This wine is also referred to as "still" as opposed to wine with bubbles.

Table wine, no matter how many subtleties it may possess, is above all good and easy to drink. In fact, wine used in moderation aids digestion and enhances the taste of most foods whereas other alcoholic beverages often dull the taste buds and overpower the food. It is the table wines to which we now devote our attention.

TYPES OF TABLE WINES: GENERIC VS. VARIETAL

In choosing a table wine, one must first be aware of the difference between a generic and a varietal wine. A **generic wine** is a non-European wine which is patterned after European types and takes the name of an European geographic region. Generic labeling thus causes confusion for the novice wine buyer. The most common generic wines that should not be confused with the European wines by the same name are Chablis, Burgundy, Sauterne, Rhine, Chianti, and Claret.

These generics and their European namesakes are similar **in name only.** Their characteristics, tastes and qualities are quite different. We are happy to note that many American wineries are getting away from the practice of generic labeling.

A **varietal wine** is one which is named after the variety of grape from which it is produced. In all wine-producing countries there are strict laws regulating the percentage of a grape variety that must be included before a varietal name can be used. Though many varietals contain 100% juice of one grape variety, the percentage may vary within limits. Examples of varietal wines are: Chardonnay, Cabernet Sauvignon, Zinfandel, Pinot Noir, and Johannisberg (white) Riesling.

While the best California wines are varietals, awareness of the reputation and style of the winery is equally important in selecting a table wine. The quality of each wine is the result of several very important factors. The variety of grape, the soil on which it is grown, the climate (ever-changing and unpredictable, as we all know) and the winemaker are the determining factors in every bottle of wine. Change any one of these elements in the slightest and your finished product will vary. Thus, a Pinot Noir grape grown in Burgundy, France, and one grown in Napa Valley, California, will be different, though similar, due to soil and climate differences. The varying style of the vintners will also produce differences in the two wines.

To list the labeling practices of the many wine-producing regions of the world would only confuse the majority of readers. We will summarize and say that some areas use generic names, some use varietal names, and some use their own proprietary name on their wines. While few generalities can be made about wine production, it is widely believed that the smaller the area in which grapes are grown, the higher the quality the wine will be.

THE TASTE OF WINE

Wines vary in sweetness from syrupy nectar-type wines to bone dry ones. Wine also contains varying amounts of acidity, fruit and alcohol which affect the overall taste. Since these components are so variable, a reputable wine merchant is your best resource in choosing from wines you haven't experienced. The food you are serving as well as your own palate will determine which wine will be enjoyable in a given instance.

WHICH WINE TO SERVE

The basic rule of thumb, in serving wine with food is to serve red wine with red meat, white wine with white meat, and rosé with either, though rosé is better substituted for white wine. Also, the richer the food, the richer the wine. Therefore, bear in mind that sauces and stuffings should be the determining factor in selecting a wine, not just the meat itself.

Multiple course meals should be accompanied by more than one type of wine if possible. What is best with a light cream soup will not usually be best with a roast lamb entrée. In serving more than one wine during a meal, the following hints are useful — serve white wine before red, young before old, dry before sweet, and modest before great.

The above guidelines are merely that and need not be adhered to so strictly that you find yourself drinking a wine you don't care for just because someone else says you should. The most important rule in serving wine is to relax, serve a wine that is pleasing to you, at the temperature you wish and with the food you like.

The following is a list of a few specific recommendations for serving wine with food. These pairings have been proven over and over again to be mutually complimentary. There are many, many wines that could be served with each food, so don't feel compelled to choose only those listed.

Aperitif — A medium dry to dry white wine such as California Johannisberg Riesling, Gewurtztraminer, Chenin Blanc, California generic whites, or German wines.

Fish and Shellfish — When served without a sauce or with a butter-based sauce, use a light dry white wine such as French Muscadet, Chablis, Alsatian, Graves, Italian Verdicchio or Frascati or a California Sauvignon Blanc. When served with a rich cream sauce or highly flavored sauce, fish and shellfish are best accompanied by a more full-bodied dry white wine such as California Chardonnay, French White Burgundy, or Italian Soave.

Chicken and Turkey —These are extremely versatile meats. Depending on the preparation, either white, red or rosé can be very complimentary. Simply roasted meat is best served with a good light red wine such as Beaujolais, or a well-aged Bordeaux, a Cabernet Sauvignon, or any good dry white wine. If a cream sauce is used, a fuller-bodied white wine is best.

Pork and Veal —When meat is unsauced, serve a full-bodied white wine such as Chardonnay or Soave, or a good rosé, or a light red such as Beaujolais. If the meat is served richer with cream sauce, serve a full-bodied white. If the sauce is sweet, a medium dry white wine such as Chenin Blanc or a Spätlese or lesser quality German wine is appropriate.

Beef and Lamb —These meats are definitely enhanced by red wines rather than white. Although any red wine to your liking would be satisfactory, a guideline is to use well-aged and full-bodied wines with the tender, more expensive cuts of meat. Among these would be the French Bordeaux and Burgundies, Cabernet Sauvignon, and the fuller-bodied Beaujolais. Lighter bodied red wines are complimentary to the less expensive cuts of beef and lamb. Beaujolais, Côtes-du-Rhône or Bardolino wines would also be good.

Game —Strong game with sauce requires full-bodied red wine such as for the expensive cuts of lamb and beef. Château-neuf-du-Pape or California Petite Sirah would be good also. Light-flavored game deserves a soft, well-aged red wine—the best you can find and afford. A Zinfandel or Cabernet Sauvignon would be pleasant.

Cheese —Any wine that pleases you is fine, but red wines and Port are usually wonderful with cheese. Use a fine wine only with milder cheeses such as Brie or Camembert. Very strong-flavored cheeses tend to overpower the smoother, well-aged wines. Cream cheeses are best with a sweeter white or rosé wine.

Dessert —Sweeter white wines such as the German Spätlese or Auslese, French Sauternes or Vouvray and the late harvest Johannisberg Riesling from California are delicious dessert wines. A sweet champagne, Asti Spumante, sweet Sherry or Madeira are also good accompaniments to most desserts.

When Not to Serve Wine
Wine does not go well with the following foods:

Mint Sauce	Citrus Fruits
Cocktail Sauce	Curry
Chocolate	Oil and Vinegar dressing

SERVING WINE

If your budget is limited, it is better to serve an adequate amount of inexpensive wine than to serve a skimpy amount of costly wine. Besides, the best wine is not necessarily the most expensive. For best results, serve red wine at room temperature (65-70 degrees). Some light red wines such as Beaujolais may be served slightly chilled. Most red wines improve in flavor if allowed to "breathe" in a decanter or glass for at least 30 to 60 minutes prior to drinking. The younger the red wine is, the more breathing time it needs. White and rosé wines are best served after about two hours of chilling. They should not be icy cold as this interferes with the flavor of the wine.

COOKING WITH WINE

For cooking wine, we generally use whatever dry white or red is open in the refrigerator. Cooking wines need not be expensive—there are many good jug wines that are quite pleasant for both cooking and sipping. Never cook with anything you wouldn't drink, and avoid using "cooking wines" from the supermarket unless a recipe specifically calls for it. Such "cooking wine" has added salt and seasonings that often are incompatible with the rest of your ingredients. If no other wine is available, cook with some of the wine you plan to serve with your meal. This will certainly be complimentary, though possibly more expensive. Wine used correctly in cooking can add a whole new dimension to tired-out dishes.

STORING WINE

You don't have to have an elaborate, temperature controlled cellar to keep wine on hand at home. For short-term storage (less than 3 years), even an apartment dweller can find a place to store a wine collection. An extra closet is often a good resting place for wines.

There are three important things to remember for proper wine storage. First, be sure to keep the cork moist by laying the bottle on its side. This prevents the cork from drying out, and contracting and allowing air to enter the bottle. The second thing to remember is to try to keep the temperature constant, if not the ideal 55 degrees. This generally eliminates the kitchen as a good storage place for wine. Fluctuations in temperature cause improper development and eventual deterioration of the wine. Lastly, be sure to store your wine in a dark, quiet place, away from vibrations and possible jarring.

Leftover wine which has been opened can be re-corked and stored in the refrigerator for several days. Pasteurized wines will last a little longer.

While most wines, especially reds, improve with age, some wines do not and should be drunk young. Even reds reach a peak in the aging process and then begin to decline. A knowledgeable wine merchant can tell you how long to keep specific wines in your "cellar."

A VOTRE SANTÉ

After spending time planning and preparing a meal, choosing an appropriate accompanying wine, and perhaps inviting guests to share them, you are more than ready to relax and enjoy yourself. Sharing wine with others is one of the most delightful ways to socialize and enjoy oneself. Wine can turn any meal into a festive, elegant occasion. So raise a glass and keep in mind that "wine puts life into a man if he drinks it in moderation. What is life to a man deprived of wine? Was it not created to warm men's hearts? Wine brings gaiety and high spirits . . ." (Ecclesiasticus 31:27-28)

A Votre Santé!

Mr. and Mrs. Howard M. Schramm, Jr.

SOUPS & GUMBO

CONSTANTINE'S RESTAURANT
A Mobile tradition for lunch, dinner and supper after the ball, Constantine's is the place to go for Creole Gumbo.

Cold Cucumber Soup

Yield: 1 quart

4 cups cucumber, peeled, sliced, seeded
1 large onion, sliced thin
5 chicken bouillon cubes (do not substitute)
2-3 sprigs parsley or 1 teaspoon, chopped
2 tablespoons margarine
1 teaspoon salt
1/2 teaspoon pepper
1 (8 ounce) carton sour cream or plain yogurt

Cook all ingredients except sour cream until tender. (Can be put into a pressure cooker for 5 minutes instead). Blend in blender and strain. Chill and add sour cream or yogurt. Sour cream makes a thicker soup than yogurt.

Mrs. Jeff Pettiss, Jr.

Cream of Gazpacho

Serves 10-12

1 can (46 ounce) tomato juice
1 cup cucumber, finely chopped
1 cup green pepper, finely chopped
2 teaspoons Worcestershire sauce
2 teaspoons celery salt
1 teaspoon onion salt
1/2 teaspoon garlic salt
1/8 teaspoon freshly ground pepper
2 cups half and half cream

Combine juice, vegetables and seasonings. Chill at least 4 hours. Stir the mixture into the cream. Serve immediately. Garnish with scored cucumber slices. This is a good, easy, summertime dish.

Mrs. Danner Frazer, Jr.

Low-Calorie Gazpacho (No Oil)

Serves 4-8

6 medium tomatoes (only good summer ones)
1 stalk celery
2 small cucumbers (seed if you prefer)
2 small green peppers, seeded
1/2 small onion or 2 green onions (very small)
3 cloves garlic, minced
1 tablespoon wine vinegar
1 (12 ounce) can tomato juice
1 dash Worcestershire
Salt and pepper to taste

Put vegetables through food processor in individual groups (process onion and celery together because of small amount) or dice by hand. Combine all in a large bowl. Place tomato juice, garlic, vinegar, Worcestershire and salt and pepper in bowl of processor or blender. Run for a few minutes until thoroughly blended and pour over chopped vegetables. Serve very cold in soup bowls with an ice cube and a thin slice of lime in each one. This entire amount is 308 calories.

8 servings — 35 calories
6 servings — 52 calories
4 servings — 77 calories

Mrs. David A. Richards

Cold Squash Soup

Serves 8

2 pounds yellow squash
1 onion
3 cups chicken broth
1 cup sour cream
Salt
1/4 teaspoon white pepper
Dill weed or fresh dill

Slice squash and chop onion. Cook in 2 cups broth until soft. Purée in blender and place in bowl. Stir in 1 cup more chicken broth, 1 cup sour cream, salt and pepper. Let cool and chill for at least 4 hours. Garnish with dill.

Mrs. Frank Frazer

Reed Green's Black Bean Soup

Serves 6

1	pound black beans
2/3	cup olive oil
3	cloves garlic, minced
1	large green pepper, chopped
1	large onion, chopped
	Ham or ham hock
	Salt to taste
	Cooked rice
	Green onions, chopped

Wash and pick over beans. Place in large kettle, cover with fresh, cold water. Cook beans for 3 hours or until tender, adding water as needed. Heat olive oil in skillet. Add minced garlic, green pepper and onion. Sauté until vegetables are tender. Add drained vegetables to beans along with ham. Cook until beans are soft and juice is thickened. Add salt to taste. Serve over cooked rice, topped with chopped green onions.

Mrs. Byron Green

To tame over-salted soup, add a few slices of raw potato.

Broccoli Soup

Serves 4

1	bunch fresh broccoli, washed, peeled and cut up
1	stalk celery, chopped
1	onion, chopped
3	cups chicken broth
	Mustard, a pinch
	Salt and pepper to taste
1	cup cream

Combine all of the above ingredients in a saucepan. Cook until vegetables are tender. Then purée in batches in food processor or blender. Return to saucepan and add a pinch of mustard, salt and pepper to taste, and the cup of cream. Reheat and serve.

Mrs. Greer Megginson

Creamy Cauliflower Soup

Serves 6

1 medium cauliflower
2 chicken bouillon
    cubes
2 tablespoons butter
2/3 cup onion, chopped
2 tablespoons flour
2 cups half and half
    cream
1/2 teaspoon
    Worcestershire sauce
3/4 teaspoon salt
1 cup Cheddar cheese,
    grated
    Parsley, chopped

Chop the cauliflower into small pieces and cook in 3 cups boiling water about 15 minutes. Remove from heat and add bouillon cubes. Set aside. In a 3 quart saucepan melt butter and add onion. Cook until soft. Blend in flour; add cauliflower and broth gradually, stirring constantly until mixture comes to a boil. Stir in half and half, Worcestershire sauce and salt. Heat to boiling and stir in cheese until melted. Garnish with parsley and serve.

Mrs. Harry G. Sparks, III

Leek Soup

Yield: 1 quart

1/2 stick butter (4
    tablespoons)
3 medium onions
1 package leeks or 2
    packages green
    onions
4 medium potatoes
6-8 Wyler's chicken
    bouillon cubes
2½ quarts water
    Black pepper to taste

Melt the butter in a large saucepan. Add onions and leeks, chopped. Sauté until wilted and add the potatoes, peeled and chopped. Add bouillon cubes, water and pepper and cook until reduced by about 1/3 and the potatoes are tender. Blend in a food blender. The soup may be served hot as is. You may also add cream and 2 tablespoons Sherry, chill and serve as Vichyssoise.

Mrs. William B. Inge

Mushroom Bisque

Yield: 6

4	tablespoons butter
1	cup onion, chopped
1	pound fresh mushrooms, chopped
4	tablespoons flour
3	cups chicken stock
1	cup milk
1	cup whipping cream
1/2	teaspoon salt
1/8	teaspoon pepper
	Cayenne pepper, pinch
3	tablespoons Sherry
1/4	cup parsley, chopped

Melt butter and sauté onions about five minutes. Add mushrooms and sauté two more minutes. Sprinkle flour over vegetables and stir a minute or two. Add chicken broth and parsley and stir until well combined. Simmer over low heat for twenty minutes. Stir in milk, cream, salt, pepper, and Sherry. Do not boil.

Mrs. Victor H. Lott, Jr.

Janet's Mushroom Soup

Serves 6

3	tablespoons butter
1/2	pound fresh mushrooms, sliced
1	bunch (5-6) whole green onions, chopped
	Garlic salt, optional
2	tablespoons flour
2	cans clear chicken broth (13¾ ounces each)
1	cup whole milk
	Salt and pepper
1	cup (1/2 pint) whipping cream

Melt butter in heavy, deep pan. Sauté mushrooms and onions. Stir until mushroom juice covers bottom of pan. (Optional—then add several shakes of garlic salt.) Sprinkle in flour and stir well. Stir in chicken broth and bring to a boil. Stir in milk, turn to low heat, and add salt and pepper to taste. Simmer ten (10) minutes, stirring often. Set off heat. When ready to serve, heat and stir in whipping cream.

This is a real treat to take to a friend who is "under the weather." Just take off heat and cool slightly before adding cream. Pour into a 32 ounce jar with top (reserve 2 cups for home use) and put in friend's refrigerator. Will heat well.

Mrs. Virginia B. Baumhauer

Minestrone

Serves 10-12

1/4	pound lean salt pork, diced
2	quarts hot water
1½	cups tomato juice
2	(15 ounce) cans kidney beans
1	can bean with bacon soup, undiluted
6	beef bouillon cubes
1	cup carrots, diced
1	cup cabbage, shredded
1	cup green onions, chopped
1	package frozen chopped spinach
1	teaspoon basil
1/2	teaspoon salt
1/2	teaspoon pepper
3/4	cup uncooked regular rice
	Grated Parmesan cheese (optional)

Sauté salt pork in a deep large saucepan until crisp and brown. Add remaining ingredients except rice and cheese, bring to a boil. Cover and simmer over low heat one hour, stirring occasionally. Add rice and simmer an additional 30 minutes. Ladle into soup bowls, and sprinkle with cheese. May be frozen.

Mrs. Carl E. Jones, Jr.

For a small bouquet garni, tie in a piece of cheesecloth two parsley springs, 1/3 of a bay leaf and 1/8 teaspoon thyme.

Spinach Soup

Serves 8-10

Chicken pieces
3-4 cups chicken broth
2 large onions, chopped
4 stalks celery, chopped
1/4 cup spinach, fresh or frozen
1 cup parsley, chopped
1-2 chicken bouillon cubes (optional)
1 cup creamed potatoes, instant or regular
1 quart skim milk
3/4 teaspoon salt (optional)

Boil bony pieces of chicken that have been skinned. Pick off meat from bones to make 1 cup or more. Put broth in refrigerator. Cool and skim off fat. Put broth in a 2 quart boiler. Add onion, celery, spinach and parsley. Cook 8 to 10 minutes. Purée vegetables and chicken in blender and return to the pot. Chicken bouillon cubes may be added to make the soup richer. Add creamed potatoes and skim milk. Add salt if necessary. Serve hot or cold. (Additional potatoes and milk may be added if desired.)

Mrs. J. Mac Bell

Tomato Curry Soup

Serves 6

3 cups tomato juice
2 tablespoons tomato paste
4 scallions, minced
Salt to taste
Pinch of powdered thyme
1/2 teaspoon curry powder
Freshly ground pepper
2 tablespoons lemon juice
1 cup yogurt or sour cream
Chopped parsley for garnish

Mix all ingredients except yogurt and parsley. Refrigerate. Before serving, blend in yogurt. Sprinkle each portion with parsley.

Mrs. Norman E. Waldrop, Jr.

Chicken Curry Soup

Serves 6-8

3	cups onion, chopped
4	cloves of garlic, minced
3	tablespoons butter
3	tablespoons Italian olive oil
1½	to 2 teaspoons curry powder from freshly opened jar
2	cans (10¾ ounce size) cream of potato soup
2	cups chicken broth
2	cups sour cream
	Parsley

Sauté onions, garlic, butter, olive oil and curry powder in 3 quart saucepan until soft. Put all in blender. Whirl until completely blended. Gradually add the following to blender mixture and continue blending until smooth: potato soup, chicken broth and sour cream. Return all to pan and heat slowly until mixture thickens on sides of pan and flavors are blended. Stir often. Garnish with sprigs of parsley. Serve in soup mugs or bowls. This is a very rich soup. Grand served as a first course.

Mrs. Hugh M. Doherty

Quick Brunswick Stew

Serves 6

1	small fryer
3	cups water
2	small or 1 large onion
2-3	ribs celery with leaves
1/2	teaspoon orégano
1/2	cup parsley, chopped
	Salt and pepper to taste
1	package frozen baby limas
1	package frozen corn
1	medium can stewed tomatoes
1	package frozen okra (optional)

Simmer chicken until tender in water with onion, celery, orégano, parsley, salt and pepper. Remove from broth and cool. Bring broth to full boil and add limas and corn. When vegetables are tender add stewed tomatoes and okra (optional). Cook on medium heat for 15 minutes. Broth should be the consistency of thick gumbo. If you wish, thicken at this point with a little flour. Last, add deboned chicken, cut in large pieces. Serve with white rice in gumbo dishes, with cornmeal muffins and a green salad. Note: this is such a nice dish to take to a sick friend.

Mrs. Ray Miller, Jr.

70

Smoked Turkey Soup

Serves 8-10

Carcass and skin from smoked turkey
1 large onion, chopped
5 ribs celery, chopped
1 pound split peas, washed but not soaked
1 large carrot, grated
Pepper to taste

Cover bones and skin with water in a large kettle. Add onion and celery. Bring to a boil, add peas, then lower heat and simmer for 2 hours, stirring occasionally. Remove bones and skin. Skim any fat from the surface of soup. Return any meat from bones (cut up finely). Add carrots and simmer 45 minutes, stirring to smooth the soup. Season to taste.

Mrs. John Wilson

Yankee Doodle Clam Chowder

Serves 4

2 slices bacon, chopped
1/2 medium onion, chopped
2 tablespoons butter, divided
1 (6½ ounce) can minced clams
1 (10¾ ounce) can cream of potato soup
1 soup can milk
Salt and pepper to taste

Sauté chopped bacon and onion in 1 tablespoon butter until onion is golden. Add clams and juice and simmer for 3 minutes. Add soup, then add milk slowly, stirring. Add salt and pepper. Heat thoroughly but do not boil. Right before serving add other tablespoon of butter and stir well.

Mrs. John Wilson

Crab Soup

Serves 6

1	bunch green onions, chopped fine
1	stick butter
1	can condensed tomato soup
2	cans cream of mushroom soup
1/3	cup Sherry
	Half and Half
1	pound of fresh crabmeat
	Tabasco to taste

Sauté onions in butter. Blend soups, add to onions. Add Sherry. Fold in crab. Add cream to consistency desired, and season to taste with Tabasco. Heat and serve.

Mrs. O. M. Otts, III

Shrimp Celery Bisque

Serves 4

1	cup water
1	cup celery, chopped
1	cup potatoes, diced
1/4	cup onion, chopped
1/2	teaspoon salt
	Dash white pepper
2	cups milk
2	tablespoons all-purpose flour
1½	to 2 cups peeled and deveined shrimp, coarsely chopped
2	tablespoons butter
	Snipped parsley

In a large saucepan, combine water, celery, potatoes, onion, salt and pepper. Bring to a boil, reduce the heat and simmer, covered, for 15 minutes or until potatoes are tender, stirring occasionally. Combine the milk and flour until smooth; stir into the potato mixture along with the shrimp and butter. Cook and stir until thickened and bubbly. Garnish with snipped parsley. Do not leave out parsley.

Mrs. William J. May

Crab Chowder

2½ cups onion, chopped
1 cup green onions, chopped
1½ cups celery, chopped
1/3 cup oil
4 cups chicken broth
2 pounds canned tomatoes with juice
1 teaspoon basil
1/4 teaspoon thyme
1 package frozen green peas or 1 pound fresh peas, shelled, optional
Salt and pepper
1 pound lump crabmeat, picked over
1/3 cup dry Sherry or Chablis

Cook vegetables in oil slowly for 15 minutes, covered. Add broth, tomatoes and seasoning and simmer for 1¼ hours. Add peas, salt and pepper to taste and simmer 15 minutes, until peas are just tender. Add crabmeat and Sherry or Chablis and simmer 5 minutes. Serve from a heated tureen. This is *not* a gumbo. but a nice change when you don't have a lot of time to spend in the kitchen.

Mrs. Wade Faulkner

Commercial stocks are saltier than homemade varieties and may need to be diluted with wine, beer or tomato juice.

Gumbo

1   whole chicken breast
1   chicken bouillon
     cube
1   (8 ounce) can tomato
     sauce
1   (1 pound) can stewed
     tomatoes
2   tablespoons
     Pickapeppa sauce
2   bay leaves
1   clove garlic, crushed
     Salt and cayenne
     pepper to taste
1   pound claw crabmeat
1½   pounds cleaned
     shrimp
1   package frozen cut
     okra

Roux:
2/3 cup oil
2/3 cup flour
1   cup white onion,
     chopped
1   cup green onions,
     chopped
1   cup celery, chopped
1/4 cup bell pepper,
     chopped
1/4 cup fresh parsley (or
     2 tablespoons, dried)

Boil chicken breast in water seasoned with celery leaves. Save broth and add to it the bouillon cube and enough water to make 3 cups. Dice chicken and set aside. Put broth, diced chicken and all ingredients except seafood and okra in large pot. Bring to boil, then lower heat and simmer for 30 minutes. While this is simmering, make a roux.

Brown oil and flour slowly in iron skillet for about 30 or 45 minutes, or until roux is caramel colored. Add chopped vegetables and okra and stir until wilted. Remove from heat and transfer to 4 cup Pyrex container. Add hot water, stirring, to bring roux to 4 cup mark. Add hot roux and vegetables to simmering soup. Simmer, covered, about 1 hour. (At this point, gumbo can be frozen for later use). Add crabmeat and shrimp and continue simmering for 20 minutes. Turn off fire, and let sit on stove, lid on, until ready to serve, at least an hour. Serve over rice and garnish, if desired, with fresh parsley or chopped green onions. At any point, gumbo may be thinned or increased by adding hot water or chicken broth.

Mrs. John Wilson

74

Seafood Gumbo

Serves 8

1   cup flour
1   cup bacon grease or margarine
1   cup onions, chopped
1   cup celery, chopped
1/2   green pepper, cut up fine
3   cups hot water
1   large can tomatoes, mashed
2   tablespoons catsup
3   bay leaves
3   tablespoons parsley, chopped
4   tablespoons Worcestershire
8-10   drops Tabasco
    Salt and pepper to taste
2   cups okra, sliced or 1 box frozen okra
3   pounds shrimp, cleaned and raw
1   pound dark crabmeat (claw)
1   pint oysters
2   teaspoons gumbo filé

First, make a dark roux by browning flour in bacon grease. Add the chopped vegetables and cook slowly for a few minutes. Then add water, tomatoes, catsup and seasonings. Cook *very slowly* for about an hour. Add okra and cook until it is soft. Now add the seafood and cook until the shrimp is done. At the very last, add the gumbo filé, a New Orleans seasoning. This is optional, but adds a lot to the taste if you have it. One or more teaspoons of Kitchen Bouquet seasoning can be added now to give it color. Don't cook after these are added. You have to play with the making of gumbo. I have also put in bouillon cubes to give it more flavoring. Serve with a spoonful of cooked rice in a large soup bowl.

Mrs. Vernon M. Dukes
From "A Good Cook's Book"

Duck Gumbo

Serves 8

3	ducks
1/2	pound smoked sausage
1/2	pound bacon
5	tablespoons bacon grease
5	tablespoons flour
1	cup green onions, chopped
1	cup celery, chopped
1/2	cup green pepper, chopped
2	cloves garlic, thinly sliced
2	cups duck stock
1	quart chicken stock
2	tablespoons chili powder
1	tablespoon Worcestershire
	Salt and pepper
1/4	cup fresh parsley, minced
	Cooked rice

Boil ducks in enough water to cover until tender (about 1 hour). Debone and cut into bite size pieces. Reduce stock to 2 cups. Slice the smoked sausage diagonally and brown it. Cook bacon and reserve 5 tablespoons bacon grease. Brown flour in bacon grease until it reaches a dark brown color. Add green onions, celery, green pepper and garlic. Cook 2 minutes, then add duck stock and chicken stock. Season with chili powder, Worcestershire, salt and pepper. Simmer 1 hour. Add duck, bacon and sausage. Continue to cook for 30 minutes more. Before serving, stir in parsley and serve over rice.

Mrs. Floyd Fraser

Asparagus Sandwich

Yield: 9 sandwiches

1   loaf Pepperidge Farm
    Sandwich Bread
1   small package (3
    ounces) cream cheese
1   small can asparagus
    tips (Squeeze all the
    juice out)
    Seasoned salt
    Worcestershire sauce
    Tabasco
    Garlic salt
    Melted butter
    Parmesan cheese

Mix ingredients together and spread in between slices of Pepperidge Farm Bread. Spread melted butter on outsides of bread and sprinkle Parmesan cheese and then toast in oven broiler on both sides.

Mrs. Richard Murray, III

Avocado, Bacon and Cheese Sandwiches

Yield: 4 sandwiches

1   large ripe avocado,
     peeled
2   tablespoons scallions,
     minced
3   teaspoons lemon juice
1/2 teaspoon salt
12   slices of bacon
     Mayonnaise
8   slices of bread
3/4 cup medium Cheddar
     cheese, grated

Mash avocado, stir in scallions, lemon juice and salt. Put aside. Fry bacon and let drain. Spread mayonnaise on bread. Top each of 4 slices of bread with avocado mixture. Sprinkle with cheddar cheese and add 3 slices of bacon. Complete sandwiches with remaining 4 slices of bread. This sandwich is delicious made with pumpernickel bread. A special lunch or picnic treat.

Mrs. Stewart Thames, Jr.

Katie's Hot Brown Sandwiches

Serves 4

Sauce:
2	tablespoons butter
1/4	cup flour
2	cups milk
1/4	cup Parmesan cheese, freshly grated
1/4	cup sharp Cheddar cheese, grated
1/4	teaspoon salt
1/2	teaspoon Worcestershire
	Dash of Tabasco

Sandwich ingredients:
1	pound turkey, thinly sliced
4	slices ham, halved (optional)
4	slices toast, trimmed and cut in half into triangles
4	slices tomato, halved
8	strips bacon, partially cooked
1/2	cup Parmesan cheese, freshly grated

Melt butter in saucepan. Add flour and stir well. Add milk, 1/4 cup Parmesan cheese, Cheddar cheese and seasonings. Cook, stirring constantly, until thick. Place toast on baking sheet. Arrange turkey slices (and ham) on toast and cover with hot cheese sauce. Top with tomato and bacon. Sprinkle with 1/2 cup Parmesan cheese. Bake at 425° until bubbly.

Mrs. Victor Lott, Jr.

Hot Ham and Pineapple French Toast Sandwich

Butter
Bread
Sliced pineapple
Ham
French Toast mixture (egg, milk, cinnamon-sugar to taste)

Spread butter on the inside pieces of bread. Put sliced pineapple and ham in between 2 slices of bread. Dip both sides of sandwich in French Toast mixture of egg, milk, & cinnamon sugar (to taste). Sauté or pan-fry in butter in heated skillet, turning until lightly browned on both sides. Delicious and easy!

Mrs. James Hirs

Greek Salad Sandwich

Serves 4

1	package Original Ranch Dressing
1/2	pound ground beef
4	whole pita breads (pocket bread)
	Shredded lettuce
1/2	cup avocado, chopped
1/2	cup tomato, chopped
1/2	cup Feta cheese, crumbled
	Fresh alfalfa sprouts

Make dressing according to directions on package. Brown beef. Cut each bread in half and open pocket carefully with fingers. Layer ingredients in each pocket in the following order: shredded lettuce, avocado, tomato, ground beef, Feta cheese, alfalfa sprouts. Spoon dressing over all.

Tim Mulcahy
The Saratoga Trunk

Crabmeat Specials

Serves 8

1	pound crabmeat, picked over
4	green onions, minced
1	cup sharp cheese, grated
6	tablespoons mayonnaise (might need a bit more)
	Juice of 1 big lemon

Combine and set aside.

4	English muffins, split, buttered and toasted
	Thick tomato slices
1	strip bacon per sandwich, fried almost done, then broken in half

For each serving: Place toasted muffin half on a baking sheet. Top with a tomato slice, a mound of the crabmeat mixture, spread to the edges, and 2 half-pieces of bacon on top of this. Broil until crab mixture is bubbly, and serve. Note: This is an open-faced sandwich that needs a knife and fork.

Mrs. Wade Faulkner

79

Hot Ham Sandwich

Serves 4

1/2 cup mayonnaise
1   teaspoon horseradish
4   slices bread
4   slices Swiss cheese
4   slices ham
     Asparagus spears

Mix mayonnaise and horseradish in pan and heat. Layer bread, cheese, ham and asparagus and heat in oven for 10 minutes at 400° and top with sauce.

Mrs. E. B. Peebles, III

Pizza Burgers

Serves 15

2   pounds ground beef
1   large onion, chopped
2   (6 ounce) cans tomato
     paste
1   teaspoon garlic salt
1   (15 ounce) jar
     spaghetti sauce (Ragú
     meatless with
     mushrooms)
1   teaspoon orégano
     Salt to taste
     Mozzarella cheese,
     grated
     Hamburger buns
     toasted with garlic
     butter (15 buns)

Brown the beef and onion in a skillet. Add the tomato paste, garlic salt, spaghetti sauce and orégano. Cook until it boils. Chill. When ready to serve, place grated cheese on one half of a bun and spread with meat sauce. On the other half of a bun, reverse this, meat sauce then cheese. Put on a baking sheet, open face style and heat at 350° until cheese is melted, about 10 minutes. Put together like a sandwich. Great to do ahead and take to the beach. A summertime favorite!

Mrs. Marion H. Lyons, Jr.

SALADS & DRESSINGS

A GARDEN
Boston, Romaine, Bibb, Escarole — Indispensable every time!

White Wine Apricot Mold

Serves 8-10

2	envelopes unflavored gelatin
1/2	cup sugar
1/4	teaspoon salt
2	cups apricot nectar
3/4	cup water
1	cup dry white wine
1	cup sour cream
	Lettuce
	Fresh fruit

In a saucepan, combine the gelatin, sugar and salt. Stir in apricot nectar and water. Cook and stir over low heat until gelatin dissolves. Remove from heat. Stir in wine. Gradually blend into sour cream. Turn into a 5½ cup ring mold. Chill until firm. Unmold onto lettuce lined serving plate. Fill the center of the ring mold with fresh fruit. This salad goes well with melon balls, banana chunks and fresh peach slices.

Mrs. Fred Cushing

Rub a mold lightly with an unflavored salad oil or spray with a vegetable cooking spray to facilitate unmolding.

Nat Grayson's Congealed Apricot Salad

Yield: 24 squares

1	(20 ounce) can crushed pineapple (not drained)
1/2	cup sugar
2	(3 ounce) packages apricot Jello
1	(8 ounce) package cream cheese
1	cup ice water
1	cup celery, finely diced
1	cup nuts, chopped
1	(8 ounce) container Cool Whip

Bring pineapple and sugar to a boil and add apricot Jello. Mix and add cream cheese. Stir until dissolved. Add 1 cup ice water to cool. Add celery and nuts. When starting to gel, fold in Cool Whip and congeal in 9" X 13" pan. Cut into 2" squares when congealed, and serve on lettuce.

Mrs. Peter Marshall Grayson

"Lite" Pink Congealed Pear Salad

Serves 12

2   (.3 ounce) packages
    raspberry sugar free
    Jell-O
1   cup boiling water
2   cups cold water
1   container Hi/Lo
    cottage cheese
1   (29 ounce) can pears,
    drained, rinsed and
    crushed)
1   (8 ounce) container
    Cool Whip
1/2 cup pecans, chopped

This recipe is low in calories but tastes delicious. Combine gelatin and boiling water. Stir until dissolved. Add cold water and allow to thicken slightly. Add cottage cheese to pears, mix well. Add cheese-pear mixture to gelatin and whip well. Fold in Cool Whip and pecans. Chill in a Pyrex dish.

Mrs. Michael Gates

Mama Una's Frozen Fruit Salad

Serves 10-12

1   (6 ounce) can frozen
    orange juice
3   ripe bananas, sliced
1/2 cup sugar
1   (20 ounce) can
    pineapple chunks and
    juice
2   (11 ounce) cans
    mandarin oranges,
    drained
2   maraschino cherries,
    chopped

Let orange juice soften a little before combining with other ingredients. Freeze in a 9x13-inch dish. Slice and serve. This amount will fill at least two ice trays without dividers. Also good as a dessert.

Mrs. Bruce C. Finley, Jr.

Mrs. Bradshaw's Strawberry Salad

Serves 6-8

1   (8 ounce) package cream cheese
2/3 cup sugar
1   (20 ounce) can crushed pineapple
2   (10 ounce) packages frozen strawberries
2   sliced bananas
1   medium size Cool Whip

Beat the cream cheese and sugar in a bowl until creamy. In another bowl, mix pineapple, strawberries, bananas and Cool Whip. Mix all together and put in a mold or in a 2-quart rectangular pan. Freeze overnight. Put the mold over lettuce or cut into individual squares and serve over lettuce. Delicious as a summer dessert too.

Mrs. Peter Gaillard

Asparagus Congealed Salad

Serves 8-12

1   large can green asparagus, drained. Reserve juice
3/4 cup sugar
1   cup asparagus juice (add water to make a full cup, if necessary)
1/2 cup white vinegar
1/2 teaspoon salt
1   package dry Italian salad dressing mix
2½ tablespoons gelatin, softened in 1/2 cup water
1   avocado, diced Juice of 1/2 lemon
1   jar pimento, diced
1   small white onion, grated
1   cup celery, chopped
1/2 cup pecans, finely chopped

Drain asparagus. Combine the sugar, asparagus juice, vinegar, salt and salad dressing mix. Bring to a boil and add to the softened gelatin. Stir until gelatin is dissolved. Add the remaining ingredients and pour into a greased mold. Refrigerate until set.

Mrs. David Howard

85

Spinach Ring Salad

1   (3 ounce) package
     lemon gelatin
1   cup boiling water
1/2 cup mayonnaise
2   tablespoons lemon
     juice
1/2 teaspoon salt
1   (10 ounce) package
     frozen chopped
     spinach, thawed and
     drained
1   cup small curd
     cottage cheese
1   small onion, finely
     chopped
1/2 cup celery, chopped

Dissolve the gelatin in boiling water and cool. Stir in remaining ingredients (except dressing) mixing well. Pour into an oiled 1 quart mold. Chill until the salad is firm. Serve with dressing.

Dressing:
1/4 cup mayonnaise
1/2 cup sour cream
1   tablespoon vinegar
1   teaspoon sugar
     Dash salt and pepper

Combine all ingredients, stirring well. Chill.

Mrs. James Russell

Vegetable Salad Supreme

Serves 6-8

1 (12 ounce) can V-8 Juice
2 packages plain gelatin
2 teaspoons sugar
1/2 teaspoon salt
1/4 cup lemon juice
Dash of Tabasco
1 (10 ounce) can cut asparagus spears, drained
1 (14 ounce) can artichoke hearts, quartered
1/2 cup celery, chopped

In a saucepan, sprinkle the gelatin over the V-8 Juice. Stir over medium heat until gelatin is dissolved. Add the seasonings and vegetables. Fills 6 to 8 individual molds or a one quart mold. Chill 1½ hours. Serve with Sour Cream Sauce, ripe olives, and quartered boiled eggs on lettuce. Note: 55 to 75 calories per serving. This is quick and easy to make!

SOUR CREAM SAUCE:
1/4 cup sour cream
1/3 cup mayonnaise
1 teaspoon horseradish

Combine all ingredients and serve as a dressing for Vegetable Salad Supreme.

Mrs. Sam G. Ladd

Tomato Aspic

Serves 8-10

5   envelopes Knox unflavored gelatin
1   (46 ounce) can V-8 juice
1   tablespoon lemon juice
    Dash Tabasco
1/4 cup catsup
1   teaspoon salt
2   tablespoons horseradish
1   tablespoon dill pickle juice
1   teaspoon Worcestershire
2   tablespoons vinegar
1/2 teaspoon garlic salt
1   tablespoon sugar

Soften gelatin in 1 cup of the juice for 5 minutes. Combine with the remaining juice and the other ingredients. Heat everything together until the gelatin is completely dissolved, stirring. Cool, then refrigerate in a ring mold. To serve, unmold on a lettuce-lined platter and fill with shrimp or egg salad, crabmeat salad, or chicken salad. Other variations: surround with hard-boiled egg quarters, or deviled eggs, avocado, cucumber, broccoli, tomato wedges, black and green olives, asparagus, artichokes, (the latter two could be marinated). Let your imagination run wild. You might add a dressing such as Horseradish Cream, Louis Sauce, etc.

Mrs. John Brady

Super Congealed Salad

Serves 8-10

1   package lemon Jello, regular size
1   cup celery, finely chopped
1   cup cabbage, finely chopped
1   green pepper, chopped
4   pimento slices, chopped
2   tablespoons lemon juice
1/2 teaspoon salt
1/2 teaspoon prepared mustard
1/4 teaspoon paprika

Prepare Jello according to package directions. Put in refrigerator to thicken. Add remaining ingredients when starting to gel. Pour into a 2 quart mold. Especially good to add light touch to a rich entree or holiday meals. Children and men seem to like the crisp flavor.

Mrs. Virginia B. Baumhauer

Corned Beef Salad

Serves 10

1½ packages Knox unflavored gelatin
1/2 cup water
1½ cups tomato juice, heated
1 cup canned Corned Beef, broken up fine
1½ cups celery, chopped
1/2 cup cucumber, cut fine
1 small onion, cut fine
1/2 bell pepper, cut fine
1 cup mayonnaise
Salt, pepper and Tabasco to taste
3 hard-boiled eggs, sliced

Soften the gelatin in water for 5 minutes, then dissolve completely in hot tomato juice. Cool and refrigerate until the consistency of unbeaten egg whites. At this point, add all other ingredients. Grease an 8-cup ring mold with a little oil or mayonnaise. Line the mold with sliced hard-boiled eggs, then add the salad mixture. Chill until very firm, overnight, if possible. To serve, turn the mold out onto a lettuce-lined platter and garnish with tomato wedges, hard-boiled egg wedges, olives and asparagus. Pass a bowl of Horse-radish Dressing.

Mrs. Edward Roberts Leatherbury

Chicken Curry Salad

Serves 6

3 cups cooked chicken in large pieces
3 cups cooked rice (or less)
2 cups cooked English peas (or frozen petite)
2 cups celery, slivered
1/2 cup chutney
1½ teaspoons salt
3/4 cup French dressing (oil and vinegar)
1/2 to 1 teaspoon curry powder (Madras brand)
Salad greens

Combine first 8 ingredients and place on salad greens. Shrimp may be substituted for chicken. Excellent luncheon dish.

Mrs. Richard B. Cunningham

Chicken Chutney Salad in Melon Shells

Serves 8

4	whole chicken breasts
1	teaspoon salt
	Few celery tops
1	teaspoon peppercorns
2	cups celery, sliced
1/2	cup green pepper, diced
1	teaspoon salt
1	cup mayonnaise
1/2	cup sour cream
	Juice of 1/2 lemon
1/4	cup chutney, chopped
4	ripe cantaloupes, halved
	Salted pecans, watercress or lettuce

Simmer chicken breasts until tender in a covered pot with water to cover, 1 teaspoon salt, celery tops and peppercorns. Cool chicken enough to remove meat. Cube, and put into a bowl with celery and green pepper. Sprinkle with salt, then mix lightly with combined mayonnaise, sour cream, lemon juice and chutney. Cover and chill. Cut a thin slice from the bottom of each melon half after cleaning. Carve melon into balls and toss them with chicken mixture. Pile all into cantaloupe shells. Garnish with pecans, watercress or lettuce.

Mrs. Kerwin Andrews

Lincoln's Curried Chicken Salad

Serves 6-8

4 cups chicken, cooked and cubed
1 (8 ounce) can water chestnuts, sliced
1 pound seedless grapes
1 cup celery, sliced
1/4 cup almonds, sliced
1 cup mayonnaise
1-2 tablespoons curry powder
1 tablespoon soy sauce
Juice of 1 lemon

Mix all ingredients together and refrigerate. Serve on lettuce leaves.

Mrs. Mark Lyons, III

Shrimp and Caper Salad

Serves 6

2 pounds shrimp, peeled and deveined
Liquid crab boil
2 tablespoons fresh lemon juice
3/4 cup green onions, chopped
1½ cups celery, chopped
3 tablespoons capers, drained
1 cup black olives, sliced
1/2 cup oil and vinegar salad dressing
3/4 cup mayonnaise
1 tablespoon celery seed

Boil shrimp, using liquid crab boil and lemon juice. Drain shrimp, discarding liquid. Combine all ingredients and chill. This is better if made the night before. Serve on crisp salad greens and garnish with tomato wedges and hard cooked egg wedges.

Mrs. Clyde Speas

Point Clear "Greek" Salad

Serves 6

Iceberg lettuce, tossed with dressing
Tomato wedges, tossed with dressing
Paper thin sliced onion rings
Greek olives
1/2 pound Feta cheese, crumbled
1 can flat, boneless Anchovy filets
2 pounds peeled, boiled shrimp, tossed with dressing
Chopped fresh parsley

Cover a big platter with the lettuce. Place tomato wedges around the edges. Evenly distribute onion rings in center. Place olives among the tomato wedges and pile shrimp in the center. Arrange Feta cheese around shrimp. Lay anchovy filets over all, spoon more dressing over all if necessary, and sprinkle everything with parsley. Serve with warm crackers.

DRESSING:
3/4 cup olive oil
1/4 cup wine vinegar
1/8 teaspoon orégano
1/8 teaspoon basil
Salt and pepper to taste
1 clove garlic, minced

Shake together and serve. Double this if you are making a giant salad.

Mrs. Wade Faulkner

Cold Fish Salad

Lemon juice
Oil
Salt and pepper
Garlic
A large firm fish
Celery
Green olives

Make French dressing: 1 part lemon juice, 4 parts oil. Season, put in a cut clove of garlic, let stand overnight. Boil a large firm fish for 12 minutes per pound. Wrap in cheesecloth or aluminum foil to keep from separating. Remove fish from bones and put into a large bowl. Put a layer of fish, a layer of chopped celery and layer of sliced green olives. Repeat until fish is used up. Pour dressing over and marinate overnight.

SAUCE:

1   small onion, grated
1/2   pint sour cream
1/2   pint mayonnaise
1/4   teaspoon dry mustard
2   tablespoons
         dehydrated
         horseradish
1   clove garlic, chopped
1   teaspoon vinegar
2   tablespoons parsley
         or chives, chopped

Beat onion into cream and add other ingredients. Add salt and pepper to taste. Drain fish marinade. Pour on horseradish sauce to serve.

Mrs. Walter Ogburn, Jr.

Crabmeat Supreme Salad

Serves: 4

1 pound crabmeat
1 head of lettuce
1 can green asparagus
1 cup ripe olives
4 hard boiled eggs,
   sliced

Toss ingredients lightly with dressing.

LEMON DRESSING:
1 cup oil
1/4 cup lemon juice
1/2 teaspoon salt
1/2 teaspoon pepper
1/2 teaspoon curry
   powder

Mrs. Smith Downing

Low-Calorie Apple-Tuna Salad

Serves 1

1 medium-large apple,
   peeled and cubed
2 medium stalks celery,
   sliced
1 (3½ ounce) can tuna,
   drained and washed
1/4 cup dry roasted
   peanuts
1 tablespoon
   mayonnaise

Mix all ingredients well and serve cold
on lettuce leaves.

Mrs. Ernest Brown

King Mackerel Salad

Yield: about 5 cups

6 (8 pound) king
mackerel backbones,
which remain after
you filet the king
mackerel, with some
meat left on
Water
Salt
Lemon juice
2 bay leaves
1/2 cup celery, finely
chopped
4 slices onion, finely
chopped
1/2 cup stuffed olives,
chopped
1 tablespoon lemon
rind, finely minced
White pepper
Seasoning salt
Garlic salt
8 dashes Tabasco
Mayonnaise
Juice of 1/2 lemon

Be sure the meat has been skinned and trimmed of all dark meat. Boil the white king mackerel meat in water that has had salt, lemon juice and bay leaves added. Bring the water to a full boil before adding the fish and then let it boil with the fish added for 4 to 5 minutes. The meat that is left on the backbones of the fish after fileting is good to use for this but you may use filets if that is all you have. Pour the cooked fish into a colander and let it drain and cool to room temperature. Flake the mackerel to fill a quart bowl. Add celery, onion, olives, lemon rind, seasonings to taste and Tabasco. Add enough mayonnaise to moisten well, then add the lemon juice. Toss all of this together with forks and then place in the refrigerator for a couple of hours to allow the seasonings to blend. This salad may be served on a bed of shredded lettuce, in an avocado half, to fill a tomato or just to spread on crackers.

Fred Cushing

Summer Salmon Mold
with Horseradish Sauce

2	envelopes unflavored gelatin
1½	cups cold water
1	cup salad dressing (mayonnaise type)
1/2	cup French dressing
1/2	cup sour cream
1	(one pound) can salmon, drained and flaked
1	teaspoon onion, scraped
1	cup celery, chopped

Soften the gelatin in water. Stir over low heat until dissolved. Cool. Combine the salad dressing, French dressing, and sour cream. Stir in the gelatin and chill until slightly thickened. Fold in the salmon, onion, and celery; pour into a 1½ quart mold that has been sprayed well with Pam or greased with mayonnaise. Chill until firm and unmold. Serve with Horseradish sauce. Super summer luncheon dish.

Horseradish Sauce:

1	carton sour cream
1	cup mayonnaise
2-3	tablespoons horseradish
1	tablespoon cracked pepper
	Juice of 1 lemon

Combine all of the ingredients and chill well. Use with salmon mold or other seafood. Makes 2 cups.

Mrs. John P. Case, Jr.

Potato Salad Roll

3 medium potatoes
1/3 cup mayonnaise
1 teaspoon salt
1/2 teaspoon paprika
1/2 cup celery, diced
3 hard cooked eggs, chopped
2 tablespoons onion, chopped
1 cup cottage cheese
2 tablespoons mayonnaise
2 tablespoons green pepper, finely chopped
2 tablespoons pimento, diced
Parsley
Egg slices

Pare, boil and mash the potatoes, do not add any liquid. Combine with the 1/3 cup mayonnaise, salt and paprika. Stir in celery, eggs and onion. Chill. On waxed paper, pat mixture into a 12 X 9 X 1/2 inch rectangle. Combine cottage cheese, mayonnaise, green pepper and pimento. Spread atop rectangle to within 1" of edges. Roll from short side. Chill. Top with parsley and egg slices.

Mrs. Champ Lyons, Jr.

Avocado Bacon Boats

Serves 6

12 slices of bacon, cooked and crumbled
1/2 cup sour cream
2 tomatoes, peeled, seeded, and chopped
2 tablespoons sliced green onion
1 tablespoon lemon juice
1/2 teaspoon salt
3 avocados, halved and pitted

Combine bacon, sour cream, tomatoes, onions, lemon juice and salt. Scoop out the avocados, dice and mix with other ingredients. Fill avocado shells with mixture. Note: Cannot be done ahead since avocado shell darkens.

Mrs. Slade Hooks

Cold Rice Salad

Serves 4-6

1 package Uncle Ben's chicken flavor rice
1-2 green onions and tops, chopped
1/2 green pepper, chopped
12 large stuffed olives, sliced
2 (6 ounce) jars marinated artichoke hearts
1/2 teaspoon curry powder
1/2 cup mayonnaise, scant
1 pound shrimp, boiled and peeled (optional)

Cook rice according to directions and *cool*. Add onions, pepper, and olives to rice. Drain artichokes and save juice. Combine juice and curry powder with mayonnaise. Pour over rice and sliced artichokes and optional shrimp and chill. Better done the day before. If chicken flavor rice can't be obtained, cook 1 cup rice in chicken broth until done.

Mrs. John Lewis, Jr.

Avocado and Grapefruit Salad

Serves 4

2 grapefruits, sectioned
2 avocados, sliced

DRESSING:
1 cup mayonnaise
1/2 cup sour cream
1/4 cup powdered sugar
2 mint leaves
1/2 cup strawberries
Almonds (optional)

Put all ingredients for dressing in a blender, mix, and chill. Place grapefruit and avocado on lettuce leaves. Pour dressing over. You can sprinkle almonds on top (optional).

Mrs. Michael R. Bailey

Artichoke Heart Green Salad

Serves 6

1/2 cup olive oil or salad oil
1/3 cup wine vinegar
2 tablespoons water
4 thin slices onion
1 tablespoon sugar
1 clove garlic, crushed
1/2 teaspoon salt
1/4 teaspoon celery seed
Pepper
1 (9 ounce) package frozen artichoke hearts
Lettuce and tomatoes for 6 people

Bring first 9 ingredients to boil in saucepan. Add artichoke hearts and bring back to boiling. Cover, turn to low and cook 4 minutes. Chill all thoroughly. When ready to serve, drain the artichokes and reserve the dressing. Combine the artichokes, lettuce and chopped tomatoes. Toss with the dressing.

Mrs. Bruce C. Finley, Jr.

Broccoli Salad

Serves 6-8

1 (10 ounce) package frozen broccoli spears, partially thawed
2 hard boiled eggs, chopped
1 (14½ ounce) can asparagus pieces, drained
3/4 cup Italian-style salad dressing, with garlic and onion
1/2 cup Parmesan cheese
Assorted salad greens to equal one large head lettuce

Cut broccoli into bite-sized pieces. In a bowl, combine broccoli, eggs, asparagus, salad dressing, and Parmesan cheese. Marinate in refrigerator at least 2 hours before serving. May be kept in refrigerator for 4 to 5 days. Just before serving, toss with salad greens.

Mrs. C. Vearn Partridge, Jr.

Delores' Cole Slaw

1	large cabbage, shredded
1	bell pepper, chopped
3	carrots, shredded
1	small onion, (or four green onions) chopped
1	cup sugar, less 2 tablespoons
1	cup vinegar
3/4	cup oil
2	tablespoons sugar
1	tablespoon salt
1	teaspoon dry mustard

Toss cabbage, bell pepper, carrots, and onion together and sprinkle 1 cup sugar less 2 tablespoons on top but do not mix. Bring the vinegar, oil, 2 tablespoons sugar, salt and dry mustard to a boil. Pour over vegetables, mix and chill thoroughly.

Mrs. Richard O'Neill

Wilted Lettuce

Serves 6

6	slices bacon
1/4	cup vinegar
1/4	cup water
3	teaspoons sugar
1/2	teaspoon salt
	Pepper to taste
1/2	cup green onions, include tops, sliced
8	cups leaf lettuce, torn in bite size pieces
2-3	hard boiled eggs

Fry bacon until crisp—drain and crumble. Add vinegar, water, and sugar, salt and pepper to bacon drippings: Cook and stir until boiling. Toss chopped onion with lettuce and refrigerate until ready to serve. Slice eggs over lettuce; pour hot dressing over all. Sprinkle crumbled bacon over top. Should be eaten immediately.

Mrs. Peter Kenyon

Gram's Cucumbers

Serves 4

2	medium cucumbers
2	medium onions
1/2	cup sugar
1	cup vinegar
1	teaspoon salt
1/3	cup oil

Slice cucumbers and onions thin. Boil together the next 4 ingredients. Pour over the onions and cucumbers. Let sit 1½ hours. Toss together and refrigerate. Great with barbecue.

Mrs. Judson Sanders

Bacon, Lettuce and Tomato Salad

Serves 6

4	large, ripe, summertime tomatoes, peeled
	Lettuce leaves (we suggest Red leaf lettuce, Boston, or Bibb)
1	pound fresh mushrooms, cleaned and sliced
12	strips bacon, cooked crisp and crumbled coarsely
4	green onions with tops, thinly sliced
6	tablespoons vegetable oil
2	tablespoons red wine vinegar
1½	teaspoons salt
1/8	teaspoon freshly ground pepper
1/8	teaspoon garlic salt
	Swiss or Mozzarella cheese, grated

Cut 18 slices from tomatoes. Lightly salt and arrange the tomatoes in 6 lettuce-lined salad bowls. Coarsely chop the remaining tomatoes, and toss with the mushrooms, bacon, onion, oil, vinegar, salt, pepper and garlic salt. Spoon over the sliced tomatoes in lettuce-lined salad bowls. Sprinkle grated cheese on top and serve.

Note: Of course you may line a platter with lettuce, and place all the above ingredients on that, and serve your guests from this platter, rather than making the individual salads.

Also: Boiled shrimp or lump crabmeat may be added for a very special variation of this salad, really making a complete meal with the addition of some hot bread. Cold, cubed chicken or turkey may also be used.

Mrs. John Megginson

Sauerkraut Salad (Germany)

Serves 10

1　(27 ounce) can chopped sauerkraut, drained well
1　green pepper, chopped
1　cup celery, chopped
1　cup green onions, chopped
1　cup sugar
1/2　cup vinegar
1/2　cup oil

Mix the first four (4) ingredients until well combined. Mix well the sugar, vinegar and oil. Pour over the vegetable mixture. Let stand 24 hours. Great with any meats or picnic fares.

Mrs. Clyde Speas

Vegetable Salad

Serves 6

2　cloves garlic
1　cup fresh parsley
1　onion, chopped
8　tablespoons mayonnaise
1　tablespoon mustard
3/4　cup salad oil
1/4　cup red wine vinegar
　　Salt and pepper
　　Green Beans
　　Asparagus
　　Artichokes
　　Water chestnuts
　　Chopped celery

Combine first 8 ingredients in blender or processor to mix. Drain vegetables (should have about 4 cups) and marinate overnight. May be garnished with olives, tomatoes, etc. So easy to take to the beach!

Mrs. Jex R. Luce

Ann's Spinach Salad

Serves 6

1/4 cup white wine vinegar
2 tablespoons dry white wine
2 teaspoons soy sauce
1 teaspoon sugar
1 teaspoon dry mustard
1/2 teaspoon curry powder
1/2 teaspoon salt
1/2 teaspoon pepper
1/4 teaspoon garlic
2/3 cup salad oil
1 pound spinach, washed, stems removed
1/4 pound mushrooms, finely chopped
5 slices bacon, crumbled
2 hard cooked eggs, chopped

Beat together first nine ingredients. Add salad oil in a stream, beating until well-combined. In a salad bowl, combine spinach and mushrooms and toss with dressing. Top salad with bacon and eggs.

Mrs. James E. Brown, III

Spinach Salad

Serves 6-8

1   (10 ounce) bag fresh spinach
1   (11 ounce) can mandarin oranges, chilled
1   (2/3 ounce) bag slivered almonds, toasted
    Celery Seed Dressing (see Index)

Wash and drain spinach. Get as dry as possible. Drain mandarin oranges. Toss spinach, oranges and almonds with Celery Seed Dressing. This is a delicious salad as well as pleasing to the eye.

Mrs. Victor H. Lott, Jr.

Lynda's Tomatoes with Artichokes

Serves 4

6   medium tomatoes
1   (8½ ounce) can artichokes, chopped
1/2 cup celery, chopped
1/2 cup green onions, tops included, chopped
    Mayonnaise
    Salt and pepper
6   slices bacon, fried

A day ahead, mix artichokes, celery, green onions with mayonnaise, salt and pepper to taste. Before serving, peel and quarter tomatoes, and stuff with artichoke salad. Crumble strip of bacon on each tomato. Excellent luncheon dish.

Mrs. Thomas S. Damson

Korean Salad

1   bag fresh spinach
     (remove stems and
     wash)
1   can bean sprouts,
     drained
1   can water chestnuts,
     drained and sliced
     thin
6   slices bacon, fried,
     drained and
     crumbled
3   hard boiled eggs,
     sliced

DRESSING:
3/4 cup Wesson oil
1/2 cup sugar
1/2 teaspoon salt
1/3 cup ketchup
1/4 cup cider vinegar
1   medium onion, grated
1   tablespoon
     Worcestershire sauce
1   teaspoon Accent

Mix salad ingredients. Combine ingredients for dressing and pour on salad. Toss and serve.

Mrs. Wallace G. Jeffrey, Jr.

Gazpacho Salad

Serves: 4-6

2/3   cup olive oil
1/3   cup wine vinegar
1   clove garlic, minced
1   teaspoon dried basil
1   teaspoon salt
1/2   teaspoon ground pepper
2   medium cucumbers, sliced (sprinkle with salt and let stand 30 minutes)
6   small yellow squash, sliced
10   medium mushrooms, sliced
4   scallions, sliced
   Minced parsley
3   large tomatoes, sliced in wedges
1   large green pepper, thinly sliced
   Swiss cheese, cut in strips
   Hard boiled egg quarters

In a large bowl, mix olive oil, vinegar, garlic, basil, salt and pepper. Pat cucumbers dry and add to oil mixture with squash, mushrooms and scallions, Top mixture with minced parsley and mix gently. Add layer of 3 large tomatoes cut in wedges and 1 medium green pepper thinly sliced. Cover and chill for 4 hours. Before serving add Swiss cheese cut in strips and hard boiled egg quarters.

Mrs. Thomas Taul, Jr.

Spinach Salad Dressing

Yield: 1½ cups

1	cup oil (not olive)
5	tablespoons red wine vinegar
4	tablespoons sour cream
1½	teaspoons salt
1/2	teaspoon dry mustard
2	tablespoons sugar
	Black pepper, coarsely ground
2	teaspoons parsley, chopped
2	cloves garlic, crushed

Put all ingredients in a bowl and mix with wire whisk. Mix dressing at least 6 hours before using.

Mrs. J. B. Newell, Jr.

Mother's Bleu Cheese Dressing

Yield: 1½ cups

2	tablespoons white vinegar
1	(4 ounce) package Bleu Cheese
1/2	teaspoon Accent
1/2	teaspoon black pepper
1	teaspoon salt
1/2	cup green onions, finely chopped
1	(8 ounce) carton sour cream
1	cup mayonnaise

Mash vinegar and bleu cheese with fork first. Then mix all ingredients. Let sit about 2 hours in refrigerator before serving. Great on salads. Also, good as dip for chips or raw vegetables.

Mrs. McGowin I. Patrick

107

Marinated Mushrooms

Yield: 3 cups

6 tablespoons oil (I prefer vegetable to olive)

6 tablespoons pickle juice (Clausen's is the best or any kosher dill — rather than vinegar, though this is all right. If you use vinegar, use 3 tablespoons instead of 6.)

1/4 cup onion, chopped

1 small or 1/2 large garlic clove, crushed

2 teaspoons salt

1/4 teaspoon pepper
Few drops Tabasco

1/2 teaspoon orégano

1/4 teaspoon dill weed

1 tablespoon capers

1/4 teaspoon celery salt

3/4 pound fresh mushrooms, small whole ones with stems removed OR large ones sliced, including stem.

Combine first 11 ingredients and stir briskly. Pour over the mushrooms. When you pour the dressing over the mushrooms, you will have very little liquid compared with the mushrooms. Don't panic. Use a container with a tight top and gently turn the mushrooms back and forth several times during the day, and the mushrooms will make their own juice, and by serving time, you will have the amount you need as a salad dressing. When used as a dressing, you may wish to add more oil when you prepare your salad for serving. Or put a little oil on the greens first. Marinate at least 12 hours — or overnight, 24 hours. They are all right beyond this amount of time but aren't as crispy. This is a good recipe to use as a salad dressing for a green salad — or to take the mushrooms out of the dressing and serve as a cold hors d'oeuvre with cocktail picks. Very popular with men.

Mrs. John M. Scott, Jr.

Lorenzo Dressing

Yield: 6 cups

3 eggs
1 tablespoon dry mustard
1 tablespoon sugar
1/4 teaspoon salt and pepper, each
4 cups vegetable oil
1 cup white wine vinegar
1 tablespoon garlic, crushed
Juice of 1 lemon
1 tablespoon A-1 Sauce
2 tablespoons Worcestershire
1/2 teaspoon Tabasco sauce
1 tablespoon chili powder
1 cup watercress, chopped
1/2 cup fresh parsley, chopped

Beat eggs with mustard, sugar, salt and pepper. Slowly add oil, beating constantly with a wire whip. When thick, add vinegar, garlic, lemon, A-1, Worcestershire, Tabasco, and chili powder. Mix well. Fold in watercress and parsley when ready to serve. Keeps well in refrigerator.

Mrs. Larry Harless

Fruit Salad Dressing

Serves 10

1/3 cup sugar
4 teaspoons cornstarch
1/4 teaspoon salt
1 cup pineapple juice
1/4 cup orange juice
2½ tablespoons lemon juice
2 well beaten eggs
6 ounces cream cheese, softened

Mix sugar, cornstarch, salt; gradually add fruit juices. Cook 20 minutes in double boiler, stirring constantly. Add some of this to eggs, blend, then return all to double boiler and cook 5 minutes more. Beat hot mixture into cream cheese. Chill. Serve over congealed fruit salad, and pass hot mushroom sandwiches or hot pimento cheese sandwiches. This dressing may also be used over fresh fruit.

Mrs. J. B. Blackburn

Celery Seed Dressing

Yield: about 2 cups

2/3 cup sugar
1½ teaspoons salt
1 tablespoon paprika
1/2 teaspoon prepared mustard
1/2 cup tarragon wine vinegar
1/4 medium size onion, cut into chunks
1 cup salad oil (Mazola)
1 tablespoon celery seed

Put all ingredients in food processor or blender and blend until smooth. Store in tightly covered glass jar. This will keep for weeks. Delicious on fresh fruit salad or spinach salad.

Mrs. H. Eldon Scott, III

Roquefort and Oil Dressing

Serves 10

1 egg
3 cups olive oil (or 1½ cups olive oil and 1½ cups salad oil)
1/2 cup red wine vinegar
1½ teaspoons salt
1½ teaspoons dry mustard
1 teaspoon sugar
3/4 teaspoon pepper
3 drops Worcestershire sauce
1-2 drops Tabasco
3 ounces Roquefort cheese, crumbled

In a bowl, or a food processor, beat together the egg and olive oil. Stir in 1/2 cup vinegar, salt, dry mustard, sugar, pepper, Worcestershire, and Tabasco. Beat in Roquefort cheese. Keeps well and gets better all the time.

Mrs. Winston C. Patterson

MEATS

THE PILLARS RESTAURANT
The place for steak and gala celebrations.

Châteaubriand

Serves 1

Center cut of filet, 2
inches thick
Salt and pepper
Mazola oil

Sprinkle meat with salt and pepper and brush with Mazola oil. Cook over charcoal until medium rare. Serve with the following sauce.

SAUCE:
1/2 cup dry white wine
1   tablespoon onion,
     finely chopped
2   tablespoons canned
     beef bouillon
1   tablespoon butter
1/2 teaspoon tarragon
     Pinch of cayenne
     pepper
     Dash of lemon juice

Simmer wine with the onion until liquid is slightly reduced. Add remaining ingredients and heat through.

Mrs. Marion S. Adams, Jr.

Jamey's Favorite Beef Tenderloin

Serves 10

1/2 cup of butter
2   tablespoons
     Worcestershire sauce
     Juice of 1/2 lemon
2   cloves garlic, pressed
2   tablespoons vinegar
     Few dashes of
     Tabasco
3   tablespoons oil
5   pound tenderloin

Melt butter and add remaining ingredients. Take the meat out of the refrigerator, wipe, and baste with the sauce. Let stand for 1 hour, basting with the sauce several times. Sear meat on all sides over hot fire on grill. Cover and smoke from 20 to 40 minutes for desired doneness.

Mrs. Larry Harless

Tournedos With Mushrooms and Béarnaise Sauce

Serves 6

6	large mushrooms, fresh
6	small mushrooms, fresh
1/2	lemon
3	tablespoons butter
6	tournedos (filets), 1¼-inches thick
6	slices bacon
	Fresh ground pepper
6	thin slices bread
6	tablespoons clarified butter
2	tablespoons clarified butter
	Béarnaise sauce

Remove the stems from all 12 mushrooms. Flute the small caps and rub inside of all the caps with the cut lemon. Sauté the mushrooms in butter until they turn gold in color. Remove skillet from the heat and keep the mushrooms warm. Pat the steaks dry with paper towels and tie a piece of bacon around each. Season the steaks with fresh pepper, pressing it in on both sides of the meat. Cut 6 rounds from the bread the same size as the steaks and sauté them in 6 tablespoons butter until golden. Put them on paper towels to drain and arrange on a platter and keep warm. Add last 2 tablespoons butter to the skillet and sear steaks over medium high heat for 3½ to 5 minutes on each side. Remove steaks and discard bacon. Transfer steaks to a platter, arranging each on a slice of bread, and top each steak with a large mushroom cap, hollow side up. Fill the caps with Béarnaise Sauce, letting the sauce spill onto the meat. Top each filled mushroom with a small mushroom, fluted side up.

BÉARNAISE SAUCE:

1/4	cup tarragon vinegar
2	tablespoons shallots, minced
1	tablespoon dried tarragon
1/8	teaspoon white pepper
1	tablespoon cold water

In a heavy saucepan combine vinegar, shallots, tarragon and pepper. Reduce liquid over high heat to about 1 tablespoon. Remove pan from heat and add the cold water. Add the egg yolks and whisk until the sauce is thick and creamy. Whip in the butter, 2 tablespoons at a time, over low heat. Continue to whisk sauce until it is thick.

3	egg yolks, lightly beaten
1	cup clarified butter, cooled
	Salt and pepper
	Parsley, minced

Season with salt and pepper and garnish with parsley. Makes 1¼ cups. Note: This cannot be reheated as the butter and the eggs separate.

Mrs. Larry Harless

Carbonnade of Beef

Serves 4-6

2	tablespoons butter
2	tablespoons oil or bacon fat
3	pounds chuck or rump beef, cut into 1/2-inch slices
1½	pounds yellow onions, thinly sliced
	Salt and pepper
2	cloves of garlic, crushed
1	(12 ounce) bottle of beer
1	cup beef stock
1	tablespoon brown sugar
	Bouquet garni of bay leaves, thyme and parsley
2	tablespoons cornstarch
2	tablespoons vinegar

Heat butter and oil together to sizzling. Brown the beef slices well. Remove them as they brown. Reduce heat and brown onions in the same fat. Remove when browned. Season with salt, pepper and garlic. Pour in beer and stock. Stir in sugar. Drop bouquet garni into casserole dish. Cover and cook at 350° for 2½ hours or until meat is fork tender. Discard the bouquet garni. Mix the cornstarch with vinegar and stir into gravy to thicken.

Mrs. William Dumas

Sukiyaki

Serves 2

1   pound sirloin
3   tablespoons
    vegetable oil
1   onion, chopped
1/2 cup celery, chopped
4   green onions,
    chopped
    Mushrooms, sliced,
    about 1/4 pound
1/4 pound spinach,
    washed and stems
    removed
1   teaspoon sugar
3   tablespoons soy sauce
1   cup beef broth
    Chinese noodles or
    rice

Cut meat across the grain into thin slices. Using a wok, brown quickly in oil and remove. Add onions, celery, green onion and cook 2 minutes. Add mushrooms and cook 1 minute more. Return meat to wok and add spinach. Sprinkle sugar over top and add soy sauce. Pour in beef broth and stir to blend. Heat until spinach wilts and mixture is piping hot. Serve over Chinese noodles or rice. Can add bean sprouts and water chestnuts, if desired.

Mrs. Thomas Taul, Jr.

Italian Beef Roll

Serves 6

1   pound ground beef
    (chuck)
1   egg
3/4 cup cracker crumbs
1/8 teaspoon pepper
1/2 cup onion, chopped
2   (6-ounce) cans tomato
    sauce, divided
1   teaspoon salt
1/2 teaspoon orégano
1   cup Mozzarella
    cheese, shredded

Combine the meat, egg, cracker crumbs, pepper, onion, 1/3 cup tomato sauce, salt and orégano. Mix well. Shape into a flat rectangle, approximately 10" x 12", on wax paper. Sprinkle the cheese over meat. Roll up like a jelly roll by picking up one end of wax paper. Press ends and edge to seal well; otherwise cheese will cook out. Bake in a shallow dish at 350° for one hour. Drain off the fat. Pour remaining tomato sauce over the roll and bake 15 minutes more.

Mrs. Norman E. Waldrop, Jr.

Corned Beef with Orange Sauce

Serves 6

3-4 **pounds of corned beef (round or brisket)**
Onion
Celery
Garlic
Bay Leaf

Cook the corned beef in water with the onion, celery, garlic and bay leaf. Corned beef is most tender when under-cooked.

SAUCE:

1/2 **cup brown sugar, packed**
3 **tablespoons orange juice**
2 **teaspoons red wine vinegar**
1 **teaspoon Dijon style mustard**
1 **teaspoon white horseradish**
1 **teaspoon soy sauce**

Bring all ingredients to a boil. Pour over the corned beef and bake at 325° for about 15 minutes.

Mrs. W. F. D'Olive, Jr.

Indoor Barbecue Beef

Serves 8

5-6 **pounds chuck roast**
Liquid Smoke
Lea and Perrins
Salt and pepper
Onion salt
Garlic salt
Celery salt
Lawry's Seasoned Salt
1 **bottle barbecue sauce**

Rub roast with Liquid Smoke and Lea and Perrins. Season with salt, pepper, onion salt, garlic salt, celery salt, and Lawry's Seasoned Salt. Cover tightly. Let stand at least 8 hours. The next day season again and cook covered at 300° for one hour per pound. Uncover and drain off all liquid the last hour of cooking and pour a bottle of barbecue sauce over the meat.

Mrs. Edward Russell March, Jr.

Beef and Eggplant

Serves 6

1   eggplant
1½ pounds ground beef
    (chuck or tender beef
    tips)
1/2 cup onion, sliced
1   cup tomatoes, canned
1/2 cup pecans (optional)
1   cup seedless raisins
    (or canned white
    grapes)
    Salt
    Pepper
    Ripe olives
    Olive juice
    Olive oil
    Médoc wine
3   cups steamed rice
    (plain or herbed rice)

Peel and slice eggplant into 1/2" slices; sautée in olive oil. Brown ground chuck (or tender beef tips); add onions, tomatoes, raisins (or grapes) and nuts. Bring to a boil. Add the ripe olive juice. In a Dutch oven, alternate layers of the meat mixture and eggplant and rice, ending with a layer of meat mixture. Bake for approximately 10 minutes in a preheated 350° oven. Splash the top with Médoc wine. Serve on white rice or herb rice and garnish with Spanish or ripe green olives. If too dry, make a moisturizer of consommé, butter and flour plus Médoc wine to add lightly over the top.

Mrs. Emmett B. Frazer

Kitty's Dutch Meat Loaf

Serves 6

1   pound ground beef
1   onion, chopped
1/2 can bread crumbs
1   egg
1½ teaspoons salt
1½ teaspoons pepper
2   tablespoons brown
    sugar
2   tablespoons mustard
1   cup water
2   tablespoons vinegar

Mix first six ingredients. Shape into loaf and place in a baking pan. Combine last four ingredients and use as sauce to baste meat loaf while cooking. Bake at 350° for one hour. A delicious family-style recipe.

Mrs. John P. Case, Jr.

Company or Family Cabbage Rolls

Serves 6-8

1 head cabbage
1 cup water
2 pounds ground chuck
1/3 cup quick rice
2 eggs
1 small onion, chopped
1/2 teaspoon salt
1 (6 ounce) can tomato paste

SAUCE:
1/2 cup vinegar
3/4 cup brown sugar
1 (8 ounce) can tomato sauce

Boil the whole cabbage in water just until the leaves are soft. Drain and cool. Separate each leaf and carefully remove the tough center rib without splitting the leaf in half. Combine the next 6 ingredients and place a ball of the mixture on one side of each leaf and roll to enclose. Shred the remaining cabbage and place in the bottom of a 2 quart casserole dish. Place the rolls on top. Combine the remaining 3 ingredients and pour over the rolls. Bake at 325 degrees for 3 to 4 hours. This can be made a day or two ahead and refrigerated before baking.

Mrs. Jeff Pettiss. Jr.

Stuffed Peppers

Serves 4-6

4 large green peppers
1/2 cup rice, cooked
2 cups ham, diced or 2 cups ground beef, cooked and drained
2 tablespoons onion, minced
2 tablespoons celery, finely chopped
1/4 teaspoon dry mustard
1/4 teaspoon garlic salt
1/4 teaspoon pepper
1½ cups tomato juice
1/4 pound sharp cheese, sliced

Wash peppers and remove stems and seeds. Cut in half lengthwise. Drop in boiling salted water and simmer for 5 minutes. Remove, drain and reserve. If ham is used, sauté in 1/4 cup butter or margarine for 5 minutes. Combine rice with meat, onion, celery, mustard, salt and pepper. Stuff the reserved peppers with this mixture and place in a 2 quart shallow baking dish. Pour the tomato juice around the peppers and place a slice of cheese on top of each pepper. Bake at 350° for 20 minutes.

Connie Bea Hope

119

Lasagne

Serves 8-10

1 (9 ounce) package
   lasagne noodles
1 tablespoon olive oil
1 pound cottage cheese
1/2 cup Parmesan cheese
   or Romano cheese,
   grated
2 tablespoons dried
   parsley
1½ pounds ground beef
1/4 cup olive oil
1 teaspoon orégano
1/2 teaspoon salt
1 teaspoon basil
1 teaspoon dried
   parsley
1 medium onion,
   chopped
1 garlic clove, minced
1 (15½ ounce) jar meat-
   flavored spaghetti
   sauce
1 cup water
8 ounces Mozzarella
   cheese, sliced

Cook noodles in 2 quarts of rapidly boiling water with 1 tablespoon olive oil until tender (about 20 minutes). Drain, rinse with cold water and set aside. Mix the cottage cheese, Parmesan cheese, and parsley and set aside. Brown the meat in 1/4 cup olive oil. Drain in a colander, then return to the skillet. Add the seasonings, spaghetti sauce and water. Simmer for 30 minutes. To assemble: Place half of the noodles in a greased 13 x 9 x 2 inch pan. Spread half of the cheese mixture over noodles, then half of the meat mixture, finally half of the Mozzarella cheese. Repeat layers. Bake at 300° for 30 minutes. Freezes well.

Mrs. John Wilson

Enchiladas and Sauce

Serves 4-6

12   tortillas
      Oil
1   pound ground beef
1/2 clove garlic, minced
1   teaspoon salt
1/8 teaspoon pepper
1   large onion, chopped
1/2 cup ripe olives,
      chopped
3/4 pound mild Cheddar
      cheese, shredded

Brown the tortillas on both sides in oil and drain. Do not let them become crisp. Brown the beef with the garlic, salt and pepper. On each tortilla, place 2 tablespoons beef, 2 teaspoons chopped onion, 2 teaspoons ripe olives, and 1½ tablespoons cheese. Roll the tortillas tightly. Pour 1 cup of the enchilada sauce in a greased 15 x 10 x 1½ inch pan. Place the rolled tortillas, folded side down in the sauce. Spoon the remaining sauce on the tortillas and sprinkle with the rest of the cheese. Cover and bake at 350° for 20 minutes.

SAUCE:
1   medium onion,
      chopped
3   tablespoons butter
1/2 green pepper,
      chopped
2   (8 ounce) cans tomato
      sauce
1   cup water
1   teaspoon Tabasco
1   tablespoon chili
      powder

Sauté the onion in butter until brown. Add the green pepper and cook for a minute longer. Stir in the remaining ingredients. Simmer over low heat for 30 minutes. Enchiladas may be prepared and frozen ahead. Thaw before baking.

Mrs. Marvin Ussery

Mexi-Casserole

1½ pounds ground beef
1   package taco
    seasoning mix
    (reserve one teaspoon
    for topping)
1   (10¾ ounce) can
    condensed tomato
    soup
1   (15 ounce) can chili
    or kidney beans

TOPPING:
1   cup complete
    pancake mix (Hungry
    Jack Buttermilk is
    good)
1   teaspoon reserved
    taco mix
1   cup Cheddar or
    American cheese,
    shredded
1/2 cup milk
1   egg
1   teaspoon parsley
    flakes, if desired

Yield: 8 1-cup servings
Preheat oven to 400°. Brown ground beef; drain. Stir in seasoning mix, soup and beans. Simmer while preparing topping. Combine all topping ingredients except parsley and blend well. Pour meat mixture into a shallow 3 quart casserole dish or 13 x 9 inch pan. Spoon topping over meat and sprinkle with parsley. Bake, uncovered, for 15-25 minutes until golden brown.

Mrs. Kerwin Andrews

Barbecued Spareribs

1½ pounds lean
    spareribs per adult
    Salt
    Cavender's Greek
    seasoning
    Coarsely ground
    black pepper

Salt ribs heavily and sprinkle them liberally with Cavender's and pepper. Place ribs on a "water smoker" with about 3 large handfuls of hickory chips that have been soaked in water. Cook for about 3 hours. Remove pan of water and continue to cook ribs over direct heat, basting often with a mixture of 1/2 water and 1/2 vinegar. Ribs are done when meat pulls back about 1/2" from the end of the bones. Remove from grill *before* applying barbecue sauce. Slice ribs from rack and dip each rib into large saucepan of barbecue sauce. Serve while still very hot and provide bowls of extra sauce. Note: In order to get more ribs on the grill either use a rib rack or curl the ribs around and stand them on end.

BARBECUE SAUCE:

28 ounce bottle regular
    Kraft barbecue sauce
8 ounces apple cider
    vinegar
8 ounces water
1 large white onion,
    diced
    Peel of 1/2 lemon,
    minced
3 stalks celery, minced
2 cloves garlic, minced
3/4 cup brown sugar
1/2 cup Worcestershire
    sauce
    Salt and pepper
1 tablespoon mustard
    seed

Combine ingredients in a covered pot and bring to a slow boil. Simmer for 1 hour, adding water when necessary to keep sauce thin. Salt and pepper to taste.

H. E. Myers, Jr.

Curried Lamb Chops
with Stuffed Mushrooms

Serves 4-6

8	lamb chops, boned
1/4	cup butter
1	tablespoon curry powder
20	mushrooms
1	pound bulk sausage
1	small onion, minced
2/3	cup bread crumbs
2	tablespoons water chestnuts
	Thyme, salt and pepper to taste
	Canned chicken broth

Brush lamb chops with butter and curry. Broil for 8 minutes on each side. Set oven at 350° and bake chops for 20 minutes. Wipe mushrooms with damp cloth. Snap off stems. Mince stems. Sauté sausage. Drain all but 3 tablespoons of fat from pan. Add stems and finely minced onion. Stir in bread crumbs, sausage, and water chestnuts. Season with thyme, salt, and pepper. Stuff mushrooms. Place in a shallow casserole, pour on a little canned chicken broth and bake for 20 to 30 minutes. Serve with the lamb chops.

Mrs. Newland Knight

Barbecued Leg of Lamb

Serves 6

2	cups red wine (dry)
2	teaspoons poultry seasoning
2	teaspoons salt
3	cloves garlic, minced
1	leg of lamb, boned and butterflied (spread out flat)

Combine wine with seasonings; pour over lamb in glass or porcelain dish. Marinate 12 to 24 hours, turn once or twice. Barbecue over hot coals, skin side up, for 30 minutes. Turn and cook 30 minutes more. Baste often with marinade while cooking. Slice across the grain to serve and spoon on a little heated marinade. Serve with an eggplant or squash casserole, fresh steamed asparagus in lemon butter, and a salad.

Mrs. Clifton C. Inge

Gourmet Leg of Lamb

Serves 6

1   **(6 pound) leg of lamb**
2   **garlic cloves, crushed**
1/2   **teaspoon salt**
1/2   **teaspoon pepper**
2   **tablespoons vegetable oil**
1   **tablespoon dried rosemary leaves**
2   **tablespoons bacon fat**

Combine in a cheese cloth bag:
1/2   **cup onion, chopped**
1/4   **cup celery, chopped**
1/2   **cup ham or bacon, diced**
2   **small carrots, coarsely chopped**
1   **sprig fresh thyme**
1   **bay leaf**

Preheat oven to 325° Rub the lamb with garlic; season with salt and pepper, brush with oil and sprinkle with rosemary leaves. Melt the bacon fat in a roasting pan in the oven. Remove the pan from the oven and roll the lamb in the hot fat coating it evenly. Roast at 325° for 25 minutes on each side, basting often with the pan juices. Add the cheesecloth bag to pan juices. Roast uncovered for another 30 minutes. When done remove the lamb to a platter; allow to set for 15 minutes before carving.

GRAVY:
1/2   **cup dry red wine**
1/2   **cup brown stock**
1   **tablespoon cornstarch combined with 1 teaspoon water**

Drain the fat from the roasting pan and pour the drippings into a saucepan. Add the wine and brown stock and simmer for 15 minutes. Strain and return the gravy to a saucepan. Bring to a boil and stir in the cornstarch-water mixture. Bring to a boil and season with salt and pepper.

Mrs. Larry Harless

Leg of Lamb With Artichoke Hearts & Scallions

Serves 6

Leg of lamb
Several cloves of
fresh garlic
1 jar marinated
artichoke hearts
1 small bunch scallions
or green onions
Salt
Pepper

Take the leg of lamb, slit the skin in several places, and insert a part of a crushed, peeled clove of garlic between the skin and the meat. Rub the leg of lamb with salt and pepper to taste. Insert meat thermometer and roast in 325° oven uncovered until almost done. Slice the marinated artichoke hearts thinly, do the same with the scallions (including much of the green part). Sauté the scallions and the artichokes in the marinade oil until limp. Garnish the leg of lamb with the mixture and return to the oven to cook for the remaining time.

Mrs. Henry R. Seawell, III

Spareribs on the Grill

Serves 4-6

1/2 cup Cointreau
1/2 cup soy sauce
1/2 cup honey
1 cup crushed
pineapple
1/2 cup wine vinegar
1 lemon, sliced
2 teaspoons ground
ginger
2 garlic cloves, minced
5 pounds spareribs

Combine first eight ingredients. Marinate ribs at room temperature for 1 to 2 hours. Remove lemon slices. Place ribs over medium fire and grill for 20 to 30 minutes on each side, basting frequently with marinade.

Mrs. Wallace G. Jeffrey, Jr.

Marinated Pork Roast

Serves 10-12

1	(4-5 pound) pork loin roast, boned, rolled and tied

MARINADE:

1/2	cup soy sauce
1/2	cup dry Sherry
2	cloves garlic, minced
1	tablespoon dry mustard
1	teaspoon ginger
1	teaspoon thyme, crushed

Combine marinade ingredients. Place roast in a large, clear plastic bag; set in a deep bowl or pan to steady the roast. Pour marinade over the roast and close the bag tightly. Let stand 3-4 hours at room temperature or overnight in the refrigerator. Remove roast from marinade and place on a rack in a shallow roasting pan. Roast, uncovered, in a slow oven, 325°, for 2½ to 3 hours, or until meat thermometer registers 175°. Baste occasionally with marinade during the last hour of roasting time. Leftover marinade may be spooned over slices of pork when serving.

Mrs. J. B. Blackburn

Island Ribs

Serves 4-6

4	pounds country style pork ribs
	Salt
	Pepper
1	(16 ounce) can peaches, puréed
1/2	cup chili sauce or catsup
1/2	cup cider vinegar
3	tablespoons soy sauce
1/4	cup brown sugar, firmly packed
3	cloves garlic, crushed
1	tablespoon ground ginger
3	cups hot cooked rice

Rub ribs on all sides with salt and pepper. Place ribs in large baking pan and bake at 450° for 20 mintes. Spoon off excess fat. Blend remaining ingredients except rice and pour over ribs. Cover and reduce oven to 350°. Bake 1½ hours or until tender. Remove cover 20 minutes before ribs are done so meat can brown. Baste with sauce several times while browning. Serve ribs and sauce with hot cooked rice.

Mrs. Edward J. Neville

Low-Calorie Spinach Lasagne

Serves 6

1   pound lean ground beef
1   onion, chopped
1   (16 ounce) can tomato pureé
      Garlic salt
      Ground orégano
      Basil
      Salt
      Pepper
1   (6 ounce) package lasagne noodles
2   (10 ounce) packages chopped spinach, thawed
1½   cups low-fat cottage cheese
1   egg, slightly beaten
      Parmesan cheese for top

Brown meat and onion and remove all fat. Add tomatoes and season to taste. Heat to boiling, reduce heat and simmer for 5 minutes. Cook noodles as package directs and drain. Mix spinach, cheese and egg. Spray a 1½ quart oblong casserole dish with Pam. Layer spinach, noodles, sauce, and sprinkle Parmesan cheese on top. Cover with foil and bake at 350° for 40-45 minutes until bubbly. About 300 calories per serving.

Mrs. John N. Horner

Marinated Pork Tenders on the Grill

Serves 12

1/2   cup soy sauce
1/2   cup dry Sherry
2   cloves garlic
1   tablespoon dry mustard
1   teaspoon thyme
1   teaspoon ginger
5   pounds pork tenders

About 24 hours ahead, mix together all marinade ingredients. Put tenders in a large plastic bag and pour marinade over them. Close bag and put in refrigerator overnight. Shift the meat in the marinade from time to time. When the fire is ready, remove meat from marinade. Cook on grill for about an hour, depending on size of tenders. Baste with marinade while cooking.

Mac Otts, III

Pork Chops Braised in White Wine

Serves 4

4	center-cut loin pork chops, about one inch thick
1	teaspoon dried sage leaves, crumbled
1	teaspoon dried rosemary leaves, crumbled
1	teaspoon garlic, finely chopped
1	teaspoon salt Freshly ground black pepper
2	tablespoons butter
1	tablespoon olive oil
3/4	cup dry white wine or Vermouth
1	tablespoon fresh parsley, finely chopped

Combine sage, rosemary, garlic, salt and a few grinds of pepper and press a little of this mixture firmly into both sides of each pork chop. In a heavy 10 to 12 inch skillet, melt the butter with the olive oil over moderate heat. When the foam subsides, place the chops in the hot fat and brown them for 2 or 3 minutes on each side, turning them carefully with tongs. When the chops are golden brown, remove them from the pan to a platter. Pour off all but a thin film of fat from the pan, add 1/2 cup of the wine and bring it to a boil. Return the chops to the pan, cover and reduce the heat to the barest simmer. Basting with the pan juices occasionally, cook the chops for 25 to 30 minutes, or until they are tender when pierced with the tip of a sharp knife. Transfer the chops to a heated serving platter and pour into the skillet the remaining 1/4 cup of wine. Boil it briskly over high heat, stirring and scraping in any browned bits that cling to the bottom and sides of the pan, until it has reduced to a few tablespoons of syrupy glaze. Remove the skillet from the heat, taste for seasoning and stir in the parsley. Pour sauce over the pork chops and serve.

Mrs. J. B. Blackburn

Mary Miller's Sweet and Sour Pork Tenderloins

Serves 6-8

1 tablespoon Worcestershire sauce
1 jar orange marmalade or apricot preserves
1 pint jar Good Seasoning barbecue sauce, plain
1 white onion, chopped
2/3 cup soy sauce
1 cup white wine, Vermouth preferred
Salt
Pepper
3 pork tenderloins

Blend first 6 ingredients together. Salt and pepper the tenderloins. Marinate overnight in the sauce, turn once in sauce. Have barbecue fire very hot. Take the tenderloins out of sauce and place over fire for 30 minutes. Put back in sauce and cook for 2 hours in a 350° oven. Slice meat and put back in sauce. Good served for cocktail party on small hamburger-like buns. Delicious served for dinner with rice.

Mrs. Thomas G. Greaves, Jr.

Smothered Pork Chops

Serves 6

6 1-inch pork chops, center cut
1 teaspoon salt
1/4 teaspoon pepper
1/2 cup pancake mix, dry
Wesson oil
3 onions, sliced

GRAVY:
1 teaspoon salt
1/4 teaspoon pepper
1 tablespoon sugar
1/4 cup flour
2 cups boiling water

Season chops with salt and pepper, coat with pancake mix. Brown in oil and place in small covered roasting pan. Sauté onions in same fat (maybe need a bit more) along with salt, pepper, and sugar until light brown. Stir in flour. Cook and stir carefully for a minute, then add boiling water. Pour over pork chops. Cover and bake at 350° for 1 hour and 20 minutes. Skim fat and serve. Good winter supper with rice, turnip greens, and hot biscuits.

Mrs. Wade Faulkner

Ham Slice with Wine and Grapes

Serves 4

1	slice of ham at least 1 inch thick
1	tablespoon butter
1	tablespoon sugar
3/4	cup Burgundy or Rosé wine
1	tablespoon cornstarch
1/4	cup cold water
1	cup canned, drained, seedless green grapes

Melt butter in skillet. Sprinkle in sugar. Brown ham quickly on both sides. Remove ham. Add wine to skillet and bring to boil, stirring constantly. Combine cornstarch and water—add to wine mixture. Cook and stir until thick and boiling. Lower heat, add ham, cover and simmer for 15 minutes. Add grapes and cook a couple of minutes longer. Serve sauce over ham cut into portions for 4.

Mrs. Thomas O. Gaillard, Jr.

Ham Casserole

Serves 2 or 3

1½	cups ham, cut in chunks
1	(8½ ounce) can artichoke hearts, halved
2	tablespoons butter
2	tablespoons flour
1	scant cup milk
1/3	cup sour cream
1/4	cup ripe olives, sliced
1/2	clove garlic, pressed or grated
1/2	cup buttered bread crumbs
1/4	cup Parmesan cheese, grated

Put ham and artichoke hearts in a greased shallow casserole dish. Make a cream sauce with the butter, flour and milk. When the sauce has thickened, add sour cream, garlic and olives. Pour the sauce over the ham and artichoke hearts. Top with bread crumbs and cheese. Bake at 400° for 20 minutes. This is a rich casserole but great when you are tired of ham sandwiches and still have more leftover ham. Good with green salad with a tart dressing and baked tomatoes.

Mrs. Thomas O. Gaillard, Jr.

Cassoulet

1   pound Great
     Northern Beans
2   quarts water
1/4   pound salt pork,
     diced
1½   tablespoons salt
1   onion, studded with 6
     whole cloves
1   carrot, diced
1/2   teaspoon thyme
1½   pounds pork, cut into
     3/4" cubes
1/4   cup oil
1   cup onion, chopped
2   cloves of garlic,
     minced
2   pounds cooked meat,
     may use venison,
     lamb, duck, geese or
     dove
1   Polish sausage, cut
     into 1" cubes
     Salt
     Pepper
1   cup tomato juice
1/2   cup white wine
1   cup coarse bread
     crumbs
3   tablespoons butter,
     melted

This is a simplified version of a famous country French Casserole. The basic ingredients are white beans, garlic, cooked meats and link sausages. Combinations of venison, pork, lamb, duck, geese and dove are endless, but always use link sausages, such as Polish. This is a good way to use your wild game. Soak beans in the water overnight. (For quick soak, bring beans and water to a boil and boil 2 minutes; then cover and let stand 1 hour.) To the beans and soaking water add salt pork, salt, clove-studded onion, carrot and thyme. Cover and simmer until the beans are tender, about one hour. Meanwhile, brown the pork cubes in oil. Remove and drain. Sauté onion and garlic in the remaining drippings. Drain the beans, reserving liquid. Add the beans to sautéed onion and garlic. To assemble cassoulet, arrange alternating layers of beans, pork, meats and sausages in a heavy earthenware casserole dish, sprinkling each layer with salt and pepper. Add tomato juice, white wine and 1 cup of the reserved bean liquid. Combine the crumbs and melted butter. Sprinkle over the cassoulet. Cover and bake at 350° for 30 minutes. Remove cover and bake 30 minutes longer or until the top is browned. It is better if made ahead; this freezes well.

NOTE: For individual cassoulets, reduce baking time to 20 minutes, covered, and 20 minutes after removing cover. Accompanied by a crisp green salad, crusty French bread and a hearty red wine, this meal is great for a crowd.

Mrs. Kenneth Hannon

Veal Marsala

Serves 2

16	ounces milk fed veal, very thinly sliced
3	ounces pure butter
6	ounces fresh mushrooms, sliced
	Salt and pepper to taste
4	ounces Marsala

Sauté veal in butter. Remove from cooking utensil and keep warm. In same butter sauté mushrooms. Return veal to mushrooms and butter, add salt and pepper to taste and pour on the Marsala. Simmer for 8 to 10 minutes. Serve with wild rice and fresh broccoli or asparagus.

Filippo Milone
The Pillars

Veal Scallops Amandine

Serves 6

6	veal scallops (6 ounces each)
	Salt and pepper to taste
2½	cups stale bread crumbs
1½	cups almonds, blanched and sliced and lightly toasted (two 2¾ ounce packages)
1/3	cup parsley, minced
3	tablespoons lemon rind
3	egg whites
	Oil and butter for frying
	Lemon wedges for garnish
	Parsley sprigs for garnish

Flatten veal scallops between sheets of waxed paper until they are 1/4" thick. Season. Combine all other ingredients except egg whites, butter and oil in a shallow bowl. In another shallow bowl lightly beat egg whites. Dip scallops into egg whites, then into crumb mixture, pressing the mixture into the scallops. Chill 30 minutes on a baking sheet. Sauté the scallops in a large skillet in oil and butter for 1-2 minutes on each side, until just cooked and golden brown. Arrange on a platter with lemon wedges and parsley. Note: any leftovers may be broiled a few minutes. This heats veal and crisps the crumbs and almonds.

Mrs. Wade Faulkner

Ham and Broccoli Casserole

Serves 8-10

Slices of baked ham to cover a buttered 13x9" dish
4 packages frozen broccoli spears, cooked and drained
4 tablespoons butter
4½ tablespoons flour
3 cups hot milk
Nutmeg, salt and pepper to taste
1/2 pound Mozzarella cheese slices, divided
Buttered bread crumbs
Toasted almonds

Line the buttered casserole dish with the ham slices. Cover ham with broccoli. Make a white sauce by melting butter, adding flour and cooking 2 minutes, whisking constantly. Add milk all at once and stir until bubbly. Remove from heat and add seasonings and 1/3 of the cheese. Cheese may be cut into small pieces for this step. Pour sauce over broccoli. Top with remaining 2/3 of the cheese slices, bread crumbs and almonds. Bake at 350° for 40 minutes.

Mrs. Wade Faulkner

Roast Veal

Serves 12

4 pounds veal
Salt
Pepper
1/4 cup flour
Bacon strips, optional
1/4 cup celery, chopped
1/4 cup onion, chopped
1/2 stick margarine (1/4 cup)
Water

Wipe the meat; dredge with salt, pepper, and flour. Place on the rack of a roasting pan with fat side up. If a meat thermometer is used, insert it into thickest part of meat. If the cut has no fat, or if layer is thin, place strips of bacon over the top (optional). Place in a slow oven (300°) and cook uncovered until tender, 30 to 35 minutes to a pound. Baste every 15 minutes, with drippings, to which chopped celery, chopped onions, margarine, and water may be added to make gravy. Interior when done is 170°. Allow about 1/3 pound per serving.

Mrs. Marion R. Vickers

POULTRY&GAME

Chicken Crêpes Mornay

Serves 8

CRÊPES:
1 cup flour
1/8 teaspoon salt
3 eggs
1½ cups milk
    Melted butter or
    peanut oil

Beat flour, salt and eggs to form a thick paste. Slowly stir in milk and beat smooth. Let stand 1 hour. Make 18 crêpes in a 7" pan. Stack between pieces of waxed paper. Freeze 8 crêpes for another use.

FILLING AND SAUCE:
8 tablespoons butter, divided
1/4 pound mushrooms, chopped
6 green onions, chopped
2 tablespoons parsley, chopped
2 cups cooked chicken or turkey, chopped
1½ teaspoons salt, divided
4 tablespoons flour
2 cups milk
1/4 teaspoon pepper
1/2 cup Swiss cheese, grated
1/3 cup Parmesan cheese, grated
3/4 cup cream
2 tablespoons melted butter
1/3 cup seasoned breadcrumbs

Sauté mushrooms, onions and parsley in 4 tablespoons butter until tender. Add chicken and 3/4 teaspoon salt. Set aside. Melt remaining 4 tablespoons butter over medium heat. Stir in flour until smooth. Slowly pour in milk and cook until it boils and thickens. Add 3/4 teaspoon salt and pepper. Add cheeses and stir to melt. Add 1 cup sauce to chicken mixture. Stir cream into remaining cheese sauce. Fill crêpes and place in greased 8" x 11" dish. Pour sauce over crêpes. Mix together butter and breadcrumbs. Sprinkle over crêpes and bake at 350° for 20-30 minutes. A special dish. Freezes well.

Mrs. John Megginson

Chicken Pie with Cheese Crust

Serves 4

3-4	pound stewing chicken
4	sprigs parsley
1	stalk of celery in hunks
1	bay leaf
1	onion, peeled and stuck with 2 cloves
	Water
3	carrots, sliced
12	small white onions, peeled
1	can petite peas, drained
2	tablespoons butter
3	tablespoons flour
2	cups stock from chicken
1/2	cup cream
	Salt and pepper

CHEESE PASTRY:

1/2	stick butter, softened
2	cups Cheddar cheese, grated
1½	cups flour, sifted with 1/4 teaspoon each of baking powder and dry mustard

Place the chicken, parsley, celery, bay leaf and onion in a pot with water to barely cover. Bring to boil and simmer until tender. Let cool and then drain and reserve broth, and cut chicken into bite size pieces. Cook carrots and onions separately in salted water until tender. Drain thoroughly. In a saucepan, melt the butter, stir in flour and cook for 2 minutes. Add to this reserved stock and cream. Add salt and pepper to taste. Cook until thickened. Combine chicken, vegetables, and sauce in deep glass pie dish or casserole dish. In a food processor, combine butter and cheese and process until creamy. Add flour with mustard and baking powder. Process until dough forms a ball. Chill. Roll out pastry 1/4 inch thick and prick well with a fork. Cover dish with pastry and press well around the edges. Bake at 425° for 10 minutes. Lower heat to 350° and bake for 25 minutes longer.

Mrs. Thomas O. Gaillard, Jr.

Kotopits (Chicken in Phyllo)

Serves 4

4 ounces frozen phyllo (6-7 sheets)
1 cup celery, chopped
3/4 cup onion, chopped
1 tablespoon butter
2 cups cooked poultry, chopped
2 tablespoons chicken broth
2 teaspoons dried parsley
1/2 teaspoon salt
1/2 teaspoon nutmeg
1/8 teaspoon pepper
1 egg, beaten
4-5 tablespoons butter, melted

Thaw phyllo. In a covered skillet, cook the celery and onion in 1 tablespoon butter until tender but not brown, stirring occasionally. Add the chicken and broth. Cook and stir uncovered until all broth is absorbed. Stir in parsley, salt, nutmeg and pepper. Remove from heat. Stir in beaten egg. Set aside. For phyllo roll: stack phyllo, brushing each sheet liberally with melted butter. Spoon chicken mixture over phyllo to within one inch of the edges. Turn one short side over filling about one inch. Fold in long sides. Roll as for a jelly roll, starting with folded short side. Place seam side down in a lightly greased shallow baking pan. Brush with additional melted butter. Score in 6-8 portions. Bake 40 minutes at 350° until brown and crisp. Cut where scored. Arrange on a platter with hot rice. Spoon some Béchamel sauce over rolls. Pass remaining sauce. Serves 4 nicely for luncheon; 2 rolls would be needed to serve 4-6 for dinner.

BÉCHAMEL SAUCE:
2 tablespoons butter
2 tablespoons flour
2 egg yolks, beaten
1/4 teaspoon salt
1¼ cups chicken broth
4 teaspoons lemon juice

Melt the butter. Stir in flour and salt. Add broth. Cook and stir until bubbly. Combine the rest of the ingredients and stir in about half of the heated mixture. Return the rest to the pan. Cook and stir for about 2 minutes. Makes 1½ cups of sauce.

Mrs. Hugh M. Doherty

Chicken Crêpes

Serves 4-5

1/4 cup celery, chopped
2   tablespoons butter
1½   cups cooked chicken, diced
1/4 cup walnuts, chopped
1/2 teaspoon salt
1/2 cup mayonnaise
1/2 cup sour cream
2   tablespoons Sherry
1/4 cup toasted almonds

Sauté celery in butter. Add celery to mixture of chicken, walnuts, and salt. Gently toss with 1/4 cup mayonnaise. Spoon on to crêpe and place in buttered casserole. Mix 1/4 cup mayonnaise, sour cream and Sherry. Spoon sauce over crêpes and bake at 350° for 20 minutes. Sprinkle with almonds.

Mrs. E. Bailey Slaton

Chicken Special

Serves 4

4   boneless chicken breasts
     Salt, seasoned pepper
     Flour
3   tablespoons oil
2   stalks celery, finely chopped or processed
2   cloves garlic, finely chopped or processed
1/2 medium onion, finely chopped or processed
1/2 pound fresh mushrooms, sliced, or 1 small can sliced mushrooms
1   (16 ounce) can tomatoes
1/4 cup Chablis or Sauterne

Season chicken with salt and seasoned pepper. Dredge in flour, then brown in oil. (A bit more oil may be necessary.) Remove chicken from skillet, and in the same utensil sauté all the vegetables until they begin to brown. Add tomatoes, mushrooms, and chicken breasts. Cover and simmer slowly for 1 hour. Add wine and continue cooking 30 minutes longer.

Mrs. H. Eldon Scott, III

Chicken and Bourbon

Serves 6

6	boned chicken breasts, floured
1/4	cup margarine
1	tablespoon olive oil
1/4	cup scallions, chopped
1/4	cup Bourbon or more, to taste
1	cup heavy cream
1	cup mushroom caps, sautéed

Flour, salt and pepper chicken breasts. In skillet, sauté onions in oil and margarine; add chicken and brown lightly on each side. Remove chicken. Add cream and Bourbon and stir until smooth. Place chicken in gravy and cover with sautéed mushrooms. Cover and place in a 325° oven. Cook until done. Serve over rice.

Mrs. Richard O'Neill

Chicken Harpin

Serves 4

4	half chicken breasts, cooked and boned
2	(3 ounce) cans sliced ripe olives
4	tablespoons butter or margarine
1/2	pound mushrooms, sliced
4	tablespoons flour
1/2	teaspoon salt
	Dash of pepper
	Pinch of mace
1	can chicken broth
1/2	cup heavy cream
2	slices toast, quartered in triangles
	Paprika

Place chicken pieces in a shallow baking dish and sprinkle sliced olives over them. Sauté the mushrooms in butter for 10 minutes. Remove from heat and blend in flour, salt, pepper and mace. Cook, stirring constantly for 2 minutes. Add hot chicken broth and cook, stirring, until thickened. Gradually add cream and cook until hot. Pour sauce over the chicken. Sauté the toast triangles in butter until golden. Arrange over chicken breasts and sprinkle with paprika. Bake at 325° for 45 minutes.

Mrs. Thomas Gaillard, Jr.

Chicken au Cognac

Serves 4

2 medium onions, sliced
1/2 cup butter
4 chicken breasts
Salt and pepper
1 cup heavy cream
3 ounces Cognac

Brown onions in the butter until soft. Add chicken and cook over medium heat for 35 minutes, covered, or until chicken is tender. Just before serving, remove chicken and keep warm. Add cream and Cognac to pan, boil about 1 minute, and pour over chicken. This sauce may be thickened with 1 teaspoon cornstarch mixed with 1 tablespoon water, if desired. Also, canned tangerines are a nice addition.

Mrs. Clifton C. Inge

Chicken Kiev

Serves 8

1/2 pound butter, softened
1 tablespoon chives, chopped
4 whole chicken breasts, split, pounded lightly
Salt
Lemon pepper
1/3 cup fine dry breadcrumbs
1/3 cup Parmesan cheese, grated
1 can (10¾ ounce) chicken gravy
1/4 cup melted butter
1 tablespoon lemon juice

Combine softened butter and chives. Form eight butter balls and freeze. Salt and pepper the pounded chicken breasts. Place ball of butter in center of each breast and roll up, tuck in ends and fasten with skewer or tooth picks. Combine breadcrumbs and cheese. Roll chicken in 1/3 cup gravy, then in crumb mixture. Place in baking dish. Pour 1/4 cup melted butter over all. Bake at 450° for 25 minutes. Combine remaining gravy and lemon juice and serve with the breasts.

Mrs. Percy Perkins, Jr.

Cheese-Fried Chicken

Serves 4

2	whole, boneless chicken breasts, halved
4	pieces Monterey Jack cheese (1/4 x 1¼ x 3")
2	eggs
2	tablespoons Parmesan cheese, grated
1/4	teaspoon salt
1/4	teaspoon pepper
1	tablespoon parsley, minced
	Flour
	Oil

Cut a pocket in each half of chicken breast by holding knife parallel to breast and making a 2" slit in side. Do not cut all the way through the chicken. Place a piece of cheese in the slit, and secure cut edge with toothpick. Chill. Beat together eggs, Parmesan cheese, salt, pepper and parsley. Dredge breasts in flour, dip in egg mixture, then dredge in flour again. Heat oil in skillet. Sauté breasts in oil just until crisp and golden. (At this point you may refrigerate and finish just before serving.) Put chicken in baking dish and bake at 375° for 10-12 minutes, or until coating begins to brown. Garnish with parsley and lemon slices and serve. Easy — especially good for children.

Mrs. Winston Patterson

Pete's Chicken

Serves 4

4	chicken breasts (skinned and deboned)
	Salt
	Pepper
1/2	stick butter (1/4 cup)
1	can cream of chicken soup
1/2	cup beer
1	tablespoon soy sauce
1	(4 ounce) can mushrooms

Season chicken with salt and pepper. Brown in butter and place in glass baking dish. Mix remaining ingredients over burner until smooth. Pour over chicken and bake at 350° for 1 hour. Great served with hot, fluffy rice. Quick, easy and very good.

Mrs. Edward Fields, Jr.

Chicken Oscar

Serves 8

4	whole chicken breasts, skinned, boned and split to make 8 pieces
	Salt
	Flour
2	eggs, beaten
	Oil
16	asparagus spears
1	pound lump crabmeat
	Hollandaise sauce
	Fried potatoes

Pound chicken to 1/4" thickness. Dip in lightly seasoned flour, then into beaten eggs. Sauté lightly in oil. Lay chicken in baking pan. Put an asparagus spear on either side of chicken. Divide crabmeat into 8 portions and place atop each piece of chicken. Spoon Hollandaise sauce over crabmeat and place in a 400° oven for about 5-10 minutes. Broil briefly to brown, watching constantly. To serve, garnish with fried potatoes.

Bienville Club

Chris Perry's Chicken Recipe

Serves 4

4	chicken breasts, boiled and shredded
1	(8 ounce) package cream cheese
1/2	or 3/4 jar (2 ounce) diced pimentos, chopped extra fine
1	stick of butter (1/2 cup), melted and divided
8	refrigerated crescent rolls
	Garlic powder

Mix cream cheese and pimentos in a bowl with chicken pieces; pour 1/4 of melted butter into bowl and shred with hands until chicken mixture is of fine consistency. Divide into 4 parts and pat into 4 balls. Next, join 2 crescent rolls together by pinching perforations and roll into a square. This will make the dough for one portion. Put one of the chicken ball mixtures in the middle and drape dough over the top. Do this for all four. Put on greased cookie sheet and pour remaining butter over each. Sprinkle with garlic powder. Bake in preheated 350° oven for 20-25 minutes until golden brown. May be made in smaller balls.

Mrs. G. Russell Hollinger, Jr.

144

Chicken Breasts and Ham

Serves 4

1	cup butter
4	green onions
1	rib celery
4	deboned chicken breasts
4	small slices ham (to fit inside chicken breasts)
1/2	pint sour cream
	Progresso bread crumbs
1	can cream of chicken soup
	Mozzarella cheese

Sauté onion and celery in butter. Stuff chicken breasts with the above and ham slices. Roll chicken breasts in breadcrumbs. Mix sour cream and chicken soup and pour over chicken. Sprinkle breadcrumbs on top. Bake at 350° for 30 minutes covered and 15 minutes uncovered for a total of 45 minutes. You'll have gravy for rice, which would be good to serve with this dish. (A small amount of cheese can be used with the rest of the ingredients inside each chicken breast.)

Mrs. Thomas G. Greaves, Jr.

Chicken Gruyère

Serves 6

1½	cups heavy cream
	Juice of 1 lemon
	Salt and freshly ground pepper
4	tablespoons butter
6	chicken breasts, skinned, boned, and split in half
2	cups Swiss cheese, grated
1	cup boiled ham, minced

Preheat oven to 350°. In a saucepan, boil cream over high heat until reduced by one half in volume. Stir in lemon juice, salt and pepper. Set aside. In a heavy, wide skillet, heat the butter. Sauté the chicken breasts for a minute or so on each side until they begin to turn white. Place a layer of cheese and ham in a shallow, wide dish. Place chicken breasts on this layer. Sprinkle with salt and pepper and cover with remaining ham and cheese. Pour the thickened cream mixture over all. Place in a preheated oven for 10-12 minutes, uncovered, until just done. The chicken will be creamy and tender.

Mrs. Joe Gunter

145

Summer Lemon Chicken

Serves 6

6   **whole chicken breasts, boned, skinned and halved**
4   **tablespoons butter**
1/2 **cup dry Vermouth or dry white wine**
3/4 **cup fresh lemon juice**
1/4 **teaspoon salt**
1/4 **teaspoon pepper**
1½ **cups Hellman's mayonnaise**
     Ripe olives, sliced

Sauté chicken in butter in skillet until golden. Place chicken in heavy pot with a cover. Add wine to the skillet and reduce to 1/3 cup. Remove from heat and add 1/2 cup of the lemon juice and salt and pepper. Pour over chicken and bake in a 350° oven for 30 minutes, basting occasionally. When chicken is tender, remove to a platter and reduce juices in pot by half. Pour over the chicken and let cool. Cover tightly and refrigerate 6-8 hours. Beat 1/4 cup lemon juice into the mayonnaise until smooth. Spread mayonnaise over each piece of chicken, covering top and garnish tops with ripe olives. Let come to room temperature and serve. This is a good ladies luncheon dish with one of those fabulous salads with everything in it.

Mrs. Thomas O. Gaillard, Jr.

Save the broth in which chicken is cooked and use to cook rice.

Lemon Chicken Delicious

Serves 6

3	whole chicken breasts, boned
	Salt
	Pepper
1/2	cup butter or margarine
1/4	cup dry Vermouth or Sherry
3	tablespoons lemon juice
2	tablespoons lemon rind, grated
1½	cups chicken broth
1¼	tablespoons flour
1/3	cup water or chicken broth
6	thin pats butter
	Parmesan cheese, grated
	Sautéed mushrooms or artichoke hearts

Sprinkle chicken breasts with salt and pepper. Melt butter in skillet and brown chicken. Remove chicken, add Vermouth, lemon juice and rind. Stir and scrape pan. Add broth, blend in flour which has been mixed with water or broth. Stir until thickened. Pour over chicken, put pat of butter on top of each chicken breast, sprinkle with cheese and put under the broiler or bake in the oven along with sautéed mushrooms or artichoke hearts.

Mrs. Thomas S. Cowan

Marinate chicken breasts in a mixture of lemon juice, oil, tarragon and salt and pepper before you broil them.

Chicken Cashew

Serves 8

2/3 cup onion, chopped
2⅔ cups celery, sliced
2⅔ tablespoons butter
3 cans mushroom soup
1 cup chicken stock or broth
5⅓ cups chicken, boiled and diced (2 chickens)
2⅔ tablespoons soy sauce
8 drops of Tabasco
Black pepper
2⅔ cups chow mein noodles
1 cup cashew nuts

Sauté the onions and celery in the butter. Add the soup and stock, making certain it is not too soupy. Simmer this mixture until blended. Stir in the chicken, soy sauce, Tabasco and pepper to taste. Pour into a 3-quart casserole dish and sprinkle the top with noodles and nuts. Bake in a moderate oven until hot and bubbly. This can be made the day before, but add the noodles and nuts just before baking as they will become mushy if left standing.

Mrs. James R. Haas

Chicken, Pizza Style

Serves 4

4 chicken breasts, skin removed
Margarine
Salt
Pepper
1 (15 ounce) can tomato sauce
1/4 teaspoon parsley
Orégano
1 clove garlic, minced
2 tablespoons onion, minced
Mozzarella cheese

Bake chicken with salt, pepper, several pats of margarine, and a little water for 40 minutes at 350°. Mix tomato sauce with parsley, orégano, garlic and onion, and pour over chicken after baking. Pour off excess water if necessary. Place slices of the cheese on top of sauce and continue baking for 20-30 minutes. The kids love this.

Mrs. Edwin Lamberth

Chicken and Vegetables Oriental

Serves 4

2	whole chicken breasts, skinned and cut into 1" pieces
2	tablespoons soy sauce
1	tablespoon dry Sherry
1/2	teaspoon ground ginger
1	tablespoon cornstarch
1	teaspoon flavor enhancer—Accent (optional)
2-3	cloves garlic, pressed
1/4	cup oil
3-4	green onions, chopped
1/2	cup celery, sliced
1	whole onion, cut and separated in large bite size pieces
2	green peppers, cut in large bite size pieces
1	package frozen pea pods, thawed
1	package bamboo shoots, drained
1/3	cup water chestnuts, sliced
1	can bean sprouts, drained
1	cup hot chicken broth
	Rice
	Chinese noodles

Mix chicken, soy sauce, Sherry, ginger, cornstarch, flavor enhancer and garlic. Let marinate one hour at least. Heat oil over medium heat (I use an electric skillet) and sauté green onions. Then add chicken mixture and stir fry 3 minutes or until chicken is lightly browned. Add celery, onions and green pepper and stir 3 minutes more. Then add all or part of the remaining vegetables, according to taste. Stir fry 2 minutes longer and add chicken broth. Cover and simmer 2 minutes or until thoroughly heated. Serve over rice with Chinese noodles sprinkled on top.

Mrs. Theo Middleton

Chicken and Wild Rice Casserole

Serves 8-10

2-3 pound whole broiler or fryer
1 cup water
1 cup dry Sherry
1½ teaspoons salt
1/2 teaspoon curry powder
1 medium onion, sliced
1/2 cup sliced celery
1 pound fresh mushrooms
1/4 cup margarine
2 (6 ounce) packages of Uncle Ben's Wild and Whole Grain Rice
1 cup sour cream
1 (10 ounce) can cream of mushroom soup

Cook chicken with water, Sherry, salt, curry powder, onion and celery. Cook until done, about 1 hour. Remove from heat and strain broth. Refrigerate chicken and broth. When cool, cut meat off bone into bite-size pieces. Discard skin and bones. Wash mushrooms and cut if desired. Save some whole ones for top of casserole. Sauté. Drain fat from broth and measure broth to use as liquid for rice. Cook rice firmly. Combine chicken, rice, and mushrooms with sour cream and mushroom soup. Put mushrooms on top. (Can be made ahead and can be frozen.) Bake at 350° for 1 hour. Serve with a pretty vegetable and a salad. In summer try this with a marinated vegetable platter.

Mrs. T. K. Jackson, III

Hot Chicken Salad

Serves 6

1 cup mayonnaise
1 can cream of mushroom soup
1/2 cup celery, chopped
1 (7½ ounce) can water chestnuts
Salt and pepper to taste
1½ cups chicken, cooked and cubed
1 cup cooked rice
1 small-medium onion, chopped
Ritz crackers
Slivered almonds
Butter

Mix first 8 ingredients in 2-3 quart casserole dish. Top with almonds and crushed crackers, dot with the butter. Cook in a 350° oven for 45 minutes.

Mrs. D. Clay Wilson

Mama's Chicken and Yellow Rice

Serves 6

1	(3½ pound) chicken
1	large onion, minced
1	large bell pepper, minced
1	package (5 ounces) Spanish yellow rice

Boil chicken, with just enough water to cover, onion, and pepper until done. Cook rice, using broth from chicken according to directions on package. Combine chicken meat, removed from bones, and rice and place in a casserole dish. Top with cheese sauce and heat at 350° for 20 minutes or until heated through. (Reserve extra sauce to serve with meal.)

CHEESE SAUCE:

4	tablespoons margarine
4	tablespoons flour
2	cups milk
1	cup Cheddar cheese, grated
	Salt to taste
	Pepper to taste

Melt margarine. Add flour all at once. Remove from heat 5 seconds; stir with wire whisk. Add milk. Return to stove and cook over low heat until thick, stirring constantly with wire whisk. Add cheese and stir until melted.

Mrs. John P. Case, Jr.

Mother's Grilled Chicken

Serves 10

9	ounces red wine
1/3	cup hot liquid mustard (2 tablespoons dry mustard with hot water to make 1/3 cup)
1½	cups soy sauce
5	chickens, cut in half

Combine sauce ingredients and beat to blend. Marinate chickens for at least 2 hours (overnight or all day is better.) Drain marinade—grill on charcoal about 35 minutes. Chicken can be placed in marinade and reheated later.

Mrs. J. Hamilton Wright

Diddy's Company Chicken

Serves 4

1 (10 ounce) package Cheddar cheese
4 chicken breasts, boned
2 beaten eggs
3/4 cup dry bread crumbs
1/3 cup margarine
1 chicken bouillon cube
1 cup boiling water
1/2 cup onion
1/2 cup bell pepper
2 tablespoons flour
1/4 teaspoon pepper
3 cups cooked rice
1 (4 ounce) can mushrooms

Cut cheese into 8 sticks. Cut breasts in halves; flatten. Roll each piece of breast around cheese. Dip in egg and then bread crumbs. Brown each breast in margarine. Dissolve bouillon in water. Add onion, pepper, flour, and seasoning to margarine and sauté lightly. (Add more margarine, if too dry.) Add bouillon to mixture and cook until thick. Add rice and mushrooms to mixture and place in casserole. Top with chicken breasts and bake at 400° for 20 minutes. A yummy supper with curried fruit and green vegetable.

Mrs. John P. Case, Jr.

Easy Honey Chicken

Serves 6 to 8

6-8 pieces of chicken (breasts, thighs, legs, or a combination)
1/2 cup honey
1/4 cup Dijon mustard
2 tablespoons Worcestershire sauce
2 teaspoons curry powder

Place chicken, skin side down, and close together, in an oblong glass casserole dish. Mix honey, mustard, Worcestershire and curry powder. Pour over chicken. Cover and refrigerate at least 6 hours or overnight. When ready to cook, turn chicken skin side up, cover with foil, and bake at 350° for 1 hour. Remove foil, baste, and continue cooking, uncovered, for 20 minutes. Note: this do-ahead dish is easy enough for a family dinner, yet delicious enough for company. It is a different oven-barbecued chicken.

Mrs. John Wilson

Chicken and Asparagus Casserole

Serves 10

4   whole chicken
     breasts
1   onion
3-4 ribs celery
     Salt and pepper
2   large cans asparagus
     (or 2 pounds fresh,
     cooked asparagus)
1   jar pimento, drained
1   can sliced
     mushrooms, drained
     Cayenne, salt and
     pepper to taste
2   cans cream of
     chicken soup
1   (8 ounce) carton sour
     cream
     Lemon juice to taste
1/2 cup mayonnaise
2   tablespoons butter
     (1/4 stick)
     Parmesan cheese

Boil chicken with onion, celery, salt and pepper. Debone and cut into large pieces. Layer chicken, asparagus, pimento and mushrooms in a 3 quart greased casserole dish. Salt and pepper to taste. Combine soup, sour cream, lemon juice and mayonnaise and pour over ingredients in casserole dish. Dot with butter and sprinkle with lots of fresh Parmesan cheese. Bake at 350° until very hot.

Mrs. David Howard

Lemon-Butter Barbecued Chicken

1/2 pound butter
1   medium white onion,
     chopped
1   clove garlic, minced
1   small bottle
     Worcestershire sauce
1   lemon, squeezed
2   bay leaves
     Lemon slices

The sauce recipe is for 2 chickens Combine all ingredients in a pot, including some extra lemon slices. Allow to simmer slowly for about one hour before using. Salt and pepper 2 split chickens and place on the grill. Cook for 1 hour or until about half done. Then, begin to baste with the above sauce until completely done, about an hour more. Serve with additional sauce.

J. B. Blackburn

Chicken and Mushrooms

Serves 6

1½ teaspoons garlic salt or plain salt
1/4 teaspoon pepper
1/2 teaspoon paprika
8-10 boneless chicken breast halves, or 1 whole chicken, cut up
6 tablespoons butter, divided
1/2 pound fresh mushrooms, sliced (or use canned)
2 tablespoons flour
2 chicken bouillon cubes dissolved in 1 cup water
3 tablespoons white wine (optional)
1 teaspoon rosemary
1/4 teaspoon lemon pepper or 1½ tablespoons lemon juice

Mix together salt, pepper, and paprika. Sprinkle over chicken. Brown in 4 tablespoons butter. Place in flat dish. Add 2 tablespoons butter to drippings and sauté mushrooms. Stir in flour, chicken bouillon, wine, rosemary, lemon pepper or lemon juice. Cook for a few minutes and pour over chicken. Cover. Bake at 375° from 40 to 60 minutes, until tender. Makes 6 servings. Can make ahead of time and bake when ready to serve.

Mrs. J. Tyler Turner, Jr.

Always dissolve cornstarch first in a small amount of cold liquid before adding to a hot liquid.

Chicken and Artichoke Casserole

Serves 10

1	(3 pound) fryer and 2 to 3 extra breast halves
1	cup butter
1/2	cup flour
3½	cups milk
3	ounces Gruyère or Swiss cheese
1/8	pound rat cheese (mellow Cheddar)
1	tablespoon Accent
2	cloves garlic, pressed
1/2	tablespoon red pepper (or less)
2	large cans button mushrooms, drained
2	large cans artichoke hearts, drained

Boil chicken in seasoned water. Remove skin and bones and cut meat into large pieces. Set aside. Melt butter, stir in flour until blended. Slowly add milk and stir until the sauce is smooth. Add cheese (cut into small pieces or grated) and seasonings. Stir until cheese melts and sauce bubbles, then add chicken, mushrooms, and artichokes to the sauce. Check the seasonings. Put the combined mixture in a casserole dish and bake 30 minutes at 350°. Lobster, crab, or shrimp may be substituted. This is good served with buttered noodles.

Mrs. E. Burnley Davis

Pineapple Chicken

Serves 6

6	chicken breasts (or 4 cups cut up chicken)
	Salt
	Pepper
	Curry powder
1	large onion, sliced
2	bell peppers, sliced in thin strips
1	large can crushed pineapple
1/2	cup brown sugar
1	can water chestnuts, sliced
1	cup raisins

Sprinkle breasts with salt, pepper and curry powder. Brown in small amount of oil. Place breasts in casserole dish. To chicken drippings, add onions, peppers, pineapple, sugar, water chestnuts and raisins. Cook at low heat for 15 minutes and pour over chicken. Bake covered at 350° for one hour.

Mrs. Clarke Irvine, Jr.

Low Calorie Chicken (One Dish Meal)

Serves 2

2 chicken breasts,
 skinned
 Salt and pepper
 Garlic powder
 Greek seasoning
 Herbs, optional
1 small potato,
 quartered
1 squash, cut in 1"
 pieces
1 stalk celery, cut into
 1" pieces
1 medium onion,
 quartered
1/2 green pepper, cut in
 pieces
1 carrot, sliced
 Worcestershire sauce
 Water

Season chicken with salt, pepper, garlic powder and Greek seasoning. You may add a few herbs. Place in a casserole dish or baking pan. Add vegetables on top and sprinkle with salt, pepper and Worcestershire sauce. Add approximately 1/4 to 1/2 cup water. Cover tightly with a lid or foil and bake 1½ hours in a preheated 300° oven, or until vegetables are done but not overcooked. 215 calories for each serving.

Mrs. David A. Richards

Chicken Spaghetti

Serves 12-14

1 (5 to 6 pound) hen or 2
 (3 pound) fryers
1 pound spaghetti
1 pound bacon
3-4 medium onions,
 chopped
1 large can tomatoes
2 (4 ounce) cans
 mushrooms, drained
2 (4 ounce) cans pitted,
 ripe olives, drained
 Grated American
 cheese

Cook chicken and remove meat from bones. Cook spaghetti in chicken stock. Fry bacon and drain half of bacon grease. Cook onions in bacon fat. Add tomatoes, mushrooms and olives. Crumble bacon. Add all ingredients and pour into 2 (2 quart) casserole dishes. Sprinkle grated American cheese on top. Bake at 350° for 30 minutes.

Mrs. Carl A. Torbert, Jr.

Chicken Tetrazzini

Serves 6-8

1	(3 or 4 pound) hen
3	tablespoons butter
2	cups celery, chopped
2	cups onion, chopped
1/4	cup green pepper, minced
1	pod garlic, minced (optional)
1/2	pound mushrooms, sliced OR
1	(4 ounce) can sliced mushrooms, drained
1	small package spaghetti
3	cans mushroom soup, undiluted
3	tablespoons dry Sherry
	Salt
	Pepper
1	cup Cheddar cheese, grated, for topping

Boil chicken in salted water. Reserve chicken broth. Cut chicken into pieces. In 3 tablespoons butter, sauté celery, onions, green pepper, garlic and mushrooms. Set aside. Boil spaghetti in chicken broth. Drain. Mix all ingredients together except grated cheese. Place in two 1½ quart casserole dishes and sprinkle the grated cheese on top of each. Cook at 400° until bubbly. This may be frozen.

Mrs. J. Michael Druhan, Jr.

Low-Calorie Spicy Chicken Breasts

Serves 4

1	clove garlic, cut in half
4	(10 ounces each) chicken breasts, skinned
1	(16 ounce) can tomatoes
1	(6 ounce) can V-8 Spicey Hot
1	teaspoon sweet basil
1	teaspoon rosemary
	Salt and pepper to taste
1/4	teaspoon powdered horseradish
1	medium yellow onion, sliced thin
2	teaspoons brown sugar replacement
1	tablespoon cornstarch
2	tablespoons water

Place garlic at each end of baking dish. Add chicken and rest of ingredients. Cover and bake at 350° for 50-60 minutes. Remove chicken to a platter and keep warm. Thicken liquid with cornstarch and water, mixed together, and cook until thickened. Pour over chicken.

Mrs. Ernest Brown

Stuffed Cornish Hens

Serves 6

3 Cornish hens
   Lime juice
1/2 cup chicken broth or
   stock
1 teaspoon butter

An hour before cooking, wash hens and dry with paper towels. Sprinkle the cavities with lime juice. Prepare stuffing and just before cooking, stuff hens. Truss hens, securing the legs and wings to the body. Brown hens in 1 teaspoon butter in a non-stick skillet. Place in a 5 quart casserole dish or Dutch oven. Pour the chicken broth over the hens. Cover the hens with foil and make a small hole to release steam. Bake at 350° for one hour. Baste every 15 minutes. Remove cover for last 15 minutes of cooking time. Halve the hens and place on a platter surrounded by cooked vegetables such as braised carrots and celery. Spoon sauce over hens and serve.

Stuffing:
1 teaspoon butter
1/2 cup onion, chopped
   Livers from Cornish
   hens
1 (10 ounce) package
   frozen, chopped
   spinach, cooked and
   drained
1 (10¾ ounce) can
   cream of mushroom
   soup
   Salt
   Pepper
   Orégano
   Tabasco

Melt the butter in a non-stick skillet and sauté the onions and livers for 5 minutes. Remove the skillet from the heat and mince the livers. Return the minced livers to the skillet and add the spinach (well-drained) and the soup. Season to taste with salt, pepper, orégano and Tabasco.

Mrs. R. O. Blackwell, III

Turkey Florentine

Serves 6

1/4 cup margarine or butter
1/2 cup onion, chopped
1/4 cup unsifted flour
1/2 teaspoon salt
1/8 teaspoon pepper
Dash nutmeg
1½ cups milk
1/2 cup light cream
1 egg yolk
1/2 cup Swiss or Parmesan (I use both), grated
2 packages frozen chopped spinach
3 cups turkey or chicken cut in 1 inch pieces
2 tablespoons Parmesan cheese, grated

Melt margarine or butter and sauté the onion until golden, about 5 minutes. Remove from heat and add flour, salt, pepper and nutmeg. Stir until smooth. Add milk, then cream and return to heat. Over medium heat bring to boil, stirring constantly. Reduce heat and simmer 3 minutes, stirring. In small bowl beat egg yolk and add 1/2 cup of the hot sauce and mix well. Return egg mixture along with 1/2 cup of grated cheese to the rest of the sauce, stirring constantly. Cook over low heat until thickened and cheese is melted. Cook spinach as directed and drain well. Mix with 3/4 cup of the cheese sauce. Layer spinach in a 2 quart baking dish and arrange turkey or chicken over spinach and cover with remaining sauce. Sprinkle with 2 tablespoons grated Parmesan cheese and bake at 350 degrees until hot. Run under broiler until lightly brown.

Mrs. Theo Middleton

Turkey Casserole

Serves 35 generously

Meat from 2 cooked turkey breasts, thinly sliced

16 yellow onions, thinly sliced

SAUCE:
4 cups Parmesan cheese, grated
8 cans cream of chicken soup
1 pint sour cream
1 quart mayonnaise
Milk to make sauce creamy, not runny

In 2 greased 13 x 9" baking dishes, put layers of turkey, then onions and pour sauce over all. Bake at 350° for 1 hour. Delicious with cheese grits for brunch. Note: for 1 casserole, use 1 cup cheese, 2 cans soup, 1/2 pint sour cream, and 1/2 to 3/4 cup mayonnaise. Reheats beautifully. Great made with smoked turkey, too.

Mrs. John P. Case, Jr.

Turkey Salad Soufflé

Serves 6

5 slices white bread
2 cups cooked turkey, diced
1/2 cup celery, chopped
1 teaspoon dehydrated onion flakes
1/2 cup mayonnaise
Salt and pepper to taste
2 eggs, beaten
1½ cups milk
1 can cream of chicken soup

Cube 2 slices of bread (easier if frozen) and place in bottom of greased 8" x 8" baking dish. Combine turkey, celery, onion, mayonnaise and salt and pepper. Spoon over bread cubes. Trim crusts from remaining 3 slices of bread and arrange on top of turkey. Combine eggs and milk and pour over mixture. Cover and chill 2½ to 3 hours. Spoon soup over top of casserole dish and bake at 325°, or until set, or about 1 hour. Great way to use leftover chicken, ham or turkey.

Mrs. John Wilson

Sugar Smoked Turkey

1 (12 pound) thawed,
   pre-basted turkey
3/4 cup salt
   Salad oil
3/4 cup brown sugar,
   packed

3 Days Ahead
Rinse bird well with cold running water
and drain (do not pat dry). With hands,
rub salt well inside and out of bird.
Wrap with plastic and refrigerate 24
hours.

2nd Day
Rub bird with salad oil and bake in foil
"tent" approximately 4½ hours in 325
degree oven or when meat thermometer
reaches 180 degrees. Breast side up.
Allow bird to stand until room temperature, cover and refrigerate overnight. (Discard drippings as they will
be too salty to use).

3rd Day
Prepare grill for Barbecue. Make a
"tray" from heavy duty foil and
sprinkle with brown sugar. Place tray
directly on coals and turkey on grill;
cover grill and "smoke" for 20 minutes.
Remove turkey and refrigerate 4 hours
to mellow flavor. Then slice turkey and
serve cold.

Mrs. Harry Gordon Sparks, III

Smoked Turkey (Gas Grill)

1/4 cup salad oil
1/2 cup salt
10-12 pound turkey
1 cup vinegar
1/4 cup lemon pepper
2 tablespoons parsley, chopped
Hickory chips, soaked in water

Make a paste of the salad oil and salt and rub 1/4 cup inside the turkey. Mix remaining paste with vinegar, pepper and parsley and use to baste turkey often. Bake turkey on rack in a pan over low heat on grill with hickory chips. Bake for 6 to 8 hours. Outside will be very salty and crusty.

Jack Horner

Dove Kabobs

Serves 8-10

Doves
1/3 cup vinegar
1/3 cup lemon juice
1/4 cup soy sauce
1½ cups vegetable oil
1 tablespoon Worcestershire sauce
6 dashes Tabasco
2 garlic cloves, chopped
1/4 teaspoon pepper
1/4 teaspoon paprika
1 cube chicken bouillon dissolved in 1 cup water

Skin out the dove breasts and marinate overnight in a large bowl in the above mixture. The next day, remove doves from the mixture and place on square skewers (tend to spin on round skewers). Broil over hot charcoal, basting frequently with the marinade mixture. Turn often to prevent scorching. Do not overcook. Serve medium rare for full flavor. This marinade is enough for 2 dozen doves.

Mrs. Lewis Beville

Lucille's Dove Pie

Serves 6

15-20 doves (25 if small)
    Salt
    Pepper
    Celery tops
    Water
    Worcestershire sauce
    Flour, instant
    blending type
1   can cream of
    mushroom soup
4   tablespoons butter
4   hard boiled eggs,
    thinly sliced

PASTRY:
2½ cups sifted flour
1⅛ teaspoons salt
1/2 cup shortening
    Ice water to moisten
2   tablespoons butter,
    melted for topping

Simmer birds in seasoned water with a handful of celery tops until meat is ready to fall off the bones. While birds cook, make pastry as follows: Sift together flour and salt. Cut in shortening and add enough ice water to moisten and make mixture come away from the sides of the bowl and form a mass. Chill. Roll out pastry and cut a circle to fit the top of your casserole dish. Prick it well and set it aside in the refrigerator. Line bottom and sides of dish with pastry. Set aside in refrigerator. Bake any pastry scraps to use later. When birds are done, remove from liquid and remove as much meat as is possible from bones, leaving breasts in large pieces. Set aside. Strain stock and measure. Season stock with more salt, pepper and Worcestershire to taste. Thicken with about 5-6 tablespoons flour for 5-6 cups stock. In a large saucepan whisk together soup, seasoned, thickened stock and butter. Heat until butter melts. To assemble dish, place half the dove meat in pastry lined casserole dish, add half the eggs and half the soup-stock mixture. Place baked pastry scraps on top and repeat the meat-eggs-soup ingredients. Place reserved pastry top over the mixture, seal, and brush with melted butter. Bake at 350° for about 1 hour, or until pastry is golden brown. (Use a 3-quart casserole dish.)

Mrs. Palmer Gaillard

Pecan Island Ducks

Serves 4

1	stick butter
2	ducks, stuffed with onion and heavily salted and peppered
1	banana pepper, finely chopped
1/2	cup celery, chopped
1/2	cup onions, chopped
1/2	cup carrots, chopped
1/2	cup parsley, chopped

Cook ducks with the vegetables and butter in a heavy, covered skillet on medium heat for 60 minutes. Then brown in a hot oven.

Wythe Whiting, III

Wild Ducks

Serves 4

	Salt and pepper
4	tablespoons bacon drippings
4	duck breasts
4	tablespoons flour
2	onions, sliced
1	large can sliced mushrooms
3	cups water
1	can mushroom soup
1	can chicken broth
	Garlic salt
1	cup Sherry, optional

Salt, pepper, and flour ducks and brown in bacon drippings. Add onions and mushrooms and sauté until limp. Add water, soup, broth and garlic salt and season to taste. Add Sherry, if desired. Cover and simmer several hours until done.

Mrs. John N. Horner

Quinton's Country Duck

Serves 6

6   **wild duck breasts**
    Green pepper, garlic,
    onion and celery
    OR
    Wine (Sauterne)
    Flour
    Pepper, salt, onion
    salt and garlic salt to
    taste
    Deep fat
1   **can cream of**
    mushroom soup
    Additional sliced
    onions
1/4   **cup additional wine**

Parboil duck breasts 3 minutes in highly seasoned salted water with green pepper, garlic, onion and celery OR marinate overnight in wine in a covered container. Remove from boiling water or marinade and shake in a bag of flour seasoned with pepper, salt, onion salt and garlic salt. Brown in deep fat. Pour off fat, leaving 1 tablespoon in the pan. Add soup and 1 can water. Return breasts to skillet with sauce and simmer for 30 minutes or more, until very tender. Additional onions and wine may be added before duck breasts are added for the final simmer.

Mrs. James A. Yance

Joe Sneed's Ducks

Serves 2-4

2   **Mallards or 3 Wood**
    ducks
    Salt and pepper
    Vermouth
    Onion
    Raw carrots
    Celery

Liberally salt and pepper the ducks inside and out. Stuff cavities with one part onion, one part carrot and one part celery. Place in an electric skillet with 3/4 cup of Vermouth. Add enough water so that 2/3 of the ducks are submerged in liquid. Cover and cook at 350°. When liquid comes to a boil lower to 200°-225°. Continue cooking until meat begins to pull away from the breast, approximately 3-4 hours. You will need to add water from time to time. Serve with wild rice.

Mrs. Thomas Twitty, Jr.

Spiced Wild Duck

Serves 4

2	wild ducks
3	ounces butter
	Salt
	Black pepper, freshly ground
1/2	teaspoon ground ginger
1	bouquet garni
1	clove garlic, finely chopped
8	small apples
1-2	ounces butter
4	tablespoons red currant jelly
2	tablespoons wine vinegar
1	glass Port wine, about 4 ounces
	Juice of 1 medium orange

Brown the ducks lightly in the butter in a large deep pan or a skillet. Season with salt and pepper and add the ginger, bouquet garni and garlic. Cover and cook for about 50-60 minutes on medium heat, basting from time to time. While the ducks are cooking, peel and core the apples. Bake the apples with the butter at 350° until golden brown. Melt the jelly in the vinegar and keep warm. Remove the ducks from the pan and place on a serving platter. Place the apples around the platter and coat each one with a spoonful of the jelly. Skim the fat from the pan juices and add the Port and orange juice. Bring to a boil and adjust the seasonings. Strain into a sauce boat and serve with the ducks.

Mrs. Barry Bruckmann

Simple Duck Supper

Serves 4

4	wild ducks
	Bacon drippings
	Salt and pepper
1	apple, quartered
2	small onions, halved
4	celery chunks
	Water to almost cover ducks
4	beef bouillon cubes
1	cup red wine
6	green onions, chopped
1	(4 ounce) can mushrooms, undrained
1	(5 ounce) can water chestnuts, drained
	Cooked rice

Rub the ducks inside and out with bacon drippings, salt and pepper. Put a piece of apple, onion and celery in each duck. Put ducks in a Dutch oven and add water, bouillon cubes and half of the wine. Cook over medium heat until liquid is reduced by half. Add the rest of the wine. Cook until tender, at least 2 hours. Remove the ducks and cut in half, discarding the apple, onion and celery. Keep warm. Add the green onions, mushrooms and water chestnuts to the pan. Simmer a few minutes until onions are cooked. Put the duck halves on rice and pass the sauce.

Mrs. Thomas O. Gaillard, Jr.

Vernon's Wild Duck

Serves 4

2	Mallards or 4 Teal
2	onions, chopped
1	rib celery, cut up
1/2	bell pepper, cut up
1/4	cup salad oil
1	cup water
1	cup Sherry
1	tablespoon flour
1/4	cup water
4	tablespoons parsley, chopped
	Lemon, salt, and black pepper to taste

Salt and pepper ducks well inside and out. In the cavities of the ducks place equal amounts of 1 chopped onion, celery, and bell pepper. Brown ducks in an open, heavy roasting pan at 400° in the oil, about 30 minutes. Wilt the second onion (chopped) in the fat around the duck. Add a cup of water and a cup of Sherry. Reduce heat to 350°, cover and cook until done, about 1½-2 hours. Baste and add more liquid if needed. Toward the last, make a paste of flour and water. Add this to the drippings. Add chopped parsley and more Sherry to taste. Excellent served with currant jelly and wild rice.

Mrs. E. Burnley Davis

Baked Quail Supreme

3	oysters per quail
	Butter, melted
	Cornmeal
	Quail
	Flour
	Salt and pepper to taste
	Bacon, 1 slice per quail
	Mushroom soup and water
	Mushrooms

Dip the oysters in melted butter, then roll in cornmeal and place 3 oysters in each quail. Make a paste of butter and flour and rub breasts with paste. Salt and pepper. Put quail in a baking dish with breast on top, add a strip of bacon across each breast and bake until brown, approximately 30 minutes, uncovered. Make a gravy from cream of mushroom soup and water and as many additional mushrooms as desired. Pour gravy into bottom of container, cover and steam birds for about an hour or until tender when pricked with a fork. Serve with rice or grits.

Mrs. H. Eldon Scott, III

Quail with White Wine

Serves 8

8 quail
1/2 cup butter or margarine
2 cups mushrooms, sliced
1/2 cup green onion, chopped
1 cup dry white wine
2 tablespoons lemon juice
Salt and pepper to taste

Brown the quail in butter. Remove and set aside. Sauté mushrooms and onion in the butter. Place the quail, mushrooms and onion in a shallow pan and cover with heavy-duty aluminum foil. Bake at 350° for 1 hour. The last 15 minutes of cooking time, remove foil. Combine wine, lemon juice, salt and pepper; baste quail often. Serve hot with wild rice.

Mrs. Joe Little, Jr.

Mama's Tender Birds

Serves 6

1/4 cup Worcestershire sauce
1 dozen birds, dove, quail, etc.
Salt and pepper
Sprinkling of instant gravy flour
3/4 stick butter or margarine
1 bouillon cube in 1½ cups water
1/4 cup white wine
6 slices of ham
6 pieces of toast

Sprinkle Worcestershire sauce over birds and coat them. Salt and pepper and then top with flour. Heat butter and brown birds. Add water with bouillon and wine. Bring to a boil, cover and simmer for 1½ hours. Serve 2 birds on each slice of ham on toast.

Mrs. Mark Lyons, III

Pheasant in Red Wine

Serves 2

1	pheasant
	Salt and pepper
	Flour
2	tablespoons butter
	Oil
	Apple
4	ounces red wine
8	ounces chicken stock
4	ounces cream or 4 ounces sour cream

Salt and pepper the pheasant. Dredge in flour and brown quickly in heavy skillet in 2 tablespoons of butter and a little vegetable oil to keep butter from burning. Transfer to a roaster and place a few apple slices at either end or along the sides of the pan. Add the red wine to the skillet and simmer, scraping brown bits from the bottom and sides. Add the chicken stock and cook for 5 minutes. Add this to the pheasant in the roaster. Cover and cook at 375 degrees for 30 minutes. Reduce heat to 350 degrees and cook one hour longer (or test for doneness by sticking with a fork.) Juice should spurt out a clear yellow. If pinkish, cook a little longer until the juice clears. Remove the pheasant to a platter to set for 10 minutes before serving. Meanwhile, add the cream to juices (or sour cream) and simmer until cooked together. Pour over the pheasant and serve at once.

Mrs. George D. Cunningham

Venison Wellington

Serves 4 to 6

1   3-3½ pound venison
     filet or saddle of
     venison
     Lawry's seasoned salt
     Cavender's Greek
     seasoning
     Bacon slices

Place 4 slices of bacon lengthwise on filet before roasting. Roast ahead of time the seasoned filet with all tallow trimmed off in a preheated 425° oven, until desired doneness is reached (17 minutes for rare, 20 minutes for medium rare.) Cool the roast and reserve any juices for gravy.

Pastry:
1/4 pound cream cheese
1/4 pound butter
1   cup flour
     Ice water

Cream together cheese and butter. Cut in flour as for pie dough. Sprinkle ice water into mixture until dough is easy to manage. Put in refrigerator for 2 hours.

Forming Wellington:
1   recipe pastry (above)
     French paté
1   teaspoon Cognac
     Mushrooms (sliced,
     canned, in butter)
1   egg yolk
1   teaspoon water

Roll out pastry in a rectangle to wrap around roast. Cover roast with paté, mushrooms and Cognac. Completely encase roast with pastry overlapping the dough on bottom side. Any extra dough may be made into decorative cut-outs and put on top by moistening with water. Make small slits in dough for steam to escape. Paint entire surface with mixture of egg yolk and water. Place seam side down on roasting pan and bake at 400° for 30 minutes or until crust is golden brown. Serve with the following sauce.

Sauce:

	Reserved juices
1	cup red wine
1	cup beef consommé, canned
1	tablespoon flour
	Salt and pepper
	Sliced fresh mushrooms

Make sauce while pastry is in refrigerator. Mix juices with wine and consommé. Season with salt and pepper. Let simmer until thickened. Make a paste of flour and some sauce and gradually return to sauce stirring constantly. Add mushrooms and simmer until thickened. Note: This recipe is a little bit of trouble but well worth the time involved. This can be frozen if there is anything left. Two 3 pound filets will feed 5 couples as this is a very rich dish. Venison is best if cooked rare before adding pastry.

Mrs. Jere Austill, Jr.

Venison Hindquarter

1	venison hindquarter, ham or haunch — any size
1	large (16 ounce) bottle Italian salad dressing
1	10-12 ounce jar currant jelly
1	cup red wine

In refrigerator, in covered glass or enamel container, marinate meat for 24 hours in salad dressing. Turn several times. Next day, drain meat, put in uncovered pan in a pre-heated 250° oven. Heat together jelly and wine until jelly is melted. Bake meat 40 minutes to the pound, basting every hour with wine and jelly mixture. If meat begins to get too brown, cover with "tent" of foil. Serve with barbecue sauce if desired. Good leftover on hamburger buns, too!

Mrs. John Wilson

173

Party Venison

MARINADE:

2   tablespoons salt
1   tablespoon freshly
     ground black pepper
1   teaspoon garlic salt
1/2 cup vinegar
1/3 cup catsup
1/2 cup Worcestershire
     sauce

Marinate 1 whole "ham" of venison in a plastic bag in refrigerator for 2 to 3 days, turning frequently. Place meat on foil in barbecue oven with several strips of bacon on top to prevent drying out. Cook *very* slowly to desired doneness (venison does not have to be well done). Slice very thin and put in chafing dish with a very mild barbecue sauce of your choice. Serve with homemade rolls. If cooked in a regular oven, roast 40 minutes per pound at 250°.

Mrs. J. Michael Helmsing

174

SEAFOODS

WINTZELL'S OYSTER HOUSE
From raw oysters to fried shrimp, with hush puppies in
between, Wintzell's must be enjoyed at one's leisure to
absorb the unusual atmosphere.

Frog Legs

Serves 4

8	legs
	White wine
	Salt
	Pepper
	Flour
1	stick butter
2	cloves garlic, minced
1/4	cup shallots or green onions, chopped
	Juice of 1/2 lemon
1	cup parsley, chopped
1/4	cup Brandy or Cognac
1	small can sliced mushrooms

Marinate the frog legs in white wine overnight. Drain and reserve 1/2 cup of the wine. Salt and pepper the legs and dredge in flour. Sauté the legs in the butter until browned. Add the garlic and cook for 3 minutes. Add the reserved wine and remaining ingredients. Cook for 5 minutes or until legs are done. Serve with wild rice.

Mrs. Byron Green

Crabmeat Imperial

Serves 6

4	tablespoons mayonnaise
1½	tablespoons Durkees dressing
1½	tablespoons Lea and Perrins
1/3	cup lime juice (lemon may be substituted)
	Pinch of dill weed
	Salt and pepper to taste
1	pound lump crabmeat
1/2	stick butter
1	cup coarsely rolled cracker crumbs
1	teaspoon paprika

Combine mayonnaise, Durkees, Lea and Perrins, lime juice, dill weed, salt and pepper. Mix well. Carefully add crabmeat. Melt butter in sauce pan, add cracker crumbs and paprika. Mix 1/3 of buttered crumb mixture with crab mixture. Fill 4 or 5 crab shells or 1 shallow casserole dish with crab mixture. Sprinkle remaining crumbs on top. Bake in 350° oven for 12 to 15 minutes.

Mrs. Sam W. Pipes, III

Seafood Pie

Serves 6-8

2	tablespoons butter or margarine
1/4	cup green pepper, chopped
1/4	cup green onions, chopped
1/4	cup celery, chopped
1	(3 ounce) can mushrooms
1/2	pound lump crabmeat
1/2	pound shrimp, boiled and peeled
1	cup Cheddar cheese, grated
1/4	cup Parmesan cheese, grated
1	can artichoke hearts, sliced and quartered
1	can water chestnuts, sliced
1	tablespoon lemon juice
1/8	teaspoon Tabasco sauce
1	egg, beaten
	Lea and Perrins sauce, to taste
1/4	cup mayonnaise
1	9-inch deep dish pie shell, partially baked
1/4	cup almonds, slivered

Melt the butter in a large skillet and sauté green pepper, green onions, celery and mushrooms. Add crabmeat, shrimp, 3/4 cup Cheddar cheese, Parmesan cheese, artichoke hearts, water chestnuts, lemon juice, Tabasco sauce, egg, Lea and Perrins, and mayonnaise. Stir well to combine. This mixture should be moist but not juicy, so drain off any excess liquid. Pour into pie shell. Bake at 350° for about 20 minutes. Add almonds and remaining 1/4 cup Cheddar cheese. Bake 10 minutes longer. If fresh seafood is not available, canned seafood can be used.

Mrs. Paul Brock

Crab au Gratin

4 tablespoons butter
1 onion, finely chopped
4 tablespoons flour
2 cups hot milk
1½ cups sharp cheese, grated
3 drops Tabasco
1 tablespoon Worcestershire
Salt and pepper, to taste
1/2 cup mushrooms, sautéed in butter (or more mushrooms if you like)
1/4 cup Chablis
1 pound lump crabmeat, picked over
Buttered bread crumbs
Additional grated cheese, for crêpes

Melt butter in a 2 quart saucepan and sauté onion until it is limp. Stir in flour and cook 2 minutes. Add hot milk all at once and stir until mixture comes to a boil. Add cheese, seasonings, mushrooms, wine and crabmeat. Stir gently. Pour into a greased 2 quart casserole dish and top with buttered bread crumbs. Bake in a 350° oven for 30 minutes. The sauce may be strained to remove the sautéed onion if you like, but do this before you add seasonings, cheese, etc. Instead of baking this in a casserole dish, it may be used nicely as a crêpe filling. In this case, omit bread crumbs, and use additional grated cheese to sprinkle over the top of crêpes, returning them to the oven just long enough to let the cheese melt. Mixture should fill at least 12 crêpes.

Mrs. David A. Richards

Shrimp and Crab Coquille

Serves 6

1/2 cup green onions, chopped
1 clove garlic, minced
1 cup celery, chopped
4 tablespoons butter
1/2 cup flour
3 cups light cream
1 cup dry white wine
1½ pounds shrimp, boiled and peeled
1 pound crabmeat
1 cup breadcrumbs
8 tablespoons Swiss cheese, grated fresh
8 tablespoons parsley, chopped
6 tablespoons melted butter
Lime slices

Sauté vegetables in butter until they are limp. Add the flour and stir for 2 minutes. Remove from heat and stir in cream all at once, place back over heat, and stir constantly as you bring the mixture to a boil. Boil for 1 minute, continuing to stir. Add wine, shrimp and crabmeat. Put in individual buttered shells. Combine breadcrumbs, cheese, parsley and butter. Top seafood mixture with this crumb mixture and bake at 350° for about 20 minutes. Serve garnished with lime slices.

Mrs. A. Clifton Worsham

Fran's Crab Mornay

Serves 4-6

4 tablespoons butter
8 tablespoons flour
3/4 cup chicken stock
3/4 cup milk
2 egg yolks
1 pound crabmeat
1/2 cup grated cheese
3/4 teaspoon salt

Melt butter, add flour, stock and simmer three minutes. Add milk slowly. Add 2 egg yolks and crab. Mix, put in buttered ramekins, sprinkle with cheese and place under broiler until lightly brown.

Mrs. John P. Case, Jr.

180

Crab Mousse

MOUSSE:
1   **pound crabmeat**
1/2 **teaspoon salt**
4   **eggs, separated**
2   **cups fresh bread crumbs, lightly packed**
3/4 **cup whipping cream**
    Vegetable shortening to grease the mold

To the crabmeat add the salt, egg yolks (well beaten) and the bread crumbs. Whip the cream. Beat the egg whites stiffly. Fold the cream into the crab mixture, then fold in the egg whites. Grease a 1½ quart mold heavily with vegetable shortening. Fill it with the mixture. If there is a lid, grease it also. If not, grease a sheet of foil and use it as a lid. Place the mold on a rack in a deep kettle of boiling water. Cover the kettle and simmer for 40 minutes. Meanwhile, make the sauce.

SAUCE:
2   **tablespoons butter**
3   **tablespoons flour**
    Salt
    Cayenne pepper
1½ **cups milk**
1   **egg yolk**
3/8 **cup Sherry**
4-5 **mushrooms, cut into quarters**
6   **whole shrimp, cooked and cleaned**

Melt the butter. Remove from heat and stir in flour, salt and cayenne. Add milk and return to heat. Stir until sauce comes to a boil. Turn down the heat; add the mushrooms and continue cooking for 10 minutes at a simmer. Strain off mushrooms, setting them aside. Place the sauce in a blender; add the egg yolk and Sherry and blend until well combined. Place again over heat and cook, stirring, until thick. Do not boil. Return mushrooms to sauce, correct seasonings. Unmold mousse on serving platter. Pour sauce over it, with mushrooms in the center, and garnish with whole shrimp and parsley. Serve hot.

Mrs. Winston C. Patterson

Crab Casserole

Serves 12

2 bunches green
onions, chopped
1 stick margarine
8 tablespoons flour
1 quart milk
1 tablespoon
Worcestershire sauce
1 tablespoon parsley
flakes
1/2 pound mild cheese,
grated
1 (8 ounce) can
mushrooms
2 pounds crabmeat
1/2 box Ritz crackers
1/2 stick margarine,
melted

Sauté onions in 1 stick margarine. Add flour, do not brown. Add milk and cook until thick. Add Worcestershire, parsley. Stir in cheese until melted. Add mushrooms, crabmeat. Put in a greased 9" x 13" casserole dish and top with Ritz crackers that have been crushed with remaining butter or margarine. Bake at 400° for 25 to 30 minutes. Will freeze.

Mrs. John P. Case, Jr.

Molly's Crab Cakes

Serves 4

3 tablespoons flour
1 pound fresh
crabmeat
Mayonnaise, to taste
Lemon juice, to taste
Salt, to taste
Pepper, to taste
Green onions, to taste
Bread crumbs
1/4 cup butter
1/4 cup olive oil

Sprinkle flour over crabmeat, then mix in mayonnaise, lemon juice, salt, pepper, green onions, until stiff enough to form cakes about 3/4 inch thick. Lightly pat cakes in bread crumbs and refrigerate several hours. Sauté in olive oil and butter until light brown.

Mrs. John N. Horner

Sherried Crabmeat Savannah

Serves 6-8

1   pound lump crabmeat, picked over to eliminate cartilage
1/4   to 1/2 cup Sherry
3   pieces soft white bread
1/2   stick (4 tablespoons) butter, melted
1/2   cup light cream
      Juice of 1 lemon
1/2   cup mayonnaise
1   teaspoon Worcestershire sauce
      Salt and pepper to taste
1/2   cup mild cheese, grated
      Buttered bread crumbs

Marinate crabmeat in Sherry overnight. Place soft bread into a mixing bowl and pour on butter, cream, lemon juice, mayonnaise, Worcestershire, salt and pepper. Mix these ingredients together well. Carefully stir in the marinated crabmeat, along with the Sherry and the cheese, and pour the mixture into a greased casserole dish. Sprinkle with buttered bread crumbs. Bake at 350° for 20 to 30 minutes.

Mrs. William L. McDonough

Crabmeat Rockefeller

Serves 6

2	packages frozen, chopped spinach
1/4	cup onion, chopped
1/4	cup celery, chopped
	Salt and pepper to taste
	Tabasco to taste
6	tablespooons butter
6	tablespoons flour
2	cups milk, heated
	Salt and pepper to taste
	Grated onion
1	pound lump crabmeat
	Parmesan cheese

Cook spinach and drain well. Sauté onion and celery in 2 tablespoons butter and add to spinach. Season with salt and pepper and a touch of Tabasco. Spread in a greased 2 quart casserole dish. Make a cream sauce as follows: Melt butter and stir in flour. Cook 2 minutes, stirring constantly. Do not let the flour brown. Add hot milk all at once. Stir over heat with a whisk until thick and bubbly. Add salt and pepper to taste and a little grated onion. Fold in the crabmeat. Spoon this mixture over the spinach and sprinkle Parmesan cheese all over the top. Bake in a 350° oven until bubbling hot. Great with tomato aspic for lunch.

Mrs. George Fuller

Vic's Oven Shrimp

Serves 12

1	pound butter
1	pound margarine
1	teaspoon rosemary
6	ounces Worcestershire sauce
5	tablespoons black pepper
4	teaspoons salt
4	lemons, sliced thin
1	teaspoon Tabasco sauce
10	pounds washed, headless shrimp in the shell (medium to large size)

Heat the first 8 ingredients to the boiling point. Pour over the shrimp in a large, shallow pan. Bake at 400° for 20 minutes. Serve with a green salad and French bread. The juice is delicious with the bread.

Mrs. Victor Lott

Spicy Grilled Shrimp

Serves 10

1 teaspoon chili powder
1 tablespoon vinegar
1/4 teaspoon pepper
1 clove garlic, minced or mashed
1 teaspoon salt
1 teaspoon basil
1 tablespoon finely chopped fresh mint
3/4 cup salad oil
2 pounds medium shrimp or prawns, washed, shelled and deveined, or about 1½ pounds frozen deveined large shrimp (need not be thawed)

In a bowl or glass jar, blend the chili powder with the vinegar, pepper, garlic, salt, basil, and mint. Stir in the oil; shake or mix until well blended. Pour over the shrimp, cover the dish and marinate in the refrigerator at least 4 hours, or overnight. Thread the shrimp on skewers and grill for 6 to 10 minutes (depending on size), turning once and basting liberally with the marinade.

Cook these shrimp on your grill or they can be cooked in the oven. If you cook the shrimp in your broiler, they need not be strung on skewers. Arrange them on your broiler rack, and broil, turning once and basting well, time will be about the same as the grill.

Mrs. Edwin Weigel

Barbecued Shrimp

Serves 4

1 clove garlic, pressed
1/2 teaspoon salt
1/2 cup salad oil
1/2 cup soy sauce
1/2 cup lemon juice
2 tablespoons onion, very finely chopped
1/2 teaspoon pepper
2 pounds large shrimp (may be cooked in shells but better if peeled first)

Combine all ingredients except shrimp to make marinade; mix well. Place shrimp in a shallow dish, cover with marinade and refrigerate for 2 to 3 hours. Place on heavy duty tinfoil on grill and cook until pink, turning once. May also be broiled in the oven for 5 to 10 minutes, turning once.

Mrs. Champ Lyons, Jr.

Bacon Broiled Shrimp

8-10 jumbo shrimp per
person
1/2 strip of bacon per
shrimp
Equal parts lemon
juice, soy sauce, and
Lea and Perrins

Clean and devein shrimp. Wrap each with 1/2 slice of bacon. Secure with toothpick. Place shrimp in a shallow pan and sprinkle with lemon juice, soy sauce, and Lea and Perrins. No salt! Let marinate several hours or overnight in the refrigerator. Cook under the broiler about five minutes per side. Add small amount of boiling water to pan if necessary. Remove shrimp from pan and skim fat off liquid. Add about 1/2 cup boiling water to liquid. Let boil and serve as a sauce over rice. These shrimp are delicious cooked over charcoal.

Mrs. Sam W. Pipes, III

Broiled Shrimp Hollandaise

Serves 4

1 cup Hollandaise
sauce
1 pound whole, large
fresh shrimp, peeled
and deveined
1½ tablespoons lemon
juice
1 tablespoon olive oil
1/2 teaspoon salt
1/8 teaspoon freshly
ground black pepper
(grind as fine as you
can)
1/8 teaspoon cayenne

Prepare hollandaise sauce and set container in warm water in a bowl or basin. Dry shrimp thoroughly with paper towels, then arrange in a large shallow baking dish. Sprinkle with lemon juice, olive oil, salt, black pepper and cayenne. Preheat broiler. Place baking dish 3½ to 4 inches from heat and broil for 3 minutes. Turn shrimp and broil 3 minutes again. Remove the baking dish from oven and spoon 1 cup of warm hollandaise sauce evenly over the shrimp, then put the dish under broiler again for 30 seconds to a minute, just long enough for sauce to develop a light brown haze. Remove and serve immediately.

Mrs. E. B. Walker

Oven Barbecue Shrimp

Serves 6

8-10	pounds raw, large shrimp, heads on
1	pound butter
1/2	cup chives, chopped
1	bottle Tabasco (I use 1½)
1-2	teaspoons cayenne pepper
10	cloves garlic, peeled and cracked
4	tablespoons filé
4	lemons, sliced
	Paprika

Rinse raw shrimp. Mix and heat all ingredients except filé, lemon and paprika. (This can be done in the A.M.). Place layer of 1/2 the shrimp in broiler pan and pour half of heated mixture over shrimp. Place remainder of shrimp and pour remainder of mixture over. Spread sliced lemons on top. Sprinkle filé and paprika over all. Bake for 20 minutes at 400°. Stir to coat shrimp with sauce. Serve in individual bowls, with chunks of French bread (for dipping). Great dish for backyard treat — with salad — and especially to take to the beach (coals to Newcastle?). Not recommended for carpeted-room consumption. A fun dish and really not too seasoned for most. Suggestion: Common bowls for shrimp shells — perfect patio dish.

P.S. Heads lend additional flavor.

Mrs. Virginia B. Baumhauer

Sherried Shrimp Rockefeller

Serves 4

2 packages (10 ounce each) frozen chopped spinach
1 can condensed cream of shrimp soup
1 cup shredded sharp Cheddar cheese
3 tablespoons Sherry
3 tablespoons butter
2 slices fresh bread, make into crumbs
16 medium to large raw shrimp, peeled and deveined (about 1 pound)
   Paprika

Prepare spinach as directed, drain and set aside. Heat shrimp soup and stir in grated cheese and Sherry, stirring until melted. In another pan, melt butter and stir in crumbs. To assemble, place spinach in casserole dish. Top with shrimp, cover with sauce, and top with buttered crumbs. Sprinkle paprika on top. Bake uncovered at 350° for 45 minutes.

Mrs. Marion B. McMurphy, Jr.

Fried Shrimp

Serves 4

1 cup milk
1 cup white wine
1 tablespoon onion powder
1 tablespoon garlic powder
2-3 tablespoons salt
   Lemon juice
4 eggs, beaten
   Dry pancake mix
2 pounds raw shrimp, peeled

Combine milk, wine, seasonings, lemon juice, and beaten eggs. Marinate peeled, raw shrimp in this mixture for a while before cooking. Remove shrimp from marinade. Coat with dry pancake mix and fry in deep hot fat. Delicious.

Mrs. William G. Acker

188

Shrimp and Green Noodle Casserole

Serves 8-10

1   package green noodles

1   bunch green onions, chopped fine

3   pounds shrimp, cooked and cleaned

1   cup mayonnaise

1   cup sour cream

1   can cream of mushroom soup

2   tablespoons prepared mustard

2   eggs, beaten

1   cup sharp cheese, grated

1/2 cup melted butter

Cook noodles and drain. While still hot, toss with green onions. Place in a buttered casserole dish; top with the shrimp. Make the following sauce: combine mayonnaise, sour cream, soup, mustard and eggs. Cover the shrimp layer with this sauce. Then combine cheese and melted butter. Pour over the layer of sauce and bake at 350° for 30 minutes. Serve with a good salad and bread.

Mrs. Sam G. Ladd

Shrimp and Artichoke Casserole

Serves 8

1	stick margarine (not butter)
1/2	cup flour
1/4	cup white onion, grated
1/2	cup green onions, chopped
1/8	cup parsley, chopped
2	cups heavy cream
1	cup dry white wine
2½	teaspoons salt
1/2	teaspoon white pepper
1/4	teaspoon Cayenne pepper
2½	ounces Swiss cheese, minced
2	tablespoons lemon juice
2	cans artichoke hearts, halved and quartered
3	pounds boiled and peeled shrimp
1/2	pound fresh mushrooms, sliced thickly
3	tablespoons Romano cheese

Melt margarine, stir in flour, add onions. Cook for a few minutes. Stir in parsley, gradually add cream allow to heat. Add wine, seasonings and bring to a simmer. Add Swiss cheese, stir, cover. Turn off and allow to cool. Add lemon juice. Mix together in a large Pyrex dish the shrimp, artichoke hearts, mushrooms and Romano cheese. Pour the sauce over the shrimp and vegetables. Bake at 350° for 30-40 minutes until brown on top. May be served over rice.

Mrs. Thomas M. Cunningham

Mobile Shrimp Creole

Serves 4

1	large tablespoon shortening
2	tablespoons flour
2	onions, chopped fine
2	cloves garlic, chopped fine
1	large bell pepper, chopped fine
2	teaspoons fresh parsley, chopped fine
1	(16 ounce) can tomatoes
1/8	teaspoon red pepper
1	teaspoon salt
2	bay leaves
1/3	teaspoon celery seed
1/4	teaspoon powdered thyme
2	pounds raw shrimp, shelled and deveined
2	teaspoons Worcestershire

Make a good rich roux by browning the flour in the shortening. Into this, add the onion, garlic, bell pepper and parsley. Stir until the onions are soft. Add the tomatoes, including the juice. Season with red pepper, salt, bay leaves, celery seed and thyme. Add the shrimp, cover pot and simmer for an hour (preferably in an old fashioned iron pot but a heavy new pot will do if cover fits tightly). Half an hour before serving, add Worcestershire sauce. Do not add water as the juice from tomatoes and shrimp is enough. Serve with rice. Freezes very well.

Mrs. H. Michael Gates

Oysters Confederate

Step I:

1/4 stick butter

1 measured pint of oysters (without liquid)

1 large or 2 small bay leaves

1 medium onion, coarsely chopped

2 garlic cloves, sliced

2 stalks of celery, coarsely chopped

3/4 cup Vermouth or 1/2 cup dry white wine

Sauté oysters in butter in a covered saucepan (medium heat) for 4 to 5 minutes or until oysters just begin to curl. Do not overcook. Remove from heat and let stand for 10 minutes. Drain juices from oysters into a 2 quart saucepan. This will yield about 3/4 cup of oyster juice. Add bay leaves, onion, garlic, celery and wine to juice and simmer in covered saucepan for 20 minutes. This may be prepared several days in advance and stored in refrigerator. Drain juice from vegetables. Press with a spoon to drain excess juice. This should yield about 1 to 1½ cups of stock. Return stock to saucepan and keep hot.

Step II:

1 package frozen, chopped spinach

Cook chopped spinach according to directions on package. Drain thoroughly.

Step III:

3/4 stick butter (6 tablespoons)

8 level tablespoons flour

1 cup milk

1/4 cup Vermouth

1 teaspoon nutmeg

1 teaspoon salt

1/8 teaspoon Cayenne White pepper, to taste

1/2 teaspoon M.S.G.

1/2 cup cream

Make a roux — add flour to melted butter and stir with a wire whip over low heat. Pour steaming stock into roux, stirring constantly, and add milk and Vermouth. Add nutmeg, salt, Cayenne, white pepper and M.S.G. Stir. Pour in cream and stir until thickened.

Step IV:
    Butter
    Parmesan cheese
3   slices of white bread
3-4 slices of bacon

Assemble as follows in a lightly buttered 2 quart Pyrex casserole dish, dusted with Parmesan cheese. Put about 1/2 of spinach in bottom of dish, followed by a layer of oysters. Spoon thick cream sauce over first layer of oysters. Repeat layers. For topping, break 3 slices of white bread into thumbnail size pieces (including crust) and sprinkle over casserole. Cover bread crumbs with 1/2 inch sections of bacon. Place casserole dish in baking pan with 1/4 inch of water and bake in a 400° oven on middle rack for 35 to 40 minutes or until top is golden brown.

Dr. J. Mac Bell, Jr.

Eggplant and Oyster Casserole

Serves 6

1   medium eggplant
1   tablespoon onion, chopped
1/4 cup butter
1/2 cup dry bread crumbs
    Salt to taste (1 teaspoon)
1   pint oysters
1/2 cup light cream
    Additional bread crumbs

Peel, cube and cook eggplant in water until tender and drain. Sauté onion and add bread crumbs and salt. Heat oysters until they curl. Mix all ingredients and add cream. Place in two quart casserole and cover with crumbs. Bake until bubbly in a 350° oven.

Mrs. Wallace G. Jeffrey, Jr.

Oyster Casserole

Serves 4-6

1   stick margarine
1   quart oysters
1   stack pack of Ritz
      crackers
1   cup celery, chopped
1/2   cup parsley, minced
1/4   small onion, grated
      Worcestershire sauce
      Salt to taste
      Pepper to taste
      Tabasco to taste

Melt margarine in a casserole dish, put in drained oysters, crumble crackers and add with celery, parsley, onion, and seasonings; stir together. You can put some more cracker crumbs on top if it appears to have too much liquid when done. Bake at 350° for 30 minutes.

Mrs. Guy Oswalt

Red Snapper in Tomato Gravy

Serves 6

1   large red snapper,
      head on, about 3
      pounds
2   tablespoons bacon
      drippings or salad oil
2   tablespoons flour
2   large onions, chopped
      Bay leaves
2   No. 1 cans tomatoes
      Fresh parsley,
      chopped
1   bell pepper, chopped
1   clove garlic, sliced
      Salt and pepper to
      taste

Wash fish and place in baking pan. Squeeze fresh lemon juice over fish and dot liberally with butter, salt and pepper. Place in 400° oven while you make the gravy. To make the gravy, you make a roux using the drippings and flour. Get the roux as dark as possible without burning. Add tomatoes and some hot water if necessary. After this simmers for a few minutes, add other ingredients and let simmer again. Pour hot gravy over fish and bake for 1 hour in 325° oven. Gravy is delicious over rice or creamed potatoes.

Mrs. Arthur Gonzales, Jr.

Trout Filets en Casserole

Serves 6-8

4 tablespoons butter
4 tablespoons flour
2 cups hot milk
1 cup sharp Cheddar cheese, grated
6-8 trout filets, cut in 1" pieces
Salt
Water
1/2 cup almonds, sliced and toasted
1/2 cup breadcrumbs, buttered
Parsley
Rice, optional

Make a sauce by melting butter and adding flour. Cook for 2 minutes, stirring with a whisk. Add milk all at once and whisk over heat until it comes to a boil. Season to taste. Add cheese and stir until it is melted. Poach fish in a small amount of salted water until almost cooked. Gently fold drained fish into the sauce. Pour into a 1½ quart casserole dish. Top with almonds, breadcrumbs and parsley and bake at 300° for 30 minutes. This may be served over rice if you wish. It is rich and delicious.

Mrs. Evan Austill

Fried Speckled Trout

3 egg yolks
1 cup milk
Salt and pepper to taste
Speckled trout filets
Flour
Oil for frying

Use heavy cast iron skillet. Allow 1 fish filet per person. Dip filets in the batter, then coat with flour. Immediately fry in hot fat until golden brown. Serve with the following sauce.

SAUCE:
1 stick of butter, melted
Juice of 1 big lemon
1/2 small size bottle Worcestershire sauce

Combine ingredients and heat in a saucepan. Pass to pour over trout. This is very good served with a grits casserole, green salad vinaigrette, and hot bread.

Mrs. Wade Faulkner

Stuffed Flounder

Serves 8

1 pound boiled shrimp
1 cup onion, minced
1/2 cup spring onions, minced
1½ cups celery, mincéd
3 cloves garlic, minced
1 cup parsley, chopped
1/2 pound mushrooms, chopped
1/2 pound butter
2 tablespoons flour
2 cups Half and Half
1/2 pound white crabmeat
1 cup seasoned bread crumbs
Salt and pepper to taste
8 flounders (3/4 to 1 pound each)

Save 24 boiled shrimp. Chop rest. Sauté onions, spring onions, celery, garlic, parsley and mushrooms in butter. Add flour and blend well. Gradually stir in Half and Half, cooking until thickened. Add chopped shrimp and crabmeat and thicken further with bread crumbs. Season to taste. Split each flounder and fill with dressing. Top each fish with 3 whole shrimp and cook under broiler about 20 minutes or until fish is done.

Mrs. Wade B. Perry, Jr.

Baked Redfish or Bass

Serves 8-10

Salt and pepper
1 (5-8 pound) redfish or bass
Lemon juice
4 slices raw bacon
1 (1 pound) can stewed tomatoes
1 cup red piccalilli or red tomato relish
1/2 cup red wine
Pinch of tarragon

Salt and pepper the fish. Sprinkle with lemon juice. Place in a greased baking dish and cover fish with slices of bacon. Combine other ingredients and simmer for 5 minutes. Pour over fish and bake at 350° for 40 minutes, basting with sauce or a little more red wine.

Mrs. Evan Austill

Low-Calorie Baked Fish

Serves 2

1 (4 ounce) can
mushrooms, drained
(reserve liquid)
1 beef bouillon cube
2 tablespoons green
pepper, chopped
1/2 teaspoon dried onion
flakes
1/2 cup celery, chopped
1 pound fish filets
(flounder, trout,
mackerel)
1 teaspoon dried
parsley
1 tablespoon Parmesan
cheese, grated

Heat mushroom liquid and dissolve bouillon in it. Add mushrooms, green pepper, onion flakes and celery. Pour mixture over fish. Sprinkle with parsley and Parmesan cheese. Bake in a 350° oven for 20 to 25 minutes or until fish flakes easily. 255 calories per serving.

Mrs. Floyd Fraser

Mackerel Almondine

Serves 6

6 small filets of Spanish
Mackerel
Salt
1 egg, beaten
Old London Bread
Crumbs
1 stick butter
1/4 cup Mazola
1/2 package almonds,
sliced
1/4 cup butter, melted
1/2 lemon

Filet and skin Spanish Mackerel. Salt very lightly. Dip in egg, and roll in bread crumbs. Melt the stick of butter and Mazola oil in an electric frying pan (380°). Brown filets, turning once, and do not overcook. Last few minutes, pour over filets: 1/2 package sliced almonds, toasted and mixed in 1/4 cup melted butter. Squeeze 1/2 lemon over filets and serve.

Mrs. Marion S. Adams, Jr.

Low-Calorie Baked Fish
with Creole Sauce

Serves 2

12 ounces fish filets,
   (flounder, perch or
   cod)
   Butter
   Salt

Bake fish until just done, using a very small amount of butter and a dash of salt. Bake at 350° about 25 minutes or in a microwave for 3½ minutes with a turn in the middle.

Creole Sauce:
1 (15 ounce) can tomato
   sauce with herbs
1/4 cup wine vinegar
2 tablespoons
   Worcestershire sauce
1 tablespoon
   dehydrated onion
   flakes
1 teaspoon Italian herb
   flavoring
1 (4 ounce) can
   mushrooms

Boil tomato sauce, vinegar, Worcestershire sauce, onion flakes and herb flavoring until thickened, about 30 minutes. Heat, then drain mushrooms and place over fish. Pour sauce over. This is enough sauce for 2-3 pounds of fish.

Mrs. Russell Terry

Red Snapper Amoroso

Serves 4

4 filets (8-10 ounces)
   red snapper
   Butter
   Salt
   Pepper
   Lemon
8 ounces lump
   crabmeat
   Dry white wine
   Hollandaise sauce

Sauté snapper filets in pure butter. Salt and pepper to taste and sprinkle with fresh lemon juice. Sauté crabmeat in dry white wine and butter. Gently mix a light Hollandaise sauce into the crabmeat. Top the snapper filets with crabmeat mixture.

Filippo Milone
The Pillars

Fish Filets

Serves 2

2   tablespoons butter
2   tablespoons flour
2   tablespoons dry
     mustard
1   cup milk
2   tablespoons dry
     Vermouth or Chablis
1   can mushrooms
1/2 pound raw, peeled
     shrimp
     Fish filets (2)
     Salt
     Lemon juice
     Paprika

Melt butter, add flour and dry mustard, blend until smooth and add milk gradually. Stir constantly and then add Vermouth. Cook until mixture thickens and add mushrooms and raw, peeled shrimp. Set aside and salt fish (raw) filets. Squeeze lemon juice over fish then pour sauce to cover fish. Cover fish with foil and bake at 325° for 30 minutes, uncover, sprinkle with paprika and bake additional 15 minutes. (Crabmeat and small oysters may be used).

Mrs. John Flynn

Smoked Fish

Cooking oil
Mackerel, snapper or
fish of your choice
Butter
Lemon juice
Parsley
Onion, minced
Worcestershire sauce

Put heavy duty foil on grill (be sure coals are white, fire low). Punch small holes in foil with a fork or sharp pointed knife to allow smoke to get through. Rub small amount of cooking oil on the fish to keep it from sticking. Place fish on foil *skin side down.* You will not need to turn the fish, but you will need to lift edges or move slightly to keep from sticking. Cover. Cook for about 45 minutes or until fish flakes easily. Baste every 10 minutes with lemon-butter sauce prepared from next five ingredients to individual's own taste.

Mrs. Robert Wilbanks

Scamp Almondine

Serves 1

1 filet of scamp, red snapper or speckled trout
Flour
Egg-whole milk mixture
Salt and pepper to taste
Pure vegetable oil
1/8 cup butter
1-2 ounces almonds, sliced and blanched
1 cap-full Realemon
Fresh parsley, chopped

Lightly flour a filet of fish. Dip the fish in an egg-whole milk mixture. Flour the fish a second time and lightly salt and pepper to taste. Cook the floured fish filet in a shallow pan or on a griddle top. Use pure vegetable oil on the pan or griddle surface. Turn the filet one time to brown each side. Approximate cooking time (total) 15 minutes at 400°-425°. Prepare melted butter that has been heated to a light brown color. Add almonds to the butter and bring the almond pieces to a golden brown color. Add the Realemon concentrated lemon juice and mix altogether along with fresh, chopped parsley. Remove from heat. Pour the almond-butter sauce over the fish and serve. There should be enough topping to put about 3 tablespoons over each filet. Enjoy.

Weichman's All Seasons

Fried Fish Fingers

Fresh fish filets
1/2 cup sour cream
1/2 cup French mustard
1/2 cup cracker crumbs

Cut fish filets into finger strips and dip in combined cream and mustard. Roll in fine cracker crumbs and fry in deep fat.

Mrs. Mitchell A. Tanner

VEGETABLES

CRICHTON CURB MARKET
For years Southern farmers have brought fresh produce
to the local market.

Artichokes and Mushrooms

Serves 8

3 cans artichoke hearts
1½ pounds fresh
    mushrooms, sliced
1/2 stick butter (4
    tablespoons)
2 tablespoons olive oil
2 tablespoons wine
    vinegar
1/2 garlic clove, crushed
1 teaspoon celery seed
1/4 teaspoon seasoned
    salt
1/8 teaspoon pepper
2 cups cheese sauce

CHEESE SAUCE:
1/2 stick butter (4
    tablespoons)
1/4 cup flour
1½ cups hot rich chicken
    stock
1 teaspoon lemon juice
    Salt to taste
    Pepper to taste
1½ cups Cheddar cheese,
    grated
    Patty shells or
    buttered bread
    crumbs

Rinse, drain and slice the artichokes. Sauté the mushrooms in butter. Combine oil, vinegar, garlic, celery seed, seasoned salt and pepper, and toss the vegetables in this mixture. Reserve. To make cheese sauce, melt butter and blend in flour. Add the hot chicken stock and stir until thickened. Add lemon juice gradually. Add salt, pepper, and cheese, stirring until combined and smooth. Combine sauce with artichoke mixture and keep warm, or reheat over hot water. Serve either in patty shells or as a casserole. If used as a casserole, cover thickly with buttered bread crumbs and bake at 350 degrees for 30 minutes.

Mrs. Joe B. Stuart

To store mushrooms, place unwashed in a paper bag that is left open to allow the mushroom to breathe. Do not use plastic bags — the mushrooms will become soggy. Clean mushrooms just before cooking with a damp towel.

Asparagus Parmigiana

Serves 8

40	spears fresh, trimmed asparagus
1/4	pound butter
	Juice of 1 lemon
1/4	teaspoon orégano
1/4	teaspoon celery salt
	Tabasco
	Pepper
16	thin slices Mozzarella cheese
	Parmesan cheese

Steam asparagus until cooked but still crisp. Meanwhile, melt butter in a pan and add lemon juice, orégano and celery salt. Then add about 10 drops Tabasco and a dash of pepper. Keep hot. For each serving, place a slice of cheese in an individual gratin dish. Place 5 spears of asparagus on top. Pour butter sauce over this and cover with another slice of cheese. Sprinkle liberally with Parmesan cheese. Run into a preheated oven on broil until the cheese melts and browns slightly. (This is prepared best in individual gratin dishes, but it can be done in a large, Pyrex pan.)

Jimmy Hirs

Asparagus Soufflé

Serves 6

4	eggs
1	(15½ ounce) can asparagus
1	cup Cheddar cheese, shredded
1	cup mayonnaise
1	(10¾ ounce) can cream of mushroom soup
1/2	teaspoon salt

Beat the eggs in the container of an electric blender. Add remaining ingredients one at a time, blending well after each addition. Pour into a lightly greased 1½ quart casserole dish. Place in a pan of water, bake at 350° for 55 to 60 minutes or until a knife comes out clean. Easy and light. A good luncheon dish.

Mrs. James R. Haas

Louisiana Baked Beans and Sausage

Serves 8

1	pound pork sausage
1	large onion, chopped
3	cloves garlic, minced
2	large (1 pound-12 ounce) and 1 small (12 ounce) cans Pork and Beans, drained
6	ounces Kraft barbecue sauce (3/4 cup)
1/2	cup brown sugar
1	tablespoon Worcestershire Sauce
1/3	teaspoon Liquid Smoke
1	cup catsup
1/2	teaspoon dry mustard
1/4	teaspoon grated lemon peel

Fry meat, onions, and garlic. Drain. Mix with the rest of the ingredients. Bake approximately 30 minutes at 350°.

Mrs. A. A. Hory, Jr.

Low-Calorie Glazed Carrots

Serves 1

	Carrots, sliced, to equal 1 serving
1	tablespoon imitation liquid butter
1/4	teaspoon nutmeg (fresh grated is best)
1	tablespoon plus 1 teaspoon brown sugar substitute

Peel and slice carrots into 1" slices. Boil in salted water until fork tender. Drain well and add remaining ingredients. Stir well until glazed and keep warm until served.

Mrs. Ernest Brown

Green Beans

Serves 6

2   (10 ounce) packages frozen French style green beans
5   slices crisp bacon, crumbled
3   teaspoons fresh parsley, chopped
4   green onions, chopped, including tops
1/2 teaspoon Accent
1/4 teaspoon salt
    Fresh ground pepper
2   teaspoons mayonnaise
2   teaspoons sour cream
2   teaspoons bacon grease
1   tablespoon olive oil
    Dash Lawry's Seasoned Salt

Cook the green beans in boiling salted water for about 6 minutes and drain. Place in a serving bowl. Mix in bacon, parsley, onions, Accent, salt and pepper. Toss with dressing of mayonnaise, sour cream, bacon grease, olive oil and salt. Mix in the morning to serve in the evening. Cover with Saran Wrap. Do not refrigerate before serving. It should be at room temperature.

Mrs. Richard Murray, III

Low-Calorie Baked Corn

Serves 6

2   packages frozen corn
1   package Mozzarella cheese, cut up
    Salt and pepper

Mix ingredients together in a casserole dish. Bake for 30 minutes or until done. Delicious, quick and easy.

Mrs. H. Browne Mercer, Sr.

Corn Pudding

Serves 6

5-6 ears fresh corn
4 eggs
1/2 stick butter
1½ cups milk or cream
2-3 tablespoons sugar
Salt to taste

Scrape corn off cob. Beat eggs well. Add milk, sugar and salt. Stir in corn. Pour mixture into greased rectangular casserole dish. Place pats of butter along top. Set dish in larger pan of water so bottom will get done. Cook at 300° to 325° for 30-35 minutes. Test for doneness by inserting knife in center. If knife comes out clean, pudding is done.

Mrs. Robert Roberts

Green Beans with Tomato

Serves 4-6

1 pound beans, cut diagonally in one inch pieces
1/4 cup butter or margarine
1/4 cup onion, finely chopped
1 small clove garlic, crushed in a garlic press
1 tablespoon lemon juice
2 medium sized ripe tomatoes cut in pieces
1 tablespoon brown sugar
1 teaspoon salt
1/8 teaspoon black pepper
1/2 teaspoon orégano

Cook the beans in boiling salted water until tender. Drain. While beans are cooking, heat the butter in a skillet. Add the onion and garlic and cook for 3 minutes. Add remaining ingredients and heat thoroughly, stirring occasionally. Toss the tomato mixture and hot beans together. Serve immediately.

Mrs. Caine O'Rear, III

Barbra's Broccoli

Serves 6-8

1	large bunch broccoli
1	can water chestnuts
1	cup pecan halves
1	package Lipton dry onion soup mix
1	stick butter, melted

Clean the broccoli and quarter the florets. Remove the stems and slice diagonally into 1/4 inch slices. Put the broccoli in boiling water and boil gently for 10 minutes. Drain the broccoli and place in baking dish. Drain the water chestnuts and combine with the next two ingredients and pour over the broccoli. Pour the butter over all and toss gently. Cover and heat at 350 degrees for 10 minutes.

Mrs. Barry Bruckmann

Cauliflower and Broccoli Panache

Serves 6-8

2	quarts water
2	tablespoons salt
1	large cauliflower, washed and broken into florets
3	tablespoons Parmesan cheese, grated
1	large bunch broccoli, washed, with stalks peeled
2	tablespoons buter
1/4	cup sour cream
	Salt and pepper to taste
1/3	cup bread crumbs, optional

In large pot, bring salted water to boil. Add cauliflower, cover, and cook until tender (5 to 15 minutes). Drain cauliflower, (reserving cooking liquid) and place in a 1½ quart casserole dish or individual bowls. Sprinkle with Parmesan cheese. Bring reserved water to a boil and add broccoli. Cook about 8 minutes. Do not overcook or the green color will be lost. Drain. Chop broccoli coarsely and purée with butter and sour cream. Season to taste with salt and pepper. Spoon purée over cauliflower covering completely. Optional to sprinkle with bread crumbs. Bake in preheated 350° oven for 20 minutes. Beautiful in clear glass dish.

Mrs. T. K. Jackson, III

Broccoli Casserole

Serves 8

2	packages frozen broccoli or 1 bunch fresh broccoli
2	tablespoons butter
2	tablespoon flour
1	teaspoon salt
2	cups milk
1/4	teaspoon pepper
3/4	cup cheese, shredded
1/4	cup almonds, chopped
1/2	cup buttered breadcrumbs
4	slices bacon, cooked and crumbled

Cook broccoli until just tender. Drain and place in greased casserole dish. Make a sauce of the butter, flour, salt, milk, pepper and cheese. Sprinkle the almonds over the broccoli then pour the sauce over all. Sprinkle the top with breadcrumbs and bacon. Bake at 350° for 20 minutes or until bubbling hot and browned on top.

Mrs. D. Clay Wilson

Nancy Sneed's Broccoli Vinaigrette

Serves 6-8

2	(10 ounce) packages frozen broccoli spears
1	teaspoon onion salt
1	teaspoon orégano
1/2	teaspoon thyme
1	teaspoon garlic salt
1/2	teaspoon black pepper
1/2	teaspoon dry mustard
1/4	cup vinegar (tarragon or wine)
2/3	cup olive oil

Cook broccoli only until crisp tender and drain. Mix other ingredients and beat with rotary beater 1 minute. Add broccoli and toss. Cover and refrigerate overnight, turning occasionally. To serve, drain off most of the marinade. Top with chopped egg, bacon, parsley, etc.

Mrs. Thomas Twitty, Jr.

Celery Parmigiana

Serves 6

4	slices bacon
4	cups celery, diced
1/4	cup onion, chopped
1/2	clove garlic, minced
1	cup water
1	teaspoon salt
2	tomatoes, peeled and chopped
1/2 to 1 cup Parmesan cheese, grated	

Cook bacon in skillet until crisp. Drain well and crumble. Put aside. Pour off bacon fat. To same skillet add celery, onion, garlic, water and salt. Cover and simmer 20 minutes, or until tender but not mushy. Drain celery mixture; fold in tomatoes and crumbled bacon. Pour mixture into a 1½ quart casserole dish and sprinkle with cheese. Bake uncovered at 350° for 15-20 minutes.

Mrs. Hugh M. Doherty

Baked Corn and Tomatoes

Serves 8-10

1	garlic clove, chopped
1/2	cup olive or any other oil
7	tomatoes, cut in 1/2-3/4 inch slices
	Flour seasoned with salt and pepper
1	large onion, cut in thin slices
12	small ears corn, cut kernels from cob
1/2	stick butter
1	cup bread crumbs

In large skillet cook garlic in oil until it is browned. Remove garlic and add tomato slices that have been dredged in seasoned flour. Sauté tomatoes until lightly golden. Remove tomatoes and sauté onion slices for just a few minutes. In a large baking dish, layer tomatoes, onions, and corn, seasoning each layer with salt and pepper. Melt butter in a frying pan and sauté bread crumbs until golden. Sprinkle on top of casserole. Bake at 350° for 40 minutes. A terrific summertime vegetable dish.

Mrs. David A. Richards

Cabbage with Cheese and Bacon

Serves 4

1 medium head of cabbage
1/4 pound bacon or salt pork
1/4 cup flour
2 cups milk
1/4 pound sharp Cheddar or American cheese, grated (1 cup)
Salt and pepper to taste

Cut the cabbage into wedges and cook in a small amount of boiling salted water for 10 minutes or until tender. Meanwhile, fry the bacon or salt pork until crisp and remove from the pan. Drain off all but 1/4 cup of fat from the pan and stir in the flour. Gradually add milk and cook over low heat, stirring constantly, until sauce is smooth and thick. Add cheese and heat until melted. Season with salt and pepper. Drain cabbage and place on a serving platter; cover with cheese sauce and sprinkle with crumbled bacon.

Connie Bea Hope

Orange Beets

Serves 6

1 teaspoon orange peel, grated
1/2 cup fresh orange juice
2 tablespoons lemon juice
1/4 cup sugar
1 tablespoon cornstarch
1/2 teaspoon salt
2 tablespoons butter
3-4 cups beets (cooked or canned)

In a saucepan heat orange peel, orange juice and lemon juice. Mix sugar, cornstarch and salt; add to the juice mixture. Stir until thickened and clear. Add the butter and beets, and simmer for 15 to 20 minutes.

Mrs. William J. May

211

Eggplant Casserole

Serves 6

2	large eggplants
1	cup Pepperidge Farm herb dressing, divided
1	medium onion, chopped
1/2	bell pepper, chopped
1	can tomatoes (or 3 fresh), drained and chopped
8	ounces Mozzarella cheese, shredded
1/2	cup Parmesan cheese, grated

Peel, cube and cook eggplant. Drain. Grease baking pan with butter. Sprinkle 1/2 cup of the stuffing across bottom. Place half of the eggplant on top of stuffing, then spread onion, bell pepper, tomatoes, and half of Mozzarella cheese over that. Follow this with the remaining eggplant and cheese. Finally top with remaining stuffing as well as the Parmesan cheese. Bake at 350° for 30 minutes until hot and bubbly.

Mrs. Lewis E. Beville

Fran's Eggplant Casserole

Serves 8

1	large onion, chopped
1	cup celery, chopped
1	large bell pepper, chopped
1/2	stick butter
1	medium large eggplant
1	cup bread crumbs
	Salt and pepper to taste
2	eggs, beaten
1	cup milk
2	teaspoons Worcestershire sauce

Sauté the onion, pepper and celery in butter. Parboil the eggplant until tender. Drain. Add eggplant to sautéed mixture. Add the bread crumbs, salt and pepper, eggs, milk and the Worcestershire sauce and put in a buttered casserole dish and bake at 350° for 30-45 minutes. Great with a rib roast, Burgundy, oven-browned potatoes and a salad.

Mrs. John P. Case, Jr.

Eggplant Méditerranée

Serves 8

3	medium eggplants
3/4	cup olive oil
1/4	cup butter
1	cup onion, chopped
1	cup celery, chopped
1	cup tomatoes, chopped
1/2	cup bell pepper, chopped
	Orégano
	Thyme
	Ground cumin
	Garlic powder
	Salt and pepper
2	large eggs, beaten
	Bread crumbs
1/4	cup butter, melted

Slice eggplant 1/4" thick. Do not peel. Sauté in olive oil and butter in batches until slightly tender. Mix all the chopped vegetables together. Layer one third of eggplant slices in a 9x13" pan. Top with one third of vegetable mixture and sprinkle with orégano, thyme, cumin (use sparingly), garlic powder and salt and pepper. Repeat these layers two more times. Bake in a 325° oven for 15 minutes. Remove from oven and drip eggs over surface of casserole, letting eggs seep down into vegetables. Sprinkle generously with bread crumbs and melted butter. Return to oven until crumbs are brown.

Jack Stallworth,
The Casbah Restaurant

Ebbie's Eggplant Soufflé

Serves 6

1	medium eggplant
2	tablespoons butter
2	tablespoons flour
1	cup milk, heated
1/2	cup cheese, grated
3/4	cup soft bread crumbs
2	teaspoons onion, grated
1	tablespoon catsup
1	teaspoon salt
2	eggs, separated

Peel the eggplant and cut into small pieces. Cook in boiling water until tender, then mash very fine. Melt the butter. Add the flour, then milk slowly. When thick and smooth, add mashed eggplant, cheese, crumbs, onion, catsup, salt, egg *yolks* (beaten slightly). Last, fold in stiffly beaten egg whites. Pour into greased 2 quart soufflé dish. Set in pan of water. Bake at 325° for 1 hour. Serve immediately.

Mrs. Robert Wilbanks

Low-Calorie Seafood Stuffed Eggplant

Serves 4

2	eggplants, medium size
1	pound shrimp
	Lemon slices
1	cup yellow squash, grated
2	tablespoons parsley, chopped
1	small onion, chopped fine
1	teaspoon tarragon
	Salt and pepper to taste
1/8	teaspoon sugar substitute
	Juice of 1/2 lemon
1	medium stalk celery, chopped fine
	Paprika

Cut 1 eggplant in half and scoop out insides, leaving about 1/4" around edges. Reserve inside pulp. Peel and cube other eggplant. Add reserved pulp and boil in salted water until tender. Drain *very well*. Boil shrimp in salted water with slices of lemon. Drain and peel. Parboil halves of eggplant for 5 minutes. Drain well. Mash eggplant pulp very well and add squash. Mix remaining ingredients, except paprika, with eggplant pulp and shrimp. Divide in half. Fill eggplant shells and sprinkle generously with paprika. Place in baking pan and put a small amount of water in the bottom of the pan. Bake at 400° for 30-45 minutes, until heated through.

Mrs. Ernest Brown

Green Pepper Casserole

Serves 4

3   large bellpeppers,
    chopped
1   cup breadcrumbs
1   cup sharp Cheddar
    cheese, shredded and
    divided
1½ tablespoons butter or
    margarine, melted
1½ tablespoons all-
    purpose flour
1   cup milk
1   teaspoon salt
1/8 teaspoon pepper

Combine the peppers, bread crumbs and 1/3 cup cheese. Stir lightly and set aside. Combine the butter and flour in a medium saucepan. Cook until bubbly. Gradually add milk. Cook over low heat until thickened, stirring constantly. Add 1/3 cup cheese, salt and pepper and stir until the cheese melts. Add the green pepper mixture and mix well. Spoon into a well greased 1 quart casserole dish. Top with the remaining cheese. Bake at 350 degrees for 1 hour.

Mrs. John Hope, III

Mushroom Casserole

Serves 6

1½ pounds mushrooms
    Salt
    Pepper
    Accent
    Ritz crackers (3 stack
    packs)
1   pint whipping cream
1   stick butter, melted

Clean mushrooms by wiping carefully with a damp cloth. Butter a 9" x 13" baking dish. Cover the bottom of the dish with half of the mushrooms, sliced stem to button. Add salt and pepper and Accent. Cover with half of the crushed Ritz crackers. Drizzle with butter. Repeat mushrooms and crackers for a second layer. Pour (unwhipped) whipping cream very carefully around *sides* of pan between casserole and dish until it touches the top layer of crackers. Cook uncovered 30-35 minutes at 350° until very bubbly. Delicious.

Mrs. Emil Graf, III

Mushroom Pie

Yield: 6 servings

2	pounds fresh mushrooms
6	tablespoons butter, divided
	Salt
	Pepper
	Lemon juice
	Dash of soy sauce
3	tablespoons flour
1½	cups chicken stock
1/2	cup Madiera or Port wine
1/2	cup cream
1	stick pie crust mix, or a prepared pie shell, thawed

Wash, dry and remove stems from mushrooms. Heat 4 tablespoons butter and add sliced mushrooms, and sprinkle with seasonings. Cover and cook 10 minutes, stirring occasionally. Arrange mushrooms in buttered 1-quart casserole dish, piling them high in the center. To juice in pan, add remaining butter and stir in flour and stock. Cook until thick. Add wine, cream, salt and pepper to taste. Pour sauce over mushrooms. Roll out pie crust and cover mushrooms. Make a few slits and brush with beaten egg. Bake at 450° for 15 minutes, then lower temperature to 300° and bake an additional 15 minutes.

Mrs. Champ Lyons, Jr.

Mushrooms in Cream

Serves 3-4

1/2	pound mushrooms, washed and dried
2	tablespoons butter or margarine
1	cup sour cream
1	tablespoon dill seed or less if preferred
1/4	teaspoon salt
	Dash ground pepper
	Toast points, English muffins, or rice
	Paprika

Slice mushrooms through cap and stem after washing and drying. Melt the butter in a skillet, add mushrooms and cover. Cook, stirring occasionally, over medium heat about 8 minutes or until lightly browned. If a lot of liquid is left in the skillet, pour off some, then add cream and seasonings. Reduce heat, cook and stir over low heat just until heated through. Dash with paprika. Serve over toast points, muffins or rice. Nice and quick for Sunday night supper.

Mrs. Wade Lott

Swiss Mushroom Pie

Serves 6

3   tablespoons flour
5   tablespoons real
     butter, divided
1   cup light cream
1   pound fresh
     mushrooms, sliced
1   clove garlic, pressed
     Approximately 1/3
     cup green onions,
     minced
2   egg yolks
1½   teaspoons salt
1/2 teaspoon pepper
2   tablespoons white
     wine or 1 tablespoon
     Sherry
1/2 cup Swiss cheese,
     grated
1   8" or 9" baked pie
     crust

Make a thick cream sauce of the flour, 3 tablespoons of butter, and cream. Cool. Sauté the sliced mushrooms in the 2 tablespoons of butter with the garlic and onions. Drain off any excess liquid. Add the mushrooms to the cream sauce, plus the egg yolks. Blend in salt, pepper, and wine. Check for seasoning. Pour mixture into the crust and top with cheese. Bake at 425° for 20 minutes. Serve with any meat, fowl, or fish. This may be made ahead, then put in the shell just before baking. Freezes well.

Mrs. John M. Scott, Jr.

Grow your own alfalfa sprouts — they're fresher and much more economical. Make a sprouter from a glass quart jar, a lid ring, and a piece of cheesecloth or wire mesh that fits the ring. Use about a tablespoon of alfalfa seeds for a quart jar. Soak the seeds in the jar overnight in plenty of water; then drain them thoroughly and put jar on its side in a dark place. Rinse seeds twice a day, making sure to drain thoroughly to prevent mold. After they begin to sprout, they may be placed in the light (not direct sunlight) for the last day or two to green the tips. Alfalfa seeds usually take from 2 to 5 days. The sprouts will keep for up to a week in a plastic bag in the refrigerator. Experiment with different varieties — mung beans, watercress, mustard seeds, and radish. The technique is the same but the growing time varies.

Mushrooms Delwood

Serves 4

1   **pound fresh mushrooms, washed and sliced**
2   **chicken bouillon cubes dissolved in 1/4 cup hot water**
2   **teaspoons flour**
1/8 **teaspoon pepper**
1/2 **cup cream (or milk)**
1   **full teaspoon Parmesan cheese**
1   **cup Pepperidge Farm Stuffing mix Bits of butter**

Put mushrooms in buttered casserole dish. Into the bouillon, stir the flour, pepper, cream, and Parmesan cheese. Cook until thickened. Pour over mushrooms. Sprinkle with stuffing and top with bits of butter. Cover. Bake 35 minutes at 350°. Uncover; bake 5 minutes more. Good with steaks.

Mrs. J. Tyler Turner, Jr.

Country Okra and Tomatoes

Serves 6-8

1   **bell pepper, chopped**
1   **large onion, chopped**
1   **stick margarine**
1   **pound fresh okra or a package of frozen okra, sliced**
1   **(28 ounce) can tomatoes Salt and pepper Buttered bread crumbs**

Sauté, in a 10" skillet, the onion and pepper in margarine. Add the okra and cook for five to ten minutes, or until slighly brown. Add 1 can of tomatoes, and salt and pepper. Simmer for 20 minutes. Put into a casserole dish and cover with buttered bread crumbs. Bake for 30 to 40 minutes at 350°. Summer supper — okra and tomatoes, butter beans, fried trout and corn bread.

Mrs. John P. Case, Jr.

Onion Rings

Serves 6-8

4	large purple onions
3	cups buttermilk
1	egg, beaten
1	teaspoon salt
1½	teaspoons baking powder
2/3	cup water
1	cup all purpose flour
1	tablespoon salad oil
1	teaspoon lemon juice
1/4	teaspoon pepper
	Shortening (for frying)

Peel onions and slice as desired, separate into rings. Soak onion rings for 30 minutes in buttermilk. Combine egg, salt, baking powder, water, flour, salad oil, lemon juice and pepper. Stir until smooth. Heat fryer to 375°, remove onions from buttermilk and dip into batter. Fry in hot oil until golden brown.

Mrs. Paul Sheldon

Peas and Mushrooms

Serves 4-6

8	slices bacon
1	small onion, chopped
2	tablespoons bacon drippings
2	tablespoons flour
1½	cups light cream, approximately
1	can tiny green peas, drained
1	can mushrooms (sliced or button, drained and chopped)
	Salt and pepper to taste

Fry bacon, drain, crumble and set aside. Sauté onion in drippings, set aside. In 2 tablespoons of bacon drippings, cook flour for 2 minutes. Pour in the cream and stir with a wire whisk until bubbly. Add the peas and mushrooms and heat through. Season. Watch carefully. Add the bacon. May be served in a vegetable dish, or for a buffet it may be served in baked crisp pastry shells. Note: The amount of cream may be increased or decreased for thinner or thicker sauce.

Mrs. J. B. Blackburn

French Peas

Serves 4-6

2 teaspoons butter
8 pearl onions, peeled and halved
2 cups fresh green peas, shelled
1 lettuce heart, shredded
1/2 teaspoon sugar
1/4 teaspoon salt
1 teaspoon flour
1/4 cup chicken broth

Melt the butter in a 2 quart saucepan. Add onions and sauté for about 3 minutes. Add the peas and shredded lettuce, sprinkle with sugar, salt, and flour. Mix well and add chicken broth and bring to a boil. Cover and turn heat to low. Simmer for about 35 minutes and serve very hot.

Mrs. Larry Harless

Grated Potatoes au Gratin

Serves 6

1 pound boiling potatoes, peeled and grated
2/3 cup milk
2/3 cup heavy cream
1 small onion, grated (medium size is okay too)
1 large clove garlic, grated
1 teaspoon salt
Freshly ground pepper to taste
1/2-1 cup grated Swiss cheese

In a saucepan combine all the ingredients except cheese. Stirring constantly (this might stick) bring mixture to the boiling point. Pour into a greased 9" pie pan or into a greased 1½ quart gratin dish, and sprinkle with the cheese. Bake in a preheated 400° oven for 25 minutes, or until potatoes are tender and cheese is golden brown. Let stand for 10 minutes. Excellent and easy. So good with steaks, roasts, and barbecue.

Mrs. Wade Faulkner

Cheesed Potatoes in Foil

Serves 3-4

3 large baking
potatoes, pared
Salt
Cracked or coarsely
ground pepper
4-5 crisp slices bacon
1 large onion, sliced
8 ounces sharp
American cheese,
cubed
1/2 cup butter or
margarine

Slice the potatoes onto a big piece of heavy aluminum foil and sprinkle with salt and pepper. Crumble the bacon over the potatoes. Add onion and cheese. Slice the butter over all. Mix on the foil; bring the edges of foil up, leaving space for steam expansion and seal with double fold. Place the package on a grill and cook over coals for 1 hour. (May be cooked with hood down for 45 minutes.)

Mrs. John Flynn

Potato Nests

Serves 6-8

2 pounds potatoes
3 tablespoons butter
2 egg yolks
1 egg
Salt, pepper and
nutmeg to taste
1 egg mixed with 1
tablespoon cream

Boil peeled potatoes until they are tender. Drain potatoes and steam them dry. Press the potatoes through a potato ricer or sieve and stir in the butter, egg yolks and whole egg. Season mixture with salt, pepper and nutmeg. Spoon into pastry bag fitted with a large tube. Pipe small rounds onto a lightly buttered baking sheet and press a hollow in the middle of each to form a nest. Brush nests with egg and cream mixture and put under broiler until tops are light brown. Fill nests with creamed mushrooms, buttered asparagus tips, etc. Serve with beef or veal. These are nice to serve on a meat platter surrounding Tournedos with Bearnaise sauce.

Mrs. Larry Harless

221

Twice Baked Potatoes

Serves 4

4	medium potatoes
1/2	pint sour cream
1/2	cup milk
4	strips crisp bacon, crumbled
1	medium onion, chopped
1	tablespoon chives, chopped
	salt and pepper to taste
2	tablespoons Cheddar cheese, grated

Bake potatoes. Scoop potato from shell. Mash with sour cream and milk. Mix in bacon, onion, chives and seasoning. Fill shells and top with cheese. Bake at 300°-350° for 30 minutes.

Mrs. Judson Sanders

Stuffed Honey Yams

Serves 6

6	sweet potatoes, about 1/2 pound each
1/2	stick butter (4 tablespoons)
1/4	cup heavy cream
2	tablespoons honey
2	tablespoons dark Rum
1/2	teaspoon ground cardamom
	Salt and pepper
	Chopped pecans

Rub the sweet potatoes with softened butter and bake them in a preheated 425 degree oven for 20 minutes. Prick the potatoes with a fork and bake for 25 more minutes or until they are tender. Cut off the top 1/3 of each potato lengthwise and scoop out the pulp, leaving a shell about 1/4 inch thick. Mash the pulp and add butter, cream, honey, Rum, cardamom, salt and pepper. Beat the mixture until it is fluffy. Put the mixture in a pastry bag fitted with a large star tip and pipe into shells. (If you don't have a pastry bag, use a spoon.) Sprinkle with chopped pecans. Arrange on a baking sheet, and bake them in the upper third of a preheated 450 degree oven for 10 minutes.

Mrs. Larry Harless

Peachy Yams

1-2 **cans (1 pound 13 ounce can) peach halves**
2 **tablespoons butter or margarine, softened**
2½ **cups (1 pound 1 ounce can) sweet potatoes or yams, cooked and mashed**
2 **tablespoons brown sugar**
1½ **teaspoons orange peel, grated**
1/4 **teaspoon salt**
2 **tablespoons Brandy (optional)**
Nuts, chopped
Brown sugar

Drain the peach halves. Arrange halves with cut side up in a baking dish. (To make peaches stand upright, cut thin slice from bottom.) Cream the butter until very soft. Add canned mashed sweet potatoes to butter. Add brown sugar, orange peel, salt and (optional) Brandy. (If using left-over cooked sweet potatoes or canned whole sweet potatoes which have been mashed, add up to 4 tablespoons of peach syrup until of a mushy consistency.) Spoon mixture into peach halves. Sprinkle with chopped nuts and brown sugar. Peachy yams can be assembled ahead and then heated when ready to serve. Bake uncovered in conventional oven at 350°-400° for 15 to 20 minutes or in portable microwave oven for 4 minutes or until hot.

Mrs. Sam Ladd

A little lemon juice added to rice and potatoes enhances their flavor and color. It also adds a spark to many soups.

Sweet Potato Casserole

Serves 6-8

3 cups sweet potatoes, cooked and mashed (3 large potatoes)
1/2 cup butter (1 stick)
1 teaspoon vanilla
1 cup sugar
2 eggs, beaten
1/3 cup milk

Mix potatoes and next 5 ingredients and put in 9x13 inch baking dish.

TOPPING:
1 cup brown sugar
1/3 cup butter, softened
1/2 cup flour
1 cup pecans, chopped

Mix topping ingredients and sprinkle on top of casserole. Bake at 350° for 25 minutes.

Mrs. Kerwin Andrews

Spinach Casserole

Serves 4

4 slices bacon
1 (10 ounce) package frozen chopped spinach
1 egg
1/2 cup milk
1/2 teaspoon salt
1/3 cup breadcrumbs
1 teaspoon onion, minced
3/4 cup Cheddar cheese, grated and divided Paprika

Cook bacon until crisp. Drain. Cook spinach, drain. Beat egg with milk and salt. Stir in the spinach, bacon, breadcrumbs, minced onion and 1/2 cup cheese. Pour into greased 1½ quart casserole dish. Sprinkle with additional cheese and Paprika. Bake uncovered at 350° for 25 minutes.

Mrs. Hugh M. Doherty

Spinach-Rice Casserole

Serves 4-6

1	package frozen spinach, chopped
2	eggs beaten
1	cup milk
1	cup sharp cheese, shredded
1	cup cooked rice
1	teaspoon onion, chopped
1½	teaspoons salt
	Dash pepper

Cook the spinach just until tender. Drain thoroughly. Combine the eggs, milk, cheese, and rice. Stir in onion, salt, pepper, and spinach. Pour into a 1½ quart casserole dish. Top with additional cheese, if desired. Bake at 350° for 25-30 minutes. This dish may be frozen, if desired.

Mrs. Bibb Lamar

Spinach Timbale

Serves 8

1/2	cup onion, finely chopped
1	tablespoon butter
2/3	cup bread crumbs
1/2	cup Gruyère cheese, grated
1/2	teaspoon salt
	Freshly grated nutmeg and cayenne, to taste
5	eggs
1	cup milk
1/4	cup butter
3	cups cooked spinach, chopped
	Hard-boiled eggs
	Dill weed
	Melted butter
	Lemon juice

Cook the onions in butter over low heat for 10 minutes without letting them color. Combine onions with bread crumbs, Gruyère cheese, salt, nutmeg and Cayenne. Beat in the eggs, one at a time, and gradually add milk heated with butter until milk is hot and butter is melted. Fold spinach into the batter and pour into a buttered 1½ quart mold. Sprinkle with additional bread crumbs. Set the mold in a pan of boiling water and bake at 325° for 35-45 minutes or until a skewer inserted in center comes out clean. Remove, let stand 5 minutes. Run a small knife around the edge. Cover the top with chopped eggs and dill. Serve with a sauce boat of melted butter and lemon juice.

Mrs. Don S. Boughton

West Coast Spinach Casserole

Serves 6

2	packages frozen, chopped spinach
2	packages frozen Welsh Rarebit
1	can thinly sliced water chestnuts
1	can French fried onion rings (optional)

Thaw the spinach and Welsh Rarebit. Squeeze all the water from the spinach. Combine and mix well all ingredients. Place in a casserole dish and top with the French fried onion rings. Bake in a 350° oven for 30 minutes or until bubbly. Fast and delicious. Great to use in the summer, or anytime that you're in a hurry.

VARIATIONS:
Fresh mushrooms, artichoke hearts or crumbled bacon bits may be used in place of water chestnuts.

Mrs. J. B. Horst

How to Prepare Pumpkin Pulp on Halloween to Use Later for Thanksgiving

Cut the top out of a pumpkin with a sharp knife at a slant. Remove all seeds. Dig out pulp with a spoon or ice cream scoop. (Now pumpkin is ready to become a jack-o-lantern.) Boil the pulp in water about 20 minutes or until soft, tender and yellow. Drain, then mash pulp well with a potato masher or fork. Pack in freezer box or plastic bag and be sure to leave 1/2 inch at top because pumpkin will expand. Freeze until Thanksgiving or Christmas and serve your family fresh pumpkin pie or bread.

Mrs. Robert Roberts

Pumpkin Seeds

Wash seeds thoroughly to remove pulp. Spread on paper towels to dry. Spread on ungreased cookie sheet and bake in a 350° oven for 20 minutes, stirring occasionally. Remove from oven. Dot with butter; sprinkle with salt and pepper and Parmesan cheese. Return to oven for 5 minutes.

Mrs. John Wilson

Acorn Squash Casserole

Serves 4-6

4   **medium size acorn squash**
     Salt
1   **cup pecans, coarsely chopped**
1/4   **cup honey**
2   **teaspoons lemon juice**
1   **teaspoon salt**
1/2   **teaspoon ground nutmeg**
1/4   **teaspoon ground cloves**
1/8   **teaspoon pepper**

Wash squash and cut in half lengthwise. Remove the seeds and stringy portions. Scrape the cavities with a teaspoon if they are very stringy. Sprinkle cut surfaces with salt. Place squash, cut side down, in 1/2 inch water in a baking dish. Bake at 400° for 25 minutes. Turn squash cut side up and bake 30 to 35 minutes until squash is tender. Remove from oven and reduce oven to 375°. Let squash cool for a few minutes so it will be easy to handle. Peel squash and chop the pulp. Combine the pulp, pecans, honey, lemon juice, salt, nutmeg, cloves and pepper. Mix well and spoon into a 1½ quart baking dish. Bake at 375° for 20 to 30 minutes.

Mrs. J. Mac Bell

Miss Penny's Fried Squash

Serves 6-8

6   to 7 medium yellow
     squash or zucchini
1-2 cups buttermilk
     Cornmeal
     Salt and pepper
     Oil for frying

Slice squash 1/4" thick or cut into strips. In a bowl with a lid soak the squash in the buttermilk for a few minutes (10 to 20). Drain. Add cornmeal seasoned with salt and pepper, cover and shake until pieces are well coated. Pour the oil in a skillet, covering the bottom. Fry in hot oil on both sides until golden brown and crispy.

Mrs. Edward McMurphy

Cornelia's Squash Casserole

Serves 6

2   pounds yellow
     squash, sliced
1   onion, chopped
1   bay leaf
1/2 teaspoon thyme
3   tablespoons parsley
3   tablespoons butter
3   tablespoons flour
1½ cups milk
     Salt to taste
     Dash nutmeg
1   teaspoon seasoning
     salt
1   teaspoon
     Worcestershire sauce
2   egg yolks
1   cup Swiss cheese,
     grated
     Buttered bread
     crumbs

Boil squash, onion, bay leaf, parsley and thyme in a little water and drain and remove the bay leaf. Make a cream sauce of butter, flour, milk and seasonings. Gradually beat in the egg yolks and 1/2 cup Swiss cheese. Add to the squash in a casserole dish. Mix bread crumbs with rest of cheese and sprinkle on top. Bake at 350° for 35 minutes.

Mrs. John N. Horner

Squash Casserole That a Boy Will Eat

Serves 8

4   pounds yellow
     squash, cleaned
1   onion
     Salt and pepper
1   pound bulk sausage
1/2 cup celery, chopped
     Parmesan cheese

Cut up the squash and onion. Boil in a small amount of salted water until tender. Drain. Fry the sausage until well done and drain. Pour off half of the grease and sauté the celery. Combine the squash mixture with the sausage, celery and remaining grease in a shallow baking dish. Bake at 350° for 45 minutes to an hour (until dry looking). Top with Parmesan cheese and serve.

Mrs. Emil Graf, III

Carrot or Squash Soufflé

Serves 6-8

2   cups cooked carrots
     (one pound)
     OR
3   cups cooked yellow
     squash
3   eggs
1/4 cup milk
1   tablespoon parsley
1   onion
3   tablespoons butter,
     melted
2   tablespoons flour
1½ teaspoons salt
     Pepper, to taste
2   cans LeSeur peas, for
     center of finished
     ring

Mix in blender or food processor. Bake at 350° for 45 minutes in small ring pan, set in pan of water. Turn out and fill center with the two cans LeSeur peas. Looks pretty as well as tastes good!

Mrs. Arthur Pope

Squash Victor

Serves 12

12 medium yellow squash, uncooked
1 pound medium pork sausage
1/2 cup Progresso bread crumbs
   Salt, pepper, Worcestershire sauce, Tabasco to taste
1 (8 or 10 ounce) package Swiss cheese, cubed

Slice squash in half lengthwise. Dig out pulp. Crumble and fry sausage until it is almost completely cooked. Drain thoroughly. Add to sausage the squash pulp, bread crumbs and seasonings. Mix. Add cheese and cook until cheese melts. Mix. Stuff squash. Place on a cookie sheet (with sides). Fill with water 1/4 to 1/2 up the side of the cookie sheet. Bake at 350° for 20 minutes.

Mrs. Gavin Bender

Squash Soufflé

Serves 8

1 pound yellow squash, chopped
1 medium onion, chopped
1/2 stick butter
2 cups Cheddar cheese, grated and reserve 1/4 cup for topping
2 cups coarse cracker crumbs, reserve 1/4 cup for topping
   Milk
   Salt to taste
   Pepper to taste
3 eggs, beaten

Cook the squash and onions in boiling water until done. Drain. Mash well and add the butter, cheese, crackers and enough milk to make it of pudding consistency. Season to taste with the salt and pepper. Add the beaten eggs last. Sprinkle reserved cracker crumbs and grated Cheddar on top. Bake for 45 minutes at 350°.

Mrs. John P. Case, Jr.

Squash Casserole

Serves 8

1-2 pounds yellow squash, sliced
1/2 cup onion, chopped
1 cup celery, chopped
Salt and pepper
1/2 stick butter
1 egg, beaten
Small jar pimento, chopped
1 cup sharp cheese, grated
1/2 cup milk
Bread crumbs, buttered

Cook the squash, onion and celery in boiling water until tender. Drain and mash. Add the salt and pepper to taste and the butter. Stir in beaten egg, pimento, grated cheese, and milk. Pour into a 2 quart dish. Top with bread crumbs. This may be prepared ahead of time. When ready, bake for 40 minutes at 350°.

Mrs. J. Tyler Turner, Jr.

Tomatoes Stuffed with Swiss Cheese and Mushrooms

Serves 8

8 tomatoes
2 tablespoons butter
1/4 cup onion, chopped
1/8 cup parsley, chopped
1 cup soft bread crumbs
1 teaspoon dried leaf basil
1 teaspoon salt
1 8-ounce can sliced mushrooms, or fresh ones
1 cup Swiss cheese, shredded

Cut and core the stem end of tomatoes and discard. Scoop out the pulp, taking care with the shells. Save the pulp. Melt the butter in a large skillet; add onion and parsley and cook until onion is tender. Add the reserved tomato pulp, bread crumbs, basil, salt and drained mushrooms. Simmer for 5 minutes. Add the Swiss cheese and stir until melted. Spoon mixture into tomatoes. Place in a shallow baking dish and bake at 350° for 15 to 20 minutes.

Mrs. Paul Sheldon

231

Stuffed Tomatoes

Serves 6

6	ripe tomatoes (firm)
	Salt
1	package frozen spinach soufflé, defrosted
1/2	cup dry bread crumbs
1/2	cup Swiss cheese, shredded
1	teaspoon onion powder
1/8	teaspoon ground nutmeg

Slice tops and scoop out pulp and seeds of tomatoes. Sprinkle inside with salt. Place upside down to drain for about 15 minutes. Combine spinach, bread crumbs, cheese, onion powder and nutmeg. Spoon into tomato shells. Place in a dish and bake at 350° until spinach mixture is firm or about 15 minutes.

Mrs. Miller Widemire

Baked Spinach Stuffed Tomatoes

Serves 6

6	medium sized tomatoes
2	tablespoons butter or margarine
1/4	pound small fresh mushrooms, sliced
1	package (10 ounce) frozen, chopped spinach, thawed and well drained
1/2	teaspoon salt
1/8	teaspoon ground black pepper
1	cup soft bread crumbs
4	eggs, slightly beaten

Hold tomatoes at room temperature until fully ripe. Cut tops from tomatoes about 1/3 of the way down. Gently scoop out pulp from tomatoes, leaving a 1/4" thick shell. Turn shells upside down to drain. In a medium skillet, melt butter. Add mushrooms; sauté for 2 minutes. Stir in spinach, 1/2 teaspoon salt, and black pepper; cook and stir for 2 minutes. Remove from heat and stir in bread crumbs and eggs. Sprinkle tomato shells lightly with salt. Fill with spinach mixture. Stand in greased 10x6x2" baking pan. Bake in a pre-heated moderate oven (350°) until hot, about 25 minutes. If desired, sprinkle tops with buttered bread crumbs.

Mrs. John Huff

232

Tiny Baked Cherry Tomatoes

Serves 4-6

24 cherry tomatoes, washed and stemmed
4   tablespoons butter
    Salt
1   teaspoon sugar
    Parsley, minced
    Green onion, chopped (optional)

Combine all ingredients in baking dish and bake at 350° for 8-10 minutes, shaking the pan occasionally so the tomatoes turn in the butter.

Mrs. Thomas Twitty, Jr.

Ratatouille

Serves 8

2   pounds zucchini
2   pounds eggplant, several small ones
1/2 cup butter
3   green peppers, thinly sliced
2   onions, sliced
3   cloves garlic, smashed
2   pounds tomatoes, peeled, seeded, sliced
     Salt and pepper
     Basil
     Thyme
     Bay leaf (crushed)

Cut the unpeeled zucchini and eggplant into 1/2 inch slices and sauté in the butter a few at a time, several minutes on each side. Remove and drain. In the same skillet stir the green peppers, onions and garlic. Cook for 10 minutes. Remove and discard the garlic. Add the tomatoes. Layer the eggplant, zucchini, and half of the tomato mixture; season with salt, pepper and herbs. Repeat, ending with tomato sauce and seasonings. Bake, covered, at 350° for 45 minutes to an hour. Delicious either hot or cold. Serve with veal or chicken.

Mrs. Thomas B. Van Antwerp

Stuffed Zucchini

Serves 8

4   (6 inch) zucchini
    squash
1   large onion, chopped
1/2 cup ham, finely
    chopped
3/4 cup shrimp, chopped
1   bay leaf
6   tablespoons butter
1   slice of bread for each
    zucchini used
1   teaspoon thyme
1   tablespoon parsley
    flakes
1/8 teaspoon salt
1   teaspoon black
    pepper
    American cheese,
    grated
    Bread crumbs

Parboil the zucchini squash in salted water. Slice the squash lengthwise and carefully remove pulp with a spoon. Sauté the onion, ham, shrimp and bay leaf in the 6 tablespoons of butter. Simmer for 15 minutes. Combine the pulp of the zucchini with sliced bread (shredded), thyme and parsley flakes. Add the salt and pepper. Stir all ingredients and simmer for 10 more minutes. Stuff the zucchini shells and sprinkle the top with grated cheese and bread crumbs. Bake on a cookie sheet at 375° until cheese is bubbly.

Mrs. J. Michael Druhan, Jr.

Zucchini with Dill

Serves 6.

6   zucchini
1/4 cup butter
1   tablespoon chopped
    dill
1   tablespoon dill seed
1   cup sour cream
1   tablespoon lemon
    juice
1   teaspoon sugar
1   teaspoon paprika
    Salt and pepper to
    taste

Scrub zucchini and cut them into 1/4 inch slices. Melt butter in a saucepan and sauté the slices, covered over low heat with chopped dill, dill seed and salt and pepper to taste for about five minutes, or until zucchini are just tender and transparent. Add sour cream beaten with lemon juice, sugar and paprika, and also add salt and pepper to taste. Heat sauce but do not let it boil. Serve with a sprinkling of dill and paprika.

Mrs. Sam W. Pipes, III

Zucchini Parmesan

Serves 4

4-5 small zucchini squash, thinly sliced (about 3 cups)
2 tablespoons butter
1/2 teaspoon salt
Dash pepper
2 tablespoons Parmesan cheese, grated

Put the zucchini, butter and seasonings in a skillet. Cover and cook slowly for 5 minutes. Uncover and cook, turning slices until barely tender, about 5 minutes more. Sprinkle with the cheese, and toss.

Mrs. Norton Brooker

Crisp Buttered Zucchini

Serves 4

4 medium zucchini
1/4 cup butter
1/2 teaspoon garlic salt
1/8 teaspoon pepper
Pinch of sugar

Coarsely shred the zucchini. Add to the melted butter in a skillet along with all the seasonings. Cover and cook over medium heat for 8 to 10 minutes, stirring once.

Mrs. Sam W. Pipes, III

Low-Calorie Zucchini with Garlic

Serves 2

3 medium to large zucchini squash
1 pod garlic
1 lemon
Salt and pepper to taste

Wash and dry zucchini. Mash garlic. Spray Teflon skillet with non-stick ingredient. Grate squash into skillet. Mix with garlic and juice of 1 lemon. Salt and pepper to taste. Heat over medium heat until very hot and wilted. Should take only about 5-6 minutes.

Mrs. Ernest Brown

Zucchini with Cheese

Serves 6

1½ pounds zucchini
1/4 cup all purpose flour
1½ teaspoons salt, divided
1½ teaspoons dried orégano, divided
1/4 teaspoon pepper
1/4 cup olive or salad oil
2 medium tomatoes, sliced
1 cup sour cream
1/2 cup Parmesan cheese, grated

Wash the zucchini and cut crosswise into 1/4 inch slices. In a medium bowl, combine the flour, 1/2 teaspoon salt, 1/2 teaspoon orégano and 1/8 teaspoon pepper. Toss the slices in the seasoned flour and coat well. Heat the oil in a skillet and sauté the zucchini until golden brown — about four minutes on each side. Drain. Cover the bottom of a baking dish with zucchini and top with tomato slices. Combine the sour cream with the rest of the salt, orégano and pepper. Spread evenly over the tomato slices. Sprinkle with grated cheese. Bake at 350° for 30-40 minutes or until the cheese is melted.

Mrs. Edward McMurphy

Vegetable Mélange

Serves 6-8

6 large green peppers, cut into 1" squares
2 large onions, cut into strips
5 large fresh tomatoes, cut into eighths
2½ teaspoons salt
1¼ teaspoons basil
1 tablespoon butter
Cracked pepper

Arrange the vegetables in a large, shallow baking pan that has been well greased. Sprinkle with the seasonings. Top with small bits of butter and bake in a 350° oven for 35-45 minutes until tender. Delicious with steak or seafood.

Mrs. Stephen G. Lauten

Harvest Vegetable Casserole

Serves 12

2	large onions, sliced 3/4" thick
2	green peppers cut in 1" strips
2	tablespoons salad oil
1	cup water
1/2	cup barley
1	envelope beef flavor bouillon
2	large carrots, cut in chunks
2	large tomatoes, peeled and quartered
2	medium zucchini cut into 1½" chunks
3/4	pound green beans, cut in half
1	package frozen peas
1/2	cauliflower, separated into large florets
2	tablespoons lemon juice
1	clove garlic, crushed
1	tablespoon salt
1/2	teaspoon pepper
2	teaspoons paprika
1/2	cup parsley, chopped

Sauté onion rings and green pepper in hot oil until browned, about 10 minutes. Combine water, barley and bouillon in an oven-proof casserole dish. Place carrots, tomatoes, zucchini, green beans, peas and cauliflower in dish and top with onion mixture. Pour lemon juice and garlic over. Sprinkle with salt, pepper and paprika. Cover and bake at 400 degrees for 1½ hours. Stir in parsley and serve.

Mrs. Champ Lyons, Jr.

Zucchini, cucumber and eggplant should be sprinkled with salt and allowed to drain for thirty minutes, then rinsed and well dried before frying.

Succotash

Serves 6

1 medium onion, chopped
4 outside pieces celery, chopped
1 small green pepper, chopped
1 stick margarine or margarine and bacon grease
1 large can tomatoes
  Salt and pepper to taste
2 tablespoons sugar
1 teaspoon Worcestershire
1 pound fresh butter beans
1/2 pound fresh okra, diced
5 large ears of corn

Sauté vegetables in fat. Add tomatoes and seasonings and cook for 30 minutes. Add butter beans, okra and corn that has been cut from the cob. (I usually cut the kernels twice and add the corn last after the butter beans are well cooked.) Let all of this cook until it is thick. If it remains too juicy for serving, thicken with a little cornstarch mixed with water. Check seasonings before serving and adjust if necessary.

Mrs. Vernon Dukes
From "A Good Cook's Book"

My Grandmother's Succotash

Serves 8

2 pounds fresh butter beans
2 pounds fresh okra, sliced
1 stick butter
4 fresh, ripe tomatoes, chopped
5 ears of corn, cut and scraped from cob
  Salt and pepper

Put butter beans in salted water in a skillet. Cook 15 minutes. Slice okra and add to butter beans along with 1 stick butter. Cook 15 more minutes. Now add the tomatoes that have been chopped, along with salt and pepper. Cook for a few more minutes. Last, add corn that has been cut and scraped from the cob. Cook an additional 7 minutes. Note: This is a delicious summertime vegetable dish that can't be beat. Everybody *loves* it.

Mrs. Richard Murray, III

EGGS, CHEESE, PASTA & RICE

LIGNOS GROCERY STORE
Traditional Greek delicacies — Part of Mobile since 1916. Lignos is still the store for that special herb, spice or cheese.

Artichoke Frittata

Yield: 16 squares

2	jars marinated artichokes (reserve liquid)
1	bunch green onions, chopped
2	tablespoons parsley, chopped fine
4	eggs, beaten
6	saltine crackers, crushed
	Salt, pepper, Tabasco to taste
1/2	pound sharp cheese, grated

Remove artichokes from liquid. Chop artichokes and set aside. Chop onions and parsley. Sauté in the reserved artichoke liquid until tender. In another bowl beat eggs. Add crackers, artichokes, onions, parsley, seasonings and cheese. Pour into greased 8"x8" pan. Bake for 35 minutes at 325 degrees. Cut into squares and serve either warm or cold.

Mrs. Sam G. Ladd

Surprise Scramble

Serves 18

3	dozen eggs
1/2	cup butter
1/2	cup milk
1	green pepper, chopped
2	cans mushroom soup, melted
2	tablespoons Sherry
1/2	pound sharp cheese, grated
	Mushroom caps
	Paprika

Soft-scramble the eggs with butter, milk and green pepper. Make a layer of eggs in a 13x9x2" casserole dish. Mix together soup, Sherry and cheese. Pour this over the layer of eggs and top with all the remaining eggs. Place mushroom caps over all and refrigerate for 8 hours. Sprinkle with paprika. Bake at 300° for 50 minutes. This is nice for brunch served with Sausage and Rice Casserole.

Mrs. Larry Harless

Spinach and Beef Quiche

1   (10 inch) pie shell,
      unbaked
1/2 cup onion, finely
      chopped
3   tablespoons butter or
      margarine
1   pound ground beef,
      chuck or round
1   (10 ounce) package
      frozen chopped
      spinach, thawed
1   (4 ounce) can
      mushrooms, drained
      and chopped
3/4 teaspoon salt
1/4 teaspoon pepper
1/4 teaspoon ground
      nutmeg
2   large eggs
1   cup (1/2 pint) heavy
      cream
1/2 cup sharp Cheddar
      cheese, grated but
      medium or Swiss
      cheese may be
      substituted

Heat oven to 400°. Prick pie shell all over with a fork and bake 15 minutes, until lightly browned. Sauté onions in butter, add meat and brown. Drain and discard fat from the skillet. Squeeze the spinach with the hands to remove as much moisture as possible. In a bowl, thoroughly mix the beef and onion with the spinach, mushrooms, salt, pepper, and nutmeg. Beat the eggs with the cream and stir into the meat mixture. Pour into the pastry shell and sprinkle with the cheese. Turn the oven down to 375° and bake for 30 minutes, until the top is speckled brown and filling is set. Let stand 10 minutes before slicing.

Mrs. Ross Drake

Broccoli Quiche

Serves 6-8

1	10-ounce package chopped broccoli, cooked and drained
1½	cups finely shredded Swiss cheese
1	frozen Mrs. Smith's pie crust
3/4	cup milk
3	eggs
	A little onion to taste
2	tablespoons flour
	Dash of nutmeg
	Salt to taste
	Pepper to taste
	Dash of Cayenne

Layer broccoli and cheese in the pie crust. Mix the next 7 ingredients together and pour over the broccoli and cheese. Sprinkle top with Cayenne. Bake at 425 degrees until golden.

Miss Mary Herndon

Collards Quiche

Serves 8

6	slices bacon, chopped, fried, and drained
1	cup Swiss cheese, grated
1	9" partially baked pie shell
1	package frozen chopped collards, cooked and well drained
3	eggs, beaten
2	cups light cream
1	teaspoon salt
	Dash nutmeg, Cayenne, black pepper

Sprinkle bacon and cheese on bottom of pie shell. Chop drained collards again to break up any stems and pieces and combine with remaining ingredients, mixing well. Pour mixture into pie shell, over the cheese and bacon. Bake in a preheated oven at 400° for 10 minutes. Reduce heat to 350° and continue baking for 35-40 minutes until quiche is set in the middle. Let stand a few minutes before cutting into wedges.

Mrs. Elaine H. Tonsmeire

Crab Quiche

Serves 6

1   9-inch pastry shell,
    partially baked
1/2 cup mayonnaise
2   tablespoons all
    purpose flour
2   eggs, beaten
1/2 cup milk
1   cup crabmeat, or
    more
1/2 pound Swiss cheese,
    cut into 1/4 inch
    cubes
1/3 cup chopped green
    onion

Combine mayonnaise, flour, eggs and milk. Mix thoroughly. Stir in crabmeat, cheese and onion. Spoon into quiche shell and bake at 350° for 30-40 minutes, or until firm in center. Garnish with parsley. Can be used as an appetizer or with salad at luncheon. Can be frozen.

Mrs. T. K. Jackson, III

Ham and Asparagus Quiche

Serves 4-6

1-2 cups cooked ham
1   9-inch pastry shell,
    partially baked
1   (10 ounce) package
    frozen asparagus or 1
    pound fresh or 1 can
1   cup Swiss cheese
3   eggs
1   cup light cream or
    half and half
    Salt and pepper to
    taste
    Parsley sprigs,
    optional

Sprinkle ham evenly in pie shell. Arrange asparagus spears spoke-fashion evenly over ham. Sprinkle with cheese. Beat eggs, cream, salt and pepper until mixed but not frothy. Pour over ham and cheese. Bake in preheated oven, 375°, for 30 to 40 minutes or until custard is set. Garnish with parsley.

Mrs. Ross C. Havard

Swiss Quiche

Serves 6

3	eggs, slightly beaten
1	cup light cream
5	slices crisp bacon, crumbled
3	tablespoons Dijon mustard
1/4	cup onion, finely minced
1	cup Swiss cheese, grated
1/4	teaspoon salt
1/8	teaspoon pepper
1	(9 inch) pie shell, partially baked

Combine all ingredients and pour into pie shell. Bake in a 375° oven (35-40 minutes) or until inserted knife comes out clean.

Mrs. Peter Kenyon

Spinach Quiche

Serves 12-16

2	frozen pie crusts, partially baked
8	ounces Gruyere cheese, grated
2	cups heavy cream or 2 cups milk
1/2	cup flour
6	eggs
1	medium onion, minced
1½	teaspoons salt
1/2	teaspoon pepper
1	(10 ounce) package frozen spinach; let thaw and dry with towel

Preheat oven to 400°. Sprinkle grated cheese onto pie crusts. Beat cream with flour, add eggs, onion, seasonings, and beat well. Add spinach and blend. Pour into pie crusts. Bake at 400° for 40 minutes, or until a knife inserted near the center comes out clean.

Mrs. Greg Leatherbury, Jr.

Sausage and Mushroom Quiche

Serves 6

1	pound hot or sweet Italian sausage, or Kielbasa
3/4	pound mushrooms, thinly sliced
4	tablespoons butter
1	cup heavy cream
2	egg yolks, lightly beaten
1	tablespoon flour
1	tablespoon butter, melted
1	tablespoon lemon juice
1/2	teaspoon salt
	Freshly ground pepper
	10-inch pastry shell, partially baked
1/2	cup Parmesan cheese, grated

Preheat oven to 350°. Squeeze sausage out of casing and brown, breaking it up with a fork. Drain well. Sauté mushrooms in butter. Mix cream, egg yolks, flour, butter, lemon juice, salt and pepper to taste. Put sausage and mushrooms in pie shell, pour custard over, sprinkle with cheese and bake at 350° for 35 minutes until puffy and light brown. A good dish for family or company.

Mrs. William Seifert

Grits Soufflé

Serves 4

4	cups milk
1	cup grits, instant
2	teaspoons salt
1	teaspoon baking powder
1	teaspoon sugar
4	tablespoons butter, melted
6	eggs, separated

Scald milk, add grits and cook until thick. Add salt, baking powder, sugar and butter. Beat egg yolks and add to grits mixture. Beat egg whites to a soft peak and fold in the batter. Pour into a well buttered 2-quart casserole dish. Bake in 375° oven for 25 to 30 minutes. This is great with wild game dishes.

Mrs. C. R. Butler, Jr.

Cheese Soufflé

Serves 6

1/4 cup butter
3 tablespoons flour
1/4 teaspoon salt
1 cup milk
1 cup (1/4 pound) grated Gruyère or Cheddar cheese
4 large eggs, separated
Dash of Cayenne
1/4 teaspoon cream of tartar

Melt butter in a saucepan. Remove from heat and blend in flour and salt. Stir and cook 1 minute. Remove from heat and stir in milk. Cook until the sauce is of medium thickness, stirring constantly. Stir in cheese. Beat egg yolks until they are thick and lemon-colored. Add a little of the hot sauce to the egg yolks and then stir the yolks into the remaining hot mixture. Add Cayenne. Beat egg whites until they are foamy. Add cream of tartar and beat until the whites stand in soft, stiff peaks. Gently fold into the mixture. Butter the bottom (not the sides) of a 1½ quart soufflé dish and pour in the mixture. Place the dish in a pan of hot water. Bake in a preheated slow oven (325°) 1¼ hours, or until soufflé is well puffed and browned. Serve immediately.

Mrs. J. B. Newell, Jr.

Easy Never-Fail Cheese Soufflé

Serves 4

3	tablespoons quick-cooking Tapioca
2	tablespoons onion, minced
1	teaspoon salt
1	cup milk
1	cup American cheese, grated
3	egg yolks, well beaten
1	tablespoon parsley, minced
3	egg whites, stiffly beaten

Combine Tapioca, onion, salt and milk. Cook in a double-boiler for 10 minutes, stirring frequently. Add cheese and stir until the cheese melts. Add a little of the hot mixture to egg yolks. Stir a minute, then add back to the remaining hot mixture. Cool slightly and add parsley. Fold in the egg whites and pour into an ungreased 1-quart baking dish. Bake the soufflé in a pan with 1 inch of hot water surrounding it at 350 degrees for 1 hour.

Mrs. A. A. Hory, Jr.

Tomato Cheese Macaroni Casserole

Serves 6

2	cups uncooked elbow macaroni
	Salt
1/2	cup onion, finely chopped
5	tablespoons butter or margarine, divided
1	can (1 pound) whole tomatoes, with liquid
	Black pepper, to taste
1	cup dairy sour cream, at room temperature
1	cup sharp Cheddar cheese, shredded
	Grated Parmesan cheese

Cook the macaroni in boiling salted water until tender; drain. Sauté the onion in 3 tablespoons butter until tender. Add tomatoes, 1/2 teaspoon salt and pepper to taste. Cook, stirring to break up tomatoes, about 10 minutes. Add the macaroni, sour cream and Cheddar cheese and mix well. Spoon into a shallow 2-quart baking dish. Top with Parmesan cheese and bits of remaining butter. Bake in a preheated oven at 350° for about 30 to 40 minutes. A really nice "family" dish.

Mrs. Orin Wood

248

Low-Calorie Cheese Pudding
with Mushroom Sauce

Serves 1

1   slice bread, crumbled
1   egg, well beaten
1   cup skimmed milk
1/2   teaspoon dried parsley
1   teaspoon dried onion
1/4   teaspoon Dijon mustard
     Salt and white pepper to taste
1   ounce grated cheese (especially good to grate together all bits of leftovers)

Mix very well together and bake at 350° for 35-45 minutes. Time depends on your oven. It should puff up and be brown on top.

Mushroom Sauce:

5   medium or large fresh mushrooms
1   teaspoon liquid butter
1   teaspoon fresh lemon juice
1   tablespoon water
     Salt and freshly ground pepper

Sauté mushrooms in the remaining ingredients and serve hot over the cheese pudding.

Mrs. Ernest Brown

249

Cheese Casserole

Serves 6-8

1 (12 ounce) package Monterey Jack cheese, coarsely grated
1 (12 ounce) package Cheddar cheese, coarsely grated
4 egg whites
4 egg yolks
2/3 cup (1 small can) evaporated milk
2 (4 ounce) cans green chilies, drained, seeded and diced
1 tablespoon flour
1/2 teaspoon salt
1/8 teaspoon pepper
2 medium tomatoes, sliced

Mix the grated cheeses in a 9x12x2 inch baking dish. Beat the egg whites until stiff peaks form. In a separate dish, beat egg yolks, add milk, chilies, flour, salt and pepper. Fold the egg whites into the egg yolk mixture. Pour egg mixture over cheese in casserole dish and using a fork mix it through the cheese. Bake for 30 minutes at 325°. Remove from the oven. Arrange sliced tomatoes around the edge. Bake 30 minutes longer or until an inserted knife comes out clean. Something different for a brunch menu.

Mrs. Hugh M. Doherty

Wild Rice and Sausage Casserole

Serves 8

1 (6 ounce) box Uncle Ben's Long Grain and Wild Rice
2 (10 ounce) cans beef consommé
1 pound lean ground beef
1 pound hot bulk sausage
1 (4 ounce) can sliced mushrooms, drained (optional)
1 cup sharp cheese, grated

Put the rice and consommé in a casserole dish and bake for 1 hour at 350 degrees until the consommé is absorbed. Brown the ground beef and set aside. Brown the sausage and drain on paper towels. Toss the beef and sausage with cooked rice. You may add a small can of mushrooms, drained, to this mixture if you wish. Cover with the grated cheese. Heat in a 350 degree oven until warm, about 20 minutes.

Mrs. Richard Murray, III

Sausage and Rice Casserole

Serves 6-8

2 pounds Jimmy Dean hot sausage
1 cup rice, uncooked
1/2 cup celery, chopped
1/4 cup onion, chopped
2 envelopes Lipton noodle soup mix
1 tablespoon soy sauce
2½ cups water
1/2 cup almonds, slivered

Brown sausage and pour off fat. Mix together sausage, rice, celery, onion and soup mix. Place in a 2-quart casserole dish. Refrigerate at least 8 hours. When ready to bake, mix soy sauce with water and add to casserole. Sprinkle almonds on top. Cover and bake at 350° for 1 hour. Nice for brunch served with Surprise Scramble. Both recipes may be prepared ahead.

Mrs. Larry Harless

Sausage Casserole

Serves 6-8

8 slices stale bread, without crust, cubed
2 pounds bulk sausage, cooked and drained
1½ cups sharp cheese, grated
6 eggs, slightly beaten
2½ to 3 cups milk
1 tablespoon brown sugar
1/4 teaspoon paprika
1 tablespoon onion, minced
1/4 teaspoon dry mustard
1/4 teaspoon salt
1/8 teaspoon pepper
1/2 teaspoon Worcestershire
1/8 teaspoon red pepper (optional)

Layer bread cubes, sausage and cheese in a greased casserole dish (2-quart). Repeat if using a small dish. Combine beaten eggs with milk and remaining ingredients. Pour over the sausage, bread and cheese. Cover and refrigerate over night. Remove from refrigerator a while before cooking to take off the chill. Bake at 350 degrees for 45 minutes to 1 hour. (Remove cover before baking.) This is a good recipe for breakfast or brunch. Delicious served with fresh sautéed mushrooms.

Mrs. Edward Williams

Macaroni Casserole

Serves 10-12

1 (8 ounce) box macaroni, cooked and drained
1 can cream of mushroom soup
2 small cans sliced mushrooms
1 cup mayonnaise
1/4 cup pimento, chopped
1/4 cup onion, chopped
1 pound Cheddar cheese, grated
Bleu cheese crackers
3 tablespoons butter, melted

Combine ingredients and pour into a greased 13-inch Pyrex dish. Crumble cheese crackers over the mixture and pour butter over all. Bake at 375° for 25-30 minutes. This is so good, especially in the summertime with fried chicken and fresh vegetables. It is something like a hot pimento cheese sandwich, but better!

Mrs. Wade Faulkner

Armenian Rice

Serves 6

1 cup rice
2 cups chicken broth
1 stick butter
4 cloves garlic, minced
1 cup vermicelli, broken into small pieces
1 large bell pepper, diced
1 (4½ ounce) can sliced mushrooms, drained
1 (2.3 ounce) can sliced ripe olives, drained
1 (8 ounce) can water chestnuts, drained and sliced

Wash rice until water runs clear. Place the rice in a 2-quart casserole dish with cover. Cover the rice with the chicken broth. Melt the butter in a skillet and cook garlic until golden brown. Remove and discard the garlic. Add the vermicelli to the skillet and brown. Combine the vermicelli with the rice and add the remaining ingredients, mixing well. Cover and bake at 350° for 40 minutes. Stir once after 20 minutes to distribute ingredients evenly in rice. The rice will be done when all the broth has cooked away.

Mrs. Cooper Thurber

Fettuccine with Zucchini and Mushrooms

1 clove garlic, minced
1/2 pound mushrooms, trimmed and sliced
1/4 cup butter
1½ pounds zucchini, scrubbed and cut into julienne strips
1 cup heavy cream
1/2 cup butter, cut into small pieces
Salt and pepper to taste
1 pound fettuccine
7 quarts water
2 tablespoons salt
3/4 cup Parmesan cheese, freshly grated
1/2 cup parsley, chopped
Additional Parmesan cheese
Freshly ground black pepper

Sauté garlic and mushrooms in 1/4 cup butter for 2 minutes over medium heat. Add zucchini, cream and bits of butter. Simmer 3 minutes. Add salt and pepper to taste. Cook fettuccine in boiling salted water for 7 minutes until just tender. Drain well in colander, then add to vegetables in skillet along with cheese and parsley. Toss to combine. Serve on heated platter with extra cheese. Offer grinds of freshly ground black pepper.

Mrs. Fred Cushing

Grate a whole block of Parmesan cheese in the food processor with steel blade. Store in airtight jar in the refrigerator.

Noodles Romano

Serves 6

1/4 cup soft butter
2 tablespoons parsley flakes
1 teaspoon crushed basil
1 (8-ounce) package cream cheese, softened
1/2 teaspoon salt
1/2 teaspoon pepper
2/3 cup boiling water
1 (16-ounce) package fettuccine noodles or thin spaghetti
1 clove garlic, minced
1/2 cup butter
1 cup Romano or Parmesan cheese, grated

Combine first seven ingredients and keep warm. Cook noodles in large amount of salted water JUST until tender, drain. Cook garlic in 1/2 cup butter 1 to 2 minutes; pour over noodles. Toss lightly and quickly to coat well. Sprinkle with 1/2 cup of cheese; toss again. Pile noodles on warm serving platter. Top with cream cheese sauce. Sprinkle with remaining 1/2 cup cheese. Garnish with parsley. Very rich. This makes a good cold-weather supper with hot bread, a big green salad and white wine.

Mrs. Wade Faulkner

Noodles Alfredo

Serves 6

1/2 pound noodles
2 egg yolks
1/3 cup heavy cream
1/3 cup soft butter
1/3 cup Parmesan cheese
1/4 teaspoon salt, pepper and nutmeg (each)

Cook noodles in boiling water according to package directions. Drain and put them in a heated bowl. In another bowl whip egg yolks until foamy, add the cream and gradually the butter. Next mix in the cheese and season with salt, pepper and nutmeg. Pour egg mixture onto very hot noodles and mix thoroughly. Serve immediately on hot plates.

Mrs. Larry Harless

Fettuccine Romano

Serves 4

1	(8 ounce) package fettuccine or medium noodles
1/2	cup heavy cream
1/2	cup melted butter
1	tablespoon green onion, minced
1/2	cup Parmesan or Romano cheese or mixture of both, freshly grated
1	tablespoon parsley, chopped

Cook noodles according to package directions. Mix heavy cream with melted butter. Pour over hot noodles. Toss gently with onion and cheese. Sprinkle with parsley.

Mrs. David Richards

Garlic Spaghetti

Serves 8

3	cloves garlic
1/2	cup Parmesan cheese
4	tablespoons pecans, chopped
1/2	teaspoon salt
6	tablespoons olive oil or salad oil
1/2	large package very fine spaghetti
1/2	stick butter
2	tablespoons parsley, minced
	Chopped parsley

A day ahead, place garlic, Parmesan cheese, pecans, salt and oil in blender and blend to paste consistency. Chill. Before serving, boil spaghetti in salted water until tender. Drain. Add butter and toss well. Add minced parsley and paste mixture and toss. Garnish with small amount of chopped parsley. Excellent with beef roast.

Mrs. Thomas S. Damson

Green Enchiladas

Serves 6

Enchiladas:
2 dozen tortillas
1 cup cooking oil
Chopped onions
Grated cheese
(Monterey Jack or
any cheese that melts
smoothly)

Dip each tortilla in very hot oil just long enough to soften. Spread each tortilla with cheese and onion and roll up (might need toothpicks to hold.) Place in a shallow baking dish, side by side, and cover with green sauce.

Green Sauce:
1 package frozen
spinach
1 can condensed
cream of chicken
soup
3-4 green onions,
minced
2-3 jalapeño peppers (or
a can of green
chilies), chopped
1/4 teaspoon salt
1 pint sour cream
1½ cups cheese, grated

Cook the spinach as directed on box. Add the soup, green onions, peppers and salt. Put through the blender. Add sour cream and mix well. Pour over the enchiladas. Sprinkle with grated cheese, cover and bake at 350° for 30 minutes. Note: Jalapeños will make sauce spicier than chilies. This recipe may be halved easily.

Mrs. Edward Oppenheimer

PRESERVES, SAUCES & ACCOMPANIMENTS

LADY PEELING FRUIT ON PORCH
Preserving is a Southern tradition and this scene is still
typical of a Mobile porch.

Food Processor Mayonnaise

Yield: 1 pint

2   eggs
1   teaspoon salt
1   teaspoon dry mustard
2   tablespoons fresh lemon juice
  Shake of paprika
  Shake of Cayenne pepper
2   cups chilled Wesson oil
1   teaspoon onion, grated

Place in bowl of the food processor the following ingredients: eggs, salt, dry mustard, lemon juice, paprika and Cayenne pepper. Process for a few seconds with the steel blade. Then, add very slowly with machine running constantly, the chilled Wesson oil. When thick, add the grated onion. This recipe may be doubled in the Cuisinart Food Processor.

Mrs. A. A. Hory, Jr.

Curry Mayonnaise

Yield: 1 cup

1   egg, room temperature
5   teaspoons lemon juice
1½   teaspoons curry powder
1   teaspoon Dijon mustard
1   small clove garlic, crushed
1/4   teaspoon salt
1/4   teaspoon pepper
3/4   cup oil

In a food processor or blender on high, blend egg, lemon juice, curry powder, mustard, garlic, salt and pepper. Then add oil in a stream, blending while adding. Serve the sauce with meat, poultry, fish or vegetables.

Cookbook Committee

Mayonnaise Variations

Watercress Mayonnaise:
1½   cups homemade
      mayonnaise
3/4   cup watercress
      leaves, chopped
1   tablespoon snipped
      dill or 1/4 teaspoon
      dried dill
1   teaspoon lemon juice
1   teaspoon onion,
      grated
      Salt and white pepper
      to taste

Yield: 1¾ cups
In a food processor or a blender blend mayonnaise with all ingredients except salt and pepper until mixture is evenly colored. Add salt and pepper to taste.

Dill Mayonnaise:
2   cups homemade
      mayonnaise
1/3   cup sour cream
1/3   cup snipped dill or 1
      tablespoon dried dill
1   tablespoon Dijon
      mustard
1   teaspoon anchovy
      paste
1   garlic clove, crushed

Yield: 2½ cups
Blend all ingredients into mayonnaise.

Cookbook Committee

260

Tartar Sauce

Yield: 1¾ cups

1½ cups mayonnaise
3 green onions, minced
1 hard-boiled egg yolk, minced
1 teaspoon capers, minced
1 teaspoon parsley, minced
1 teaspoon onion, grated
1 teaspoon Dijon mustard
1 teaspoon lemon juice

Fold all ingredients into mayonnaise, add salt and white pepper to taste.

Cookbook Committee

Sauces such as Hollandaise and Béarnaise may be held for several hours in preheated thermos bottles.

Hollandaise Sauce

Yield: 1 cup

2 tablespoons flour
2 tablespoons butter or margarine
1 cup hot water
2 egg yolks, well beaten
Juice of 2 lemons
Salt

Blend butter and flour in a saucepan, add hot water and stir until thickened. Remove from stove — cool slightly and beat in egg yolks. Return to stove and heat but do not boil. Then add lemon juice, salt to taste, and cook until desired consistency. This can be kept in refrigerator and reheated in a jar in hot water. Good over asparagus, artichoke hearts and broccoli.

Mrs. John Flynn

Really Easy Hollandaise

1	egg
2	egg yolks
3	tablespons water
2	tablespoons lemon juice
1½	sticks butter
	Salt

Whisk egg and egg yolks together in a saucepan with a wire whisk. Heat water and lemon juice. When hot, whisk into the eggs. Cook over low heat, whisking constantly, until the mixture is too hot for your finger. Now add the butter, which has been melted, drop by drop, whisking all the while. Season to taste.

Mrs. Wade Faulkner

New Orleans Egg Dressing

Yield: 1½ cups

3	hard boiled eggs, finely chopped
1	cup mayonnaise
2	tablespoons mustard
2	tablespoons freshly squeezed lemon juice
1/4	teaspoon Tabasco
	Dash Worcestershire sauce

Mix all ingredients. This dressing is delicious on hot green vegetables, such as broccoli. It may also be used as a complement to meats and salads.

Mrs. Nicholas C. Wright

Strawberry Butter

Yield: 1 pint

1	package frozen strawberries, drained
1	cup powdered sugar
1/2	cup whipped margarine

Blend all ingredients with an electric mixer and serve on piping hot biscuits, pancakes, waffles or just plain bread.

Mrs. Richard O'Neill

Tomato Butter

Yield: 1½ cups

1/2 pound butter
1/2 cup tomatoes,
skinned, seeded and
chopped
Pinch of dry basil
1/8 teaspoon freshly
ground pepper

Combine all ingredients and blend until smooth. Press into a mold and chill. Delightful with biscuits.

Mrs. Walter Ahlborg

Cinnamon Butter

Brown sugar
Butter or margarine
Ground cinnamon

Using equal parts brown sugar and butter or margarine, cream together with a little ground cinnamon. Spread on toast and heat under the broiler

Mrs. William C. Gewin

Clarified Butter

Yield: 3/4 cup

2 sticks butter

Cut butter into one-inch pieces. Melt butter in a heavy saucepan over low heat. Remove pan from heat and let stand 3 minutes. Then skim froth from surface. Strain through cheese cloth into a small bowl. Leave milky solids in the pan. Keeps indefinitely in the refrigerator.

Mrs. Larry Harless

Turkey Basting Sauce

Yield: 1½ cups

1/2 pound margarine
1 clove garlic, minced
1 onion, minced
1 teaspoon salt
3/4 cup Tarragon vinegar
3 tablespoons brown sugar
2 teaspoons dried mixed herbs

Combine and simmer 3 minutes. Brush on turkey which is being cooked on grill or in oven. Cover turkey with foil.

Charles Graddick

Crunchy Ham Glaze

Yield: 3/4 cup

1/2 cup brown sugar
1/8 cup bread crumbs
1 tablespoon Rum
2 tablespoons ham drippings

Combine all ingredients, and when ham has about 15 minutes left to cook, pat mixture onto ham after the fat has been removed. Put the ham back into the oven and cook until brown and crusty.

Mrs. Walter Cleverdon

Applesauce and Honey Ham Glaze

Yield: 1¾ cups

1 cup applesauce
1/2 cup honey
1/4 cup brown sugar
1 teaspoon dry mustard

Combine all of the above. Pour 3/4 cup of glaze over scored ham the last 30 minutes of baking time. Heat the remaining sauce and serve with ham.

Mrs. Harry Gordon Sparks, III

Barbecue Sauce for Chicken or Pork

Serves 6

3/4 cup butter
2 tablespoons flour
3/4 cup white wine
3 tablespoons Worcestershire sauce
2 teaspoons salt
1/8 teaspoon Tabasco
1 tablespoon lemon juice
1/4 teaspoon paprika
1/2 teaspoon pepper
6 tablespoons brown sugar

Melt butter, stir in flour until smooth. Combine all other ingredients and add to butter mixture. Stir over low heat until slightly thickened. Baste on chicken or pork several times while cooking. This is especially good on chicken or pork grilled outside.

Mrs. William Seifert

Barbecue Sauce for Chicken

Proportions for 4-6 pieces chicken (large ones)

Use equal parts soy sauce and Wesson Oil
Half the amount of vinegar
Use several garlic buds, chopped
For example:
1 cup soy sauce
1 cup Wesson Oil
1/2 cup vinegar
3-4 garlic buds, chopped

Marinate chicken in mixture for 24 hours, piercing chicken and turning 3 or 4 times. Cook at 275° for about 2½ hours, covered. Then put on grill for about 30 minutes or less to brown. Note: Can freeze after browning on the grill. Let thaw and cook for 45 minutes to an hour, covered.

Mrs. Larry Sims

Marinade for Flank Steak

1/4 cup salad oil
1/4 cup Worcestershire
     sauce
1/2 cup soy sauce
1-2 pods garlic, minced
1   flank steak

Cover flank steak with garlic and marinade. Let sit for 24 hours, refrigerated, turning steak once. Grill steak and slice into thin strips against the grain to serve.

Mrs. Alex Lankford, III

Marinate steaks in a mixture of lemon juice, Dijon mustard, oil, soy sauce and dry Sherry and baste them with this mixture as they cook.

Marinade for Flank Steak, Sirloin, etc.

Serves: 6

3-4 green onions,
     chopped
2   tablespoons soy sauce
2   tablespoons salad oil
     Juice of 1/2 lemon
1/2 teaspoon thyme
     Pepper
2   pound flank steak,
     scored, or sirloin

Mix onions, soy sauce, oil, lemon juice, thyme and pepper together; brush half the mixture onto steak. Turn steak over; brush with the remaining oil mixture. Let marinate for 2 to 3 hours in refrigerator. Place on broiler pan. Broil 3 to 4 minutes on top side, 2 minutes on bottom side. Cut diagonally into thin slices. May also cook outside on grill, basting with marinade. For sirloin, double proportions for the marinade and follow above directions, increasing cooking time according to the size of your steak.

Mrs. Daniel Rencher

Venison Marinade

Yield: 4 cups

1 cup soy sauce
1 cup Worcestershire sauce
1 cup oil
1 cup sugar
3 garlic cloves
Chopped green onions to taste
Salt and pepper

Combine all ingredients. Marinate venison overnight and cook on a barbecue grill, basting as you cook with the marinade. The venison will be tender and taste similar to beef.

Mrs. Stephen G. Lauten

Otis Dunn's Venison Marinade for Smoking

Serves 16-20

2 5-ounce bottles Teriyaki meat marinade
1/2 cup vinegar
3/4 cup cooking oil
2 large onions, quartered
4 cloves garlic
1 tablespoon salt
3 tablespoons ground thyme
1 teaspoon red pepper
2 sticks butter

Put all ingredients except butter in blender and blend until onions are pulverized. Puncture meat with fork and pour marinade over meat. Let set overnight, turning one time. When meat is placed on grill, take remaining marinade, add 2 sticks butter and simmer 15 minutes. Baste meat every 20 to 30 minutes to keep moist. For an 8-10 pound venison roast or ham.

Mrs. Clarke Irvine, Jr.

Evelyn's Tomato Gravy

Serves 4

2   heaping tablespoons flour
6   tablespoons bacon grease
3   cups water
6-8 large tomatoes, peeled and diced
     Salt and pepper
1   tablespoon sugar
     Bell pepper (optional)

Brown flour in bacon grease; it doesn't need to be very dark. Add water, tomatoes, salt, pepper and sugar. At this point if desired, add chopped bell pepper. Simmer in an iron skillet about 45 minutes, adding more water if necessary. This is good for breakfast over grits.

Mrs. Thomas Twitty, Jr.

Rossini Steak Sauce

Yield: 3 cups

1   stick (1/2 cup) butter
6   shallots, peeled and chopped
1/2 cup onion, chopped
1/2 pound mushrooms, cleaned and sliced
3/4 cup red wine (Bordeaux)
1   cup beef broth
1½   tablespoons flour
1/4 teaspoon salt
     Dash of pepper
1   (2¾ ounce) can fine quality liver paté or 1 (3 ounce) can paté de fois gras

In medium saucepan, heat the butter until hot and add the shallots, onions and mushrooms. Sauté until tender, stirring occasionally, for about 5 minutes. Add the wine and simmer, uncovered, for 15 minutes. Combine the beef broth, flour, salt and pepper. Stir into the wine mixture and cook, stirring, until lightly thickened. In a small skillet over low heat, melt the paté. Add to the sauce and mix well. Serve hot.

Filippo Milone
The Pillars

Low-Calorie Horseradish Sauce

2 tablespoons powdered horseradish
4 tablespoons water
1/2 pod garlic, mashed
2 teaspoons white wine vinegar
1/2 teaspoon parsley, minced
1/2 teaspoon chives, chopped
1/2 teaspoon dry mustard
Dash of Cayenne pepper, salt, black pepper
1½ cups low fat cottage cheese

Yield: Approximately 2 cups
Place ingredients in a blender or food processor and blend until very smooth. Correct seasonings. This is great with fish, beef or as a spread for sandwiches.

Mrs. Ernest Brown

Horseradish Sauce

1 cup sour cream
1/2 cup horseradish, drained
1 teaspoon parsley, finely minced
1 tablespoon green onion, finely minced
Salt and pepper to taste
Dash of red pepper

Yield: 1½ cups
Combine all ingredients and put in refrigerator. If you like a tart flavor, add 1 teaspoon of lemon juice and serve well chilled. Good for fish, meat or poultry.

Mrs. Rex Rapier

Horseradish Mousse

Yield: 1⅓ cup mold

3	teaspoons gelatin
2	tablespoons water
1/2	cup heavy cream, whipped
1/2	cup prepared horseradish
1	teaspoon salt
1/2	teaspoon lemon juice
1	tablespoon onion, minced

Soften the gelatin in cold water and dissolve in double boiler over hot water. Cool slightly. Whip the cream and fold in the remaining ingredients. Stir in gelatin. Pour in a greased mold and put in the refrigerator to set until firm. Unmold and serve with roast beef or with cocktails as a spread.

Mrs. Robert A. Learnard

Roquefort Sauce for Meat

Yield: 1¼ cups

3/4	cup dry white wine
1	cup heavy cream
1/4	pound Roquefort cheese, softened
1	stick butter (8 tablespoons), softened

In a saucepan, reduce wine over high heat to about 1 tablespoon in volume. Add cream and reduce liquid over moderate heat by half. In a bowl, combine cheese and butter until the mixture is smooth. Whisk the cheese mixture into the cream mixture a little at a time and simmer the sauce for 3 minutes, stirring constantly. Strain the sauce through a fine sieve and add pepper to taste. Serve over steaks.

Mrs. Larry Harless

Sweet and Sour Sauce

Yield: 1¼ cups

3/4 cup sugar
2 tablespoons soy sauce
3 tablespoons wine vinegar
3 tablespoons catsup
1/2 cup water
2 tablespoons cornstarch
1 tablespoon dry white wine (optional)

Combine sugar, soy sauce, vinegar and catsup. Bring to a boil. Dissolve cornstarch in water and add to sauce. Cook over low heat, stirring until thick. Add wine. Delicious over bite-size fried chicken, shrimp or pork.

Mrs. Percy C. Fountain, Jr.

Sauce for Baked Potatoes

Yield: Approximately 3 cups

1 (8 ounce) carton sour cream
1/2 cup butter, melted
1 cup yellow cheese, grated
3 green onions, minced
8 strips bacon, fried crisp and crumbled

Mix first 4 ingredients together and chill. When ready to serve, add crisp, crumbled bacon, and spoon over hot, baked potatoes.

Mrs. Wade Faulkner

Cranberry Sauce

Yield: 3 cups

1	pound fresh cranberries
2	oranges, 1 whole and 1 peeled
2½	cups of sugar
2	apples, cored

Put all ingredients through a meat grinder or in a food processor and chop very fine. Stir and let stand overnight in refrigerator. Will keep at least a week in refrigerator.

Mary Hazen House Braswell

Cook jams and jellies in small batches. Do not double recipes. Doubled recipes do not cook the same way as the small ones.

Basic Instructions for Making Jelly

Making jelly is very simple. Like making anything else, following directions correctly is a must. You will need at least five pounds of fruit, a large clean pot of at least 6 quart capacity with no grease residue (scrub, then boil water in it to clean it thoroughly if you are in doubt.) You will also need several clean jars, half-pint or pint size. You can buy jelly jars or use ones you have saved from pickle or other products. The jars must be able to withstand heat. You may seal with paraffin or use the seal tops that come with purchased jelly jars. And of course, you will need fruit juice, sugar and fruit pectin. I generally use Sur-Jel fruit pectin. Using the pectin assures you that your jelly will gel and you will realize more jelly from the same amount of juice than the old-fashioned boiled jelly.

There are two main operations in jelly making and each can be done at different times. Rendering the juice from the fruit is first. Then the juice can be stored in the refrigerator for several days or even frozen. The next operation is the actual making of the jelly. The following instructions are for scuppernong jelly, but these general instructions can be used for any fruit such as dewberries, blackberries, crabapples, grapes or raspberries. The amounts of fruit juice, sugar and pectin may differ. There are instructions on each box of fruit pectin in the market today.

Mrs. Alex F. Lankford, III

Scuppernong Jelly

**About 5 pounds of
ripe scuppernongs**
5   **cups juice**
7   **cups sugar (3 pounds)**
1   **box fruit pectin**

Yield: 8 or 9 (8-ounce) jars
Wash fruit thoroughly and put into pot and just barely cover with water. Bring to a boil, then lower heat and cook at medium temperature for about 30 minutes, or until the fruit is soft enough to mash with a potato masher. After you have thoroughly mashed the fruit, pour through a colander into a large container, using the potato masher as you pour to be sure you have gotten as much juice from the fruit as possible. Discard the pulp, seeds and peel. Strain this juice through a cheesecloth bag to get all the residue out. A gauze diaper made into a bag is excellent for this. Dampen bag before straining juice through it. When you have finished straining the juice, you are ready to either store it or begin making jelly. Once you actually start to make the jelly make sure that you will not be interrupted. Have the sugar and juice measured, your jars clean and ready to fill and seal, and your fruit pectin ready. Heat the measured juice in the container, and stirring constantly, add the pectin. Bring to a boil, then add sugar, still stirring, and bring to a full rolling boil, that is, a boil that cannot be stirred down. Boil for a full minute. You will begin to see the juice gel as it drips from the spoon with which you are stirring. Remove from heat and skim with a large spoon the foamy substance that appears on the top of the jelly. Throw this away. Now you are ready to fill the jars and seal.

Mrs. Alex F. Lankford, III

273

Hyden Relish

Yield: About 12 pints

1 gallon ripe tomatoes, peeled and chopped
1 gallon cabbage, shredded
1 quart onions, chopped
6 ripe peppers, chopped
1 cup salt
2 teaspoons cinnamon
2 teaspoons ginger
2 teaspoons celery seed
2 teaspoons dry mustard
2 teaspoons ground cloves
3 pounds sugar
1/2 gallon vinegar
1 cup flour
2 teaspoons tumeric

Pour salt over chopped vegetables. Let stand one hour, then squeeze and drain. Add cinnamon, ginger, celery seed, mustard, cloves, sugar and vinegar. Let boil 40 minutes. Mix a little liquid from the pot with the flour and tumeric to form a paste, then add to the pot. Cook until thickened a little. Pour into jars and seal properly. Excellent with peas, beans and ham. (This recipe takes about 2 big heads cabbage and about 4 large onions.)

Mrs. Victor Lott, Jr.

My Pepper Jelly

Yield: 6 half-pint jars

3/4 cup bell pepper, seeds removed
1/4 cup hot peppers, seeds removed
6½ cups sugar
1½ cups cider vinegar
1 box (2 packages) Certo

Put peppers in grinder or blender. Combine all ingredients except Certo in a 5-quart pot. Heat and stir constantly until mixture comes to a heavy boil. Remove from heat and let stand for 10 minutes. Skim top and add Certo. Return to heat and let boil 1 minute. Add a few drops green food coloring if desired. Pour into sterilized jelly jars and top with melted hot paraffin. Wonderful accent for meats. Divine on cream cheese and crackers.

Mrs. E. Bailey Slaton

Chutney

Yield: 4 pints

18	cooking apples
3	sweet peppers
1	large onion
1½	cups raisins
1½	cups sugar
3	cups vinegar
	Juice of 3 lemons
1½	cups red currant jelly
1	tablespoon ginger
1/4	teaspoon cloves
1/4	teaspoon allspice
2	bay leaves
	Salt to taste

Slice the apples. Chop the peppers and onions. Mix together with sugar, vinegar, raisins, lemon juice, jelly, ginger, cloves and allspice. Boil until thick, add salt to taste. Remove bay leaves and pour into sterilized jars and seal immediately.

Mrs. David A. Richards

Carrot Chutney

Yield: 5 half-pint jars

3	cups carrots, cut in fine strips
5-6	cups water
2	cups brown sugar
1	cup granulated sugar
1	cup seedless raisins
1/2	teaspoon cloves, nutmeg or ginger (or a combination)
1	teaspoon cinnamon
1	teaspoon salt
1	cup vinegar
1	lemon, sliced thin with seeds removed (optional)

Parboil carrots in water until tender, about 10-15 minutes. Drain and save carrot water. To 2 cups carrot water add remaining ingredients and bring to a boil. Reduce heat and cook slowly until mixture thickens, about 2-2½ hours. Pour into hot, sterilized jars and seal. Note: This should be thick like jelly. If it thickens too much just add a little water. Don't overcook it, however.

Mrs. T. B. Snevely

Cucumber Chunks

Yield: 4 pints

14 firm cucumbers
(8 medium–1" to
1½" or14 small–¾"
to 1" diameter
2 cups sugar
1 cup vinegar
1 tablespoon pickling
spice

Cover whole cucumbers with boiling water and allow to stand overnight. Drain liquid and repeat procedure 2 more times. On the fourth day, drain and slice the cucumbers into ½ inch slices. Combine sugar, vinegar, and spices. Bring this to a boil and pour over cucumbers. Let stand one day. Next day, bring to a boil again and seal in hot jars. Additional liquid can be made if required. If used, does not need to stand overnight.

Mrs. David R. Carrington

Bread and Butter Pickles

Yield: 8 pints

12 cucumbers, sliced
thin
6 medium onions,
sliced thin
2 green peppers,
chopped
3 cloves garlic, minced
1/3 cup salt
5 cups sugar
3 cups cider vinegar
1½ teaspoons tumeric
1½ teaspoons celery seed
2 tablespoons mustard
seed

Combine first 4 ingredients. Mix in salt and cover with ice cubes. Let stand for 3 hours. Drain well. Mix sugar, vinegar and seasonings. Pour over the cucumber mixture and heat just to a boil. Seal in jars.

Mrs. Claude M. Warren, III

Pickled Onion Ring Relish

Yield: About one pint

1	tablespoon mixed pickling spices
1/2	cup water
1/3	cup cider vinegar
2	tablespoons sugar
3/4	teaspoon salt
1/4	teaspoon pepper
1	large tomato, chopped
1	large bell pepper, chopped
2	large onions, sliced and separated into rings.

Tie pickling spices in cheesecloth. In medium saucepan, heat spice bag and remaining ingredients except onions to boiling. Reduce heat to medium, cover and cook for 3 minutes. Stir in onions and cook for another 3 minutes. Remove bag. Cover and refrigerate overnight. Easy!

Mrs. Peter Gaillard

Irene's Squash Pickles

Yield: 8 pints

8	cups yellow squash, sliced
2	cups white onions, sliced
3	green peppers, sliced
2½	cups sugar
2	teaspoons mustard seeds
2	cups white vinegar
2	teaspoons celery seeds
1/2	teaspoon dried mustard

Layer squash, onions and bell pepper. Sprinkle with salt and let stand one hour. Drain off excess liquid. Heat other ingredients and pour over vegetables. Bring to a boil. Spoon into prepared Mason Jars. Cool and chill at least 24 hours before serving.

Mrs. Joe Little, Jr.

Garlic Pickles

Yield: 1 gallon

1 gallon sour pickles
5 pounds sugar
1/2 box whole black peppercorns
1/2 box whole allspice
1/2 box mustard seeds
4 pieces stick cinnamon, broken
1 tablespoon whole cloves
2 tablespoons Wesson Oil
8-10 pieces whole garlic

Drain pickles and discard juice. Cut pickles into 1/2" slices. Put into an enamel or plastic (anything but metal) crock. Add all the remaining ingredients. Let sit 3 days, mixing well twice a day. Transfer to the original gallon jar. Let sit an additional 3 days. Store in this jar, but take out some to refrigerate. Should be chilled to eat.

Mrs. Floyd Fraser

Sauce for Fresh Fruit

Yield: 2 cups

1 (8 ounce) package cream cheese, softened
1/2 cup sour cream
1/4 cup sugar
1/4 cup orange juice

Combine softened cream cheese, sour cream and sugar until well blended. Stir in orange juice and chill. Serve over fruit.

Mrs. Harry Gordon Sparks, III

Raspberry Sauce

Yield: 1 cup

1	10-ounce package frozen raspberries
1	tablespoon cornstarch
2	tablespoons Sherry

Defrost raspberries. Purée in blender; then strain to remove all the seeds. Combine with cornstarch and cook until slightly thickened. Cool. Stir in Sherry and serve. This is delicious over cheesecake, a cheese or vanilla mold, a mousse or over ice cream.

Mrs. C. H. R. Johnson

Strawberry Topping

Yield: 1 cup

1	pint strawberries
3	tablespoons sugar
1½	tablespoons lemon juice, Cognac or Rum

Wash and hull strawberries. Put all but 6 strawberries into electric blender. Add next two ingredients. Cover and process until smooth. Pour into a small bowl. Slice remaining 6 strawberries and stir into puréed mixture. Use as topping for cheesecake, ice cream or chilled fresh fruits.

Mrs. William D. Walsh

Chocolate Sauce

Yield: 1 cup

2	ounces unsweetened chocolate
1	tablespoon butter
1/2	cup water
1	cup sugar
2	tablespoons corn syrup

Melt the chocolate in a double boiler. Add and melt 1 tablespoon butter. Stir and blend well. Add 1/2 cup boiling water. Stir and blend well. Add 1 cup sugar and 2 tablespoons of corn syrup. Boil over direct heat for 5 minutes and do not stir.

Mrs. Ray Herndon

Praline Ice Cream Sauce

Yield: 2 cups

1/4 pound marshmallows
1⅓ cups brown sugar
1 cup light cream
Dash of salt
4 tablespoons butter
1 teaspoon vanilla
1/3 cup pecans, chopped

Combine first four ingredients in saucepan. Heat and stir until mixture boils. Cook over medium heat for about 10 minutes. Remove from heat and add butter, vanilla and nuts. Serve warm.

Mrs. W. Bibb Lamar

Chantilly Cream for Fresh Fruit

Yield: 1½ cups

1/2 cup whipping cream
1/2 cup dairy sour cream
3 tablespoons confectioners sugar, sifted
1/2 teaspoon vanilla

In a chilled bowl, whip the cream until stiff; fold in sour cream, then sugar and vanilla. Serve over fresh fruit. (Will keep one day in refrigerator.)

Mrs. C. Vearn Partridge, Jr.

Fried Bananas

Serves 8

8 large yellow bananas, peeled and halved lengthwise
2 tablespoons lemon juice
1/2 cup brown sugar
1/2 cup salad oil

Brush bananas with the lemon juice. Roll in brown sugar. Heat salad oil in a skillet, add the bananas and fry about 2 minutes or until golden brown. Serve hot.

Mrs. Richard Dukes

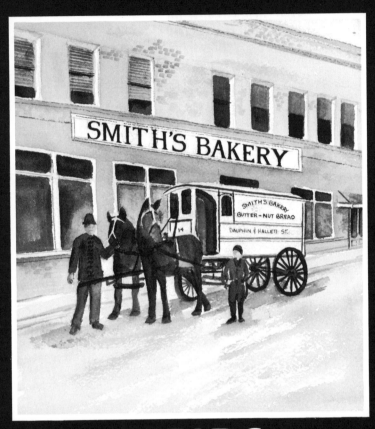

BREADS

SMITH'S BAKERY
Smith's fresh bread has graced the tables of Mobilians
for three generations.

Sour Cream Coffee Cake

Yield: 1 cake

1/4 cup brown sugar, firmly packed
2 teaspoons cinnamon
1 cup pecans, chopped
1 (18½ ounce) package yellow cake mix
3/4 cup Crisco Oil
1/4 cup sugar
1 teaspoon vanilla
4 eggs
1 cup sour cream

Grease and flour a 10 inch tube cake pan. Combine brown sugar, cinnamon, and 1/2 cup chopped pecans and set aside. Combine cake mix, oil, sugar, vanilla, eggs, and sour cream. Beat 2 minutes at medium speed of electric mixer. Stir in 1/2 cup pecans. Pour half of batter in prepared pan. Sprinkle with brown sugar mixture. Pour remaining batter into pan. Bake at 325° for 50-60 minutes. Allow cake to cool in pan 30 minutes before turning out.

Mrs. William Bibb Lamar

Sunday Morning Coffee Cake

1 cup sifted flour
1 teaspoon baking powder
1/4 teaspoon salt
2 eggs
1 cup sugar
1 teaspoon vanilla
1/2 cup hot milk
1 tablespoon butter or margarine

Sift flour, baking powder, and salt 3 times. Beat eggs well. Add sugar; beat again. Add vanilla. Stir in dry ingredients. Quickly add hot milk and butter. (Let the butter melt a little in the hot milk.) Put in greased 9" square pan at once. Bake at 375° for 20-25 minutes. After baking sprinkle with topping. Put under broiler to brown (only a few minutes — watch carefully).

Topping:
4 tablespoons butter
2 tablespoons cream
2/3 cup brown sugar
1 cup chopped nuts (optional)
1/8 teaspoon salt

Mix together the butter and cream until fluffy. Gradually add brown sugar; stir in nuts and salt.

Mrs. Sam Marshall

Cheese Braid Coffee Cake

1	cup sour cream
1/2	cup sugar
1	teaspoon salt
1/2	cup melted butter
2	packages yeast
1/2	cup warm water
2	eggs, beaten
4	cups flour
	Cream cheese filling
	Glaze

To make dough, heat sour cream, add sugar, salt and butter. Cool. Sprinkle yeast over warm water. Combine with sour cream mixture in large bowl. Add eggs. Beat. Add flour and mix. Cover in an airtight container and refrigerate overnight. Divide into 4 parts. Roll into 12 inch x 8 inch rectangles. Spread 1/2 filling, roll up starting at wide side. Place seam down on greased cookie sheet. Slit at 2 inch intervals to resemble braid. Cover and let rise double for 1 to 1½ hours. Bake at 375 degrees for 12 to 15 minutes.

Filling:

2	(8 ounce) packages cream cheese
3/4	cup sugar
1	egg, beaten
1/8	teaspoon salt
2	teaspoons vanilla

To make filling, cream cheese and sugar together. Add other ingredients beating well until combined.

Glaze:

2	cups confectioners' sugar
4	tablespoons milk
2	teaspoons vanilla

To make glaze, combine ingredients and spread on warm loaves.

Mrs. Frank E. Haas, Jr.

German Pancake

Serves 2-3

3	eggs
1/2	cup flour
1/2	cup milk
2	tablespoons butter, melted
1/2	teaspoon salt

Beat the eggs and add flour and the rest of the ingredients. Bake in a greased 9 inch pie pan at 450 degrees for 20 minutes. Sprinkle with powdered sugar and serve with melted butter. (Maple syrup is good with this, too.)

Mrs. George Fuller

Mother's Doughnut Recipe

Yield: 2 dozen

2	cups flour
2	tablespoons cornstarch
1/2	teaspoon salt
1	teaspoon baking powder
1/2	teaspoon nutmeg
1	cup sugar
2	eggs, unbeaten
1	cup buttermilk
1	teaspoon soda
5	tablespoons Crisco, melted

Sift flour, cornstarch, salt, baking powder and nutmeg. Add sugar, eggs, buttermilk, soda and shortening. Stir until smooth. Using doughnut iron, drop in molds by the tablespoon. Bake for 3½ minutes or until iron stops steaming. Sprinkle with powdered sugar when done.

Mrs. Thomas E. Sharp, Jr.

Do not put bread dough on a hot stove. The high temperature could kill the yeast.

Deli Bread

Yield: 1 loaf

1	package yeast
1/4	cup warm water
1	cup cottage cheese
1	tablespoon margarine or butter, softened
2	tablespoons sugar
1	tablespoon minced dry onion
1	tablespoon dill seed
1/2	teaspoon salt
1/4	teaspoon soda
1	egg
2¼-2½ cups flour	

Dissolve yeast in 1/4 cup warm water. Add cottage cheese, butter, sugar, onion, dill seed, salt and soda; then add egg and flour. Mix. Cover with towel and let rise 1 hour; then knead until shiny. Place in a greased loaf pan and let rise for 30 minutes. Bake at 350° for 30 minutes.

Mrs. Joseph P. Warren

285

Christmas Morning Bread

Yield: 3 loaves

1 cup sugar
1/2 cup shortening
2½ teaspoons salt
2 cups scalded milk
1/4 cup warm water
2 packages active dry yeast
2 eggs, beaten
2 cups candied fruit
1 cup golden raisins
7¾ cups flour

Put sugar, shortening, salt and scalded milk in a large mixing bowl. Cool to lukewarm. In a small cup stir yeast in warm water until dissolved. Add beaten egg and yeast to lukewarm milk mixture; blend. Add candied fruit and raisins. Add half the flour, knead until smooth. Add remaining flour gradually, mixing after each addition. Knead until smooth and elastic. Cover and let rise until double in bulk. Punch down and divide into 3 equal portions. Shape into 3 loaves. Place in 3 greased bread pans. Let rise again. Bake at 350° for 30 to 35 minutes. Delicious, light, cakelike bread, good anytime of year, especially toasted.

Mrs. Hugh M. Doherty

French Bread

Yield: 2 loaves

5-6 cups flour, divided
2 packages yeast
1 tablespoon salt
1 tablespoon sugar
1/4 cup oil
2¼ cups hot water (be careful not to kill yeast)

Put 2 cups flour, yeast, salt, sugar, shortening in water. Beat for 2 minutes on medium in mixer. Add one more cup flour. Beat one minute on high. Add as much more flour as it will take. Mix with hands. Knead. Form ball and cover with plastic wrap or a dish towel. Let stand for 20 minutes. Divide into two pieces. Beat each one down. Shape into French loaf. Put on greased cookie sheet. Oil the top of each loaf. Refrigerate for 2 to 24 hours. Bake at 350° for at least 40 minutes or until done.

Mrs. Norman E. Waldrop, Jr.

Mama's Greek Bread

2½ pounds plain flour (8 cups)
1 cup sugar
3 packages dry yeast
1½ tablespoons salt
4 cups tepid water (110°)
2 eggs, slightly beaten
1/2 cup Mazola oil
5 cups extra flour

Egg wash:
2 egg yolks
1 teaspoon sugar (scant)
3 tablespoons water
Sesame seeds and almonds for decoration (optional)

Yield: 3 large loaves

In a large mixing bowl, combine the flour, sugar, yeast and salt. Mix well with your hands. Add water, mix with hands. Cover bowl with a kitchen towel and allow mixture to rest in a draft free area for 30 minutes. This activates the yeast. Dough should be bubbly and increased in size. Add eggs and mix well. Add oil and mix well. Add extra flour until dough becomes soft and pliable. Amount of flour will depend on humidity. Turn dough out onto a floured board and knead 10-15 minutes with oiled hands and wrists. Grease dough and bowl with oil. Place bowl in a warm, draft free area. Cover well and let rise until it is double in bulk, about 2 hours. After rising, place dough on table and knead gently to bring it back down. Divide dough into 3 pieces and braid into various shapes, round or long loaves. Place on well-greased and floured baking pans. Let rise again for 40 minutes. Brush with the egg wash, made by combining ingredients and whisking. Sprinkle loaves with sesame seeds and almonds (optional). Place in a preheated 375° oven on the bottom shelf for 25 minutes and then on the top shelf for the remainder of the baking time, or until done, about 55-60 minutes.

Presvitera E. S. Haginas
(Mother of Mrs. Steve Clikas, Sr.)
From "Sophia Clikas, A Southern Lady Cooks with a Greek Accent"

Too much salt will slow the rising action of the yeast when making bread.

Sally Lunn

1 cup milk
1/2 cup margarine, room temperature
1/4 cup water
3½ cups flour, divided
1/3 cup sugar
2 teaspoons salt
2 packages dry yeast
3 eggs, room temperature

Yield: 1 loaf

Preheat oven to 350° 10 minutes before bread is ready to bake. Grease a 10 inch bundt pan. Heat milk, margarine and 1/4 cup water until very warm, about 120°. Margarine does not need to melt. Blend 1⅓ cups flour, sugar, salt and yeast in a large bowl. Blend warm liquids into the flour mixture. Beat with a mixer at medium speed for 2 minutes, scraping sides of bowl occasionally. Gradually add 2/3 cup of remaining flour and eggs and beat at high speed for 2 minutes. Add remaining flour and mix well. Batter will be thick but not stiff. Cover and let rise in a warm, draft-free place (85°) until double in bulk, about 1 hour and 15 minutes. Beat dough down with a spatula or at lowest speed on electric mixer and turn into the prepared bundt pan. Cover and let rise in a warm draft-free place until increased in bulk one-third to one-half; about 30 minutes. Bake at 350° for 40 to 50 minutes. Run knife around center and outer edges of bread and turn onto a plate to cool. This freezes well. May be warmed in foil, sliced and buttered.

Mrs. William Dumas

Plucking Bread

Yield: 1 loaf

1	package dry yeast
1/4	cup warm water
1½	cups milk, scalded and cooled
4½	cups flour
4	egg yolks
1/2	cup sugar
1/2	cup butter, melted
1	teaspoon salt

Coating: (Use 3 separate dishes)
1. 1 stick (1/2 cup) butter, melted
2. 1 cup sugar mixed with 4 teaspoons cinnamon
3. Pecans, chopped

Soften yeast in water 5 minutes. Add milk and 1 cup flour. Beat thoroughly. Let mixture stand about 20 minutes. Blend egg yolks, sugar, butter and salt. Add to yeast mixture mixing well. Then work in remaining flour and knead until smooth and elastic. Place in greased bowl, flip over to grease other side, cover, let rise in warm place until doubled. Turn out on a well-floured surface and divide in half. Form each half in a long roll and cut each into 24 or more pieces (total 40 or more). Roll each piece in a ball. Dip balls into melted butter, then cinnamon-sugar, then nuts. Place balls close together in greased tube pan lined with wax paper. Let rise 45 minutes. Bake at 350° 40-45 minutes. (Let cool 5 minutes before turning out. This will help to prevent it from falling apart!)

Mrs. Fred Cushing

Prepare bread dough with milk for a smoother texture and browner crust. Use water for a crisper crust and less cakelike texture.

Italian Bread Sticks

Yield: 28 sticks

1 package dry yeast
2/3 cup very warm water
1 teaspoon salt
1½ teaspoons sugar
2 cups all purpose
flour, sifted
1/4 cup vegetable
shortening
1 egg
1 tablespoon water
Sesame, poppy or
caraway seeds

Dissolve yeast in very warm water in a bowl. Add salt, sugar, 1 cup of the flour and shortening. Beat until smooth (about 5 minutes). Place in large greased bowl, lightly grease top of dough, cover with light cloth and let rise in a warm spot until it doubles in bulk (about 1 hour). Heat oven to 375 degrees. Pinch off pieces of dough slightly smaller than a walnut; roll on a board or between hands until strips are 8 inches long. Place one inch apart on a greased baking sheet. Beat egg with tablespoon of water, brush on sticks, sprinkle with seeds. Bake for 18 minutes or until golden. Bread sticks keep well in a covered tin; they also freeze well. To heat, place in a slow oven for 10 minutes.

Mrs. William D. Walsh, Jr.

Three Flour Bread

Yield: 2 loaves

2 packages dry yeast
3¼-3½ cups sifted all-
    purpose flour
1½ cups whole wheat
    flour
1/2 cup rye flour
2 cups milk
1/2 cup brown sugar
3 tablespoons Crisco
3 tablespoons
    granulated sugar
1 tablespoon salt

Combine the dry yeast, 1 cup of the all-purpose flour, the whole wheat flour and the rye flour. Heat together the milk, brown sugar, Crisco, granulated sugar and salt, stirring just until warm. Add to the dry mixture. Beat at low speed for 1/2 minute scraping the bowl constantly. Beat for 3 minutes at high speed. Stir in the remaining flour, enough to make a moderately stiff dough. Turn onto a floured surface. Knead 8 to 10 minutes. Place in a greased bowl turning once. Cover and let rise until doubled (1½ hours). Punch down. Let rest 10 minutes. Shape into 2 loaves. Place in greased bread pan. Let rise 45 to 60 minutes. Bake at 375° for 40 minutes.

Mrs. Joseph P. Warren

Pumpkin Bread

Yield: 2 loaves

3⅓ cups flour
3 teaspoons cinnamon
3 cups sugar
4 eggs
1 cup cooking oil
2/3 cup water
2 teaspoons soda
1 teaspoon salt
1 can pumpkin (2 cups)
1 cup raisins, optional
1 cup nuts, chopped,
    optional

Combine flour, cinnamon and sugar. Add eggs, oil and water. Mix soda, salt and pumpkin. Add to flour mixture. Mix well. Add raisins and nuts. Pour into 2 large greased loaf pans. Bake at 350° for 1 hour 15 minutes.

Mrs. Stephen Crawford

Strawberry Bread

Yield: 2 loaves

1 cup butter or margarine
1½ cups sugar
1 teaspoon vanilla
1/2 teaspoon lemon extract
4 eggs
3 cups flour
1 teaspoon salt
1 teaspoon cream of tartar
1/2 teaspoon baking soda
1 cup strawberry preserves
1/2 cup sour cream
1 cup walnuts or pecans (optional)

Cream butter and sugar. Add vanilla and lemon extract. Stir in eggs. Sift flour with salt, cream of tartar and baking soda. Combine preserves and sour cream. Add preserve mixture and creamed mixture alternately to dry ingredients. Stir in nuts. Bake in greased small loaf pans at 350° for 50 minutes.

Mrs. A. Stephen Hanes, III

Date Nut Bread

Yield: 2 loaves

1½ packages pitted dates (8-ounce size)
1½ cups boiling water
1½ teaspoons soda, dissolved in 1/2 cup warm water
2½ cups sifted flour
1 teaspoon salt
1 cup sugar
1 egg
2 teaspoons vanilla
1 cup pecans, chopped

Pour boiling water over dates and stir till they are broken in pieces. Add remaining ingredients and mix well. Pour into two well greased bread pans. Bake at 325° for about 40 minutes. Substitute orange juice for water and almond flavoring for vanilla for a great Christmas treat.

Mrs. John P. Case, Jr.

Zucchini Bread

Yield: 1 loaf

2 eggs
1/3 cup salad oil
1/2 cup granulated sugar
1½ teaspoons maple flavoring
1 cup zucchini (2 small ones), shredded
1¼ cups sifted flour
1/4 cup wheat germ
1 teaspoon salt
1 teaspoon baking soda
1/4 teaspoon baking powder
1/2 cup walnuts, finely chopped
3 tablespoons sesame seeds

In a large bowl beat the eggs with a mixer on low speed until blended. Add oil, sugar, maple flavoring and continue beating until mixture is thick and foamy. Stir in zucchini. In another bowl combine and mix the flour, wheat germ, salt, baking soda, baking powder and walnuts. Add to the oil and egg mixture, stirring just to blend. Pour into a greased and lightly floured 9x5x3-inch loaf pan. Sprinkle sesame seeds evenly over top. Bake in a preheated 350° oven for 1 hour, or until a toothpick inserted in center comes out clean. Cool, turn out, wrap and store for 1 day before slicing.

Note: Will keep in refrigerator up to 2 weeks, in freezer for 3 months.

Mrs. Thomas B. Van Antwerp

Banana Nut Bread

Yields 1 loaf

3/4 cup sugar
1/4 cup shortening
1 egg
2 cups flour
1/2 teaspoon soda
1/2 teaspoon baking powder
1/4 teaspoon salt
3 tablespoons sour milk
2 large ripe bananas, mashed
1/2 cup nuts, chopped

Cream sugar and shortening. Add egg; set aside. Sift together dry ingredients, then add to shortening mixture. Add sour milk, bananas and nuts. Pour into a greased loaf pan. Bake at 350° for one hour. Note: To make sour milk, add 1 teaspoon vinegar to 1/3 cup milk. Let stand for 15 minutes until it turns to clabber.

Mrs. Edward McMurphy

Inez's Nut Bread

Yields 1 loaf

1/2 cup margarine or Crisco
1 cup brown or white sugar
2 large eggs
1/2 cup honey
1 cup raisins
2¼ cups flour
1 teaspoon baking powder
1 teaspoon baking soda
1/4 teaspoon salt
1½ cups nuts, chopped
1-2 teaspoons vanilla
1/2 cup orange juice or wine (dry red)

Combine margarine and sugar in bowl. Add eggs and beat until thoroughly blended. Add honey. Sift together flour, baking powder, baking soda, salt. Mix well. Add raisins, nuts, vanilla, juice or wine. Blend in carefully but thoroughly. Do not beat. Overbeating makes a tight, compact loaf. Pour in greased loaf pan. Bake at 350° for one hour.

Mrs. Jack Gallalee

Herb Biscuits

Yield: 1 dozen

2 cups biscuit mix
1/4 teaspoon dry mustard
1 teaspoon parsley flakes
1½ teaspoons caraway seeds
2/3 cup buttermilk

Combine all dry ingredients. Add buttermilk and mix lightly. Turn onto a lightly floured board and knead 10 times. Roll dough to 1/2" thickness. Cut out biscuits with a cutter and bake on an ungreased cookie sheet at 450° for 10 to 12 minutes.

Mrs. Walter Ahlborg

Yeast Biscuits

Yield: 3 dozen

1 package active dry yeast
2 tablespoons very warm water
5 cups all-purpose flour
1 teaspoon soda
1 tablespoon baking powder
2 tablespoons sugar
1½ teaspoons salt
1 cup vegetable shortening
2 cups buttermilk

Dissolve yeast in warm water. Sift all dry ingredients into a large bowl. Cut in shortening with a pastry blender. Add buttermilk, then yeast mixture. Stir until moistened. Turn onto a floured board and knead a minute or two. Roll out to 1/2" and cut into rounds. Brush with melted butter and bake on ungreased pan at 400° for 12 to 15 minutes, or until lightly browned. (After kneading dough it can be stored in a plastic bag which has been floured inside for up to a week. Biscuits can then be made as needed since they need no time to rise.)

Mrs. Carl E. Jones, Jr.

Baking Powder Biscuits

Yield: 12

2 cups sifted all-purpose flour
3 teaspoons baking powder
1/2 teaspoon salt
1/4 cup shortening
3/4 cup milk

Sift dry ingredients together. Cut shortening into dry ingredients, using your hands, until mixture looks like coarse crumbs. Add milk all at once, stirring with a fork. Turn dough out onto floured surface and knead gently for about 1/2 minute. Roll dough about 1/2 to 3/4 inch thick. Dip biscuit cutter in flour and cut dough straight down. Place biscuits in greased oblong cake pan. Bake at 450 degrees for 15-18 minutes or until browned. This makes 12 tall, plump biscuits.
Note: These biscuits may be baked just until they rise. Then take them out of the oven, let cool, and freeze.

Mrs. Larry Harless

Rolls

3/4 cup milk
3 heaping tablespoons
   Crisco
1 egg, large
1 teaspoon salt
1/4-1/2 cup sugar
1 package yeast
1/4 cup warm water
3 cups sifted flour
   Melted butter

Yield: 2-2½ dozen

Warm the milk and Crisco until shortening melts. In a large bowl, beat the egg with salt and add the sugar. In the meantime dissolve the yeast in warm water. Add slightly cooled milk-Crisco mixture to egg, salt and sugar mixture. Beat with a rotary beater. Add the dissolved yeast mixture. Beat in the sifted flour. Let rise two hours until doubled. Roll out and form into rolls (clover-leaf or Parker House). Top with melted butter. Cover with a tea towel and let rise for two more hours. Bake on a greased pan at 425° for 10 to 15 minutes.

VARIATIONS:

ORANGE ROLLS: Roll out the dough, jelly-roll fashion; spread the roll with melted butter, orange rind and a little powdered sugar. Roll up and slice at about one inch intervals. Mix a little orange juice and powdered sugar and ice while hot.

CINNAMON ROLLS: Roll out flat. Spread the roll with melted butter, cinnamon and sugar (mixed). Roll up and slice. For icing use a little milk and powdered sugar.

Mrs. H. Browne Mercer, Sr.

Healthy Muffins

Yield: 20 muffins

1¼ cups whole wheat
flour
1 (16 ounce) can
applesauce
1/2 cup brown sugar,
firmly packed
1/3 cup salad oil
2 eggs
1½ teaspoons salt
1 teaspoon baking soda
1 teaspoon baking
powder
1 teaspoon cinnamon
3/4-1 cup wheat germ
(plain/sugared)
1½ cups quick cooking
oats, uncooked
1 cup dark raisins
(optional)

In mixer bowl, blend flour, applesauce, brown sugar, oil, eggs, salt, baking soda, baking powder and cinnamon. Add wheat germ, oats and raisins. Stir until well mixed. Bake in lined muffin tins at 350° for 25 minutes. Great lunch box treat.

Mrs. Hugh M. Doherty

Pecan Muffins

Yield: 1½ dozen

1/2 cup light brown
sugar
1½ cups all-purpose
flour
1/2 teaspoon salt
2 teaspoons baking
powder
1/2 cup pecans, coarsely
chopped
1 egg
1/4 cup vegetable oil
1/2 cup milk

Combine dry ingredients and mix well. Add egg, oil and milk, stirring well. Fill well-greased miniature muffin pans half full. Bake at 400° for 20-25 minutes. Remove from pans while warm. Freeze well. Versatile–great for breakfast or ladies' tea.

Mrs. William D. Walsh

Lemon Muffins

1   cup sugar
5   tablespoons butter
2   eggs
     Rind of 1 lemon,
     grated
1/2 cup milk
1/2 teaspoon salt
1½   cups flour
1   teaspoon baking
     powder
1/2 cup nuts, chopped

Glaze:
1   lemon, juiced
1/2 cup sugar

Yield: 12 muffins

Cream sugar and butter until light and fluffy. Beat eggs and add lemon rind and milk. Add to creamed mixture and mix well. Sift dry ingredients together and stir into sugar and butter mixture, stirring only until there are no traces of dry ingredients remaining. Stir in nuts and spoon batter into 12 muffin cups, either greased or lined with paper liners. Bake in a preheated 350° oven for 25-30 minutes or until golden. While the muffins bake combine lemon juice and sugar for glaze and allow to sit so that some of the sugar will dissolve. When muffins are done, poke holes into each one with a toothpick and pour the glaze over each hot muffin.

Mrs. Will Blackburn

Anytime Jam Muffins

1/2 cup butter
1   cup sugar
2   eggs
2   cups flour
1   teaspoon cinnamon
1   teaspoon nutmeg
1   teaspoon baking
     powder
1/2 cup lukewarm milk
2   teaspoons vinegar
1   cup peach preserves
     (strawberry or
     apricot preserves
     may be substituted)

Yield: 2 dozen

Cream butter and sugar until fluffy. Add eggs and beat well. Sift flour with cinnamon, nutmeg, and baking powder. Combine vinegar and milk and add alternately with dry ingredients to shortening mixture. Allow to sit for a few minutes. Stir in preserves and fill greased muffin tins 2/3 full. Bake at 375° for 20 minutes. Good for breakfast, brunch, supper or lunch! These reheat well.

Mrs. John Wilson

Blueberry Muffins

Yield: 12 muffins

1 cup sugar
1/4 cup margarine (1/2 stick)
1 cup milk
1 egg
1⅓ cups all purpose flour
2 teaspoons baking powder
3/4 teaspoon cinnamon
3/4 teaspoon nutmeg
1/2 teaspoon vanilla
1/4 teaspoon salt
1 cup fresh blueberries (or unsweetened frozen blueberries, thawed and drained)

Preheat oven to 375 degrees. In a medium bowl, cream sugar and margarine on low speed of electric mixer until smooth. Add milk, egg, 2/3 cup of flour, baking powder, spices, vanilla and salt, and mix just until thoroughly blended. Gently mix in remaining 2/3 cup flour (batter should still be lumpy). Fold in blueberries. Fill lined muffin tins 3/4 full (muffins will rise about 1 inch above pan). Bake at 375 degrees for 20-30 minutes, until golden brown. Serve hot with plenty of butter and jam.

Mrs. Wade Faulkner

Sesame Cheese Muffins

Yield: 8 muffins

2 tablespoons shortening
1¼ cups sifted self-rising flour
1/2 cup New York state cheese, grated
1/2 cup milk
1 tablespoon Wesson oil
1 egg, beaten
Parmesan cheese
1 tablespoon sesame seeds, toasted
2 tablespoons butter, melted

Cut the shortening into the flour. Add cheese. Add milk and Wesson oil to the beaten egg. Add all at once to dry ingredients and stir just until moistened. Fill greased muffin pans 2/3 full. Sprinkle tops with Parmesan cheese and sesame seeds. Drizzle melted butter over muffins and bake at 400° for 15 to 20 minutes. Delicious.

Mrs. Sam Pipes, III

Raisin-Nut Muffins

Yield: 30 muffins

1	cup shortening or butter
2	cups sugar
4	eggs, large
3	cups plain flour
3	teaspoons baking powder
1	teaspoon nutmeg
1/2	teaspoon cinnamon
1	cup milk
1	cup raisins
1½	cups nuts, chopped

Cream shortening and sugar. Stir in eggs. Combine flour, baking powder, nutmeg and cinnamon. Add shortening mixture, then milk. Add raisins and nuts. Pour into greased muffin tins. Bake at 375° for 18-20 minutes.

Mrs. C. R. Butler, Jr.

Marion's Oatmeal Muffins

Yield: 1 dozen

1	cup quick rolled oats
1	cup buttermilk
1	egg
1/2	cup brown sugar
1/2	cup melted shortening (cooled)
1	cup flour
1	teaspoon baking powder
1/2	teaspoon soda
1/2	teaspoon salt

Soak the oats in buttermilk for 1 hour. Add the egg and beat well. Add the brown sugar and shortening. Sift all dry ingredients together. Add to the first mixture and mix lightly. Fill muffin pans 2/3 full. Bake at 400 degrees for 15 to 20 minutes.

To Freeze: Grease tins well and chill them. Pour mixture in muffin tins. Freeze. Thaw and bake for 15 to 20 minutes or cook frozen 30-40 minutes.

Mrs. H. Browne Mercer, Sr.

Blueberry Muffins

Yield: 1 dozen

1/2	cup sugar
1/3	cup shortening
1	egg
1/2	cup milk
1/2	teaspoon salt
1/4	teaspoon soda
2	teaspoons baking powder
1½	cups flour
1	cup floured blueberries

Cream sugar and shortening, add egg. Add milk and mix. Combine salt, soda, baking powder and flour. Add, mixing well. Gently fold in blueberries. Spoon into greased muffin tin. Bake at 375° for 20-25 minutes until brown.

Mrs. Frank Haas, Jr.

Spoon Rolls

Yield: 20-24

1½	packages yeast
2	cups lukewarm water
1/2	stick butter, melted
2	eggs, beaten
1/4	cup sugar
4	cups self-rising flour

Dissolve yeast in lukewarm water. Add all ingredients to flour; mixture will be consistency of waffle dough. Refrigerate and let sit 24 hours. Will keep for one week in refrigerator. When ready to use, spoon into greased muffin tins. Let sit about 30 minutes to one hour before baking. Bake at 400° 10-15 minutes. These rolls freeze well.

Mrs. Floyd Fraser

Onion Popovers

Yield: 6-12

3 eggs, well beaten
1 cup milk
2 tablespoons dry onion soup mix
1 tablespoon oil
1 cup flour

Combine eggs, milk, onion soup mix and oil. Blend in the flour until smooth. Beat one minute with a mixer. Fill well greased popover pans or custard cups 1/2 full and bake at 400 degrees for 40-45 minutes until brown. Reduce heat and bake 20 minutes longer. Makes 6 large or 11 small popovers. Serve very hot with butter.

Mrs. Charles McNeil, Jr.

Popovers

Yield: 6-10

3 medium eggs
1 cup unsifted flour
1 cup milk
3 tablespoons melted butter
1/2 teaspoon salt

Beat whole eggs slightly with rotary beater. Add flour, milk, melted butter and salt, beating enough to mix after each addition. Do not over beat. Fill 8 well-greased, 6-ounce custard cups 1/3 full. If large eggs are used, fill 10 6-ounce custard cups 1/3 full. Place cups in baking pan. Bake 35 minutes at 400 degrees. Do not open door until done. Serve immediately while piping hot with butter or margarine.

Mrs. John H. Tappan

Old Fashioned Corn Bread

Serves 6-8

3   tablespoons bacon
    drippings, melted
2   eggs
1   teaspoon salt
2   tablespoons sugar
1   cup buttermilk
1½ cups self-rising corn
    meal

Melt bacon drippings in an 8" iron skillet. In a medium bowl combine eggs, salt, sugar and buttermilk. Beat a little to blend. Stir in meal. Pour most of the bacon drippings into the batter, leaving a small amount in the skillet. Stir to blend, then pour batter into the warm skillet. Bake in a preheated 425° oven for about 20 minutes, or until golden brown. Serve hot and pass lots of butter. (Plain milk may be used.)

Mrs. Y. D. Lott, Jr.

Green Corn Spoonbread

Serves 6-8

2   cups milk, scalded
     Kernels cut from 6
     ears of corn
2/3 cup cornmeal
1   teaspoon salt
1/4 pound butter (1 stick)
1   tablespoon sugar
3   egg yolks
2   cups milk
3   egg whites, beaten

Heat milk, add corn and stir in corn-meal and salt. Continue to cook and stir the mixture for 5 minutes. Remove from heat. Beat in the butter and sugar. Beat together the egg yolks and milk. Add to first mixture. Fold in beaten egg whites. Fill a buttered 2 quart baking dish and bake at 350 degrees for 1 hour. Serve immediately.

Mrs. Sam W. Pipes, III

Corn Chili Bread

Serves 8

3	ears of fresh, uncooked corn
1	cup yellow cornmeal
2	teaspoons salt
3	teaspoons double-acting baking powder
1	cup sour cream
3/4	cup butter
2	eggs, well beaten
1/4	pound Gruyère or Monterey Jack cheese, finely diced
1	(4 ounce) can peeled green chilies, finely diced

Scrape the kernels from the corn cobs and combine with remaining ingredients. Pour into well-buttered 9-inch square baking dish or 2½ quart soufflé dish. Bake in a preheated 350° oven for 1 hour. Serve with melted butter or with sauce from the main dish.

Mrs. John W. Adams, Jr.

Hush Puppies

Serves 2-4

1	cup corn meal
2	teaspoons baking powder
1/2	teaspoon salt
1	medium onion, minced
1/4-1/2-cup water or milk
1	egg
	Pepper to taste

Mix dry ingredients. Add the onion and mix in the milk. Beat in egg vigorously. Drop by spoonfuls into hot grease (the grease in which fish were fried is excellent). Fry until golden brown.

Mrs. Albert Haas

Judy's Light Corn Bread

Yield: 1 loaf

2	cups self-rising corn meal
1/2	cup self-rising flour
3/4	cup sugar
1	package dry yeast
2	cups buttermilk
1	egg beaten
3	tablespoons melted shortening or oil

Sift meal, flour, sugar and yeast. Mix buttermilk, egg and shortening. Add meal mixture and mix lightly until well blended. Pour into well-greased loaf pan. Bake at 375 degrees for 50 minutes.

Mrs. James Fibbe

Turkey Dressing

Serves 12

1	onion
1	bunch green onions
1	small green pepper
6	ribs celery
2	sticks margarine
1	pound bulk sausage (I use "Hot")
2	packages Pepperidge Farm Cornbread Stuffing mix
4	cups well seasoned chicken stock
2	eggs, slightly beaten
1½	cups parsley, minced
	Salt, pepper, Worcestershire sauce

Finely chop onions, green pepper and celery. Sauté these in butter and sausage. Be sure sausage is well done; you will have stirred it until it is in small bits. In a large bowl, combine dressing mix and chicken stock (you can make this from chicken bouillon cubes). Add sausage mixture, eggs, fresh parsley and seasonings. You may stuff the cavity of the turkey or bake all of it in a shallow baking dish. Bake for 30 minutes at 350 degrees.

Mrs. Richard Murray, III

Cornbread and Oyster Stuffing for Turkey

1	10-ounce package cornbread mix (prepared)
10	cups fresh bread cubes (14 slices, toasted)
1	teaspoon rubbed sage
2	teaspoons salt
1/8	teaspoon pepper
2	cups or 16 ounces oysters (chopped and drained)
1/2	cup butter, melted
1/2	cup water
1/2	bell pepper, cut and sautéed
4	stalks celery, cut up and sautéed
1	onion, cut up and sautéed

Mix all ingredients and stuff the turkey. Cook the turkey according to your own recipe. This is also good to stuff baked chickens.

Mrs. Ray Herndon

Sarah's Good Bread

Yield: 1 large loaf

1	large loaf French bread
1	cup whipped margarine
1	cup Parmesan cheese
1/2	cup onion, chopped
1/4	cup Worcestershire sauce
	Dash of Tabasco

Slice French bread (not all the way through) into slices of preferred thickness. Combine the remaining ingredients and spoon between each slice. Bake at 350° until bubbly brown.

Mrs. Mark Lyons, III

SWEETS

GEORGE'S CANDY SHOP
Sweets from George's are synonymous with happiness.
For special occasions or just a treat, George has cap-
tured the hearts of children from 3 to 80 since he began
making candy in 1917.

Chocolate Brownie Tarts

Serves 12

SHELL:
1¾   cups flour
1/3   cup unsweetened
      cocoa
1/4   cup sugar
1   teaspoon salt
2   tablespoons
      shortening
1¼   sticks butter, chilled
1/3   cup ice water (less if
      possible)

In large bowl of electric mixer, sift together flour, cocoa, sugar and salt. Add shortening and chilled butter which has been cut into 1/2-inch pieces. With electric mixer on low speed, mix until ingredients resemble corn meal. Gradually add ice water until dough is very pliable. Wrap in plastic wrap and refrigerate for several hours or overnight. (Dough can be frozen at this point.) On lightly floured board, roll out part of dough 1/8-inch thick. Cut out circles to fit in your muffin pan. Press dough into ungreased muffin tins (mini muffins can be made yielding 48). Set aside and prepare filling. Preheat oven to 350°.

FILLING:
1   (12 ounce) package
      semi-sweet chocolate
      morsels
2   tablespoons milk
2/3   cup sugar
2   tablespoons butter
2   teaspoons almond
      extract
2   eggs, slightly beaten
      Almonds, slivered
      and toasted

Melt chocolate in covered double boiler over simmering, not boiling water. Stir until smooth. Blend in milk, sugar, butter and almond extract. Stir and blend well. Mixture will be slightly grainy. Remove top from double boiler and add beaten eggs. Beat until mixture is smooth. Put 2½ tablespoons of chocolate mixture into each uncooked shell. Garnish with toasted almonds. Bake 22 to 25 minutes at 350°. Cool 15 minutes in pan and remove to cookie tin. Can be made a day before. Put tablespoon of whipped cream on top before serving. Very rich eating!

Mrs. Thomas E. Sharp, Jr.

Chocolate Tarts

Yield: 2 Dozen

PASTRY:
1	cup sifted flour
1/4	teaspoon salt
1/4	cup butter
1½	tablespoons vegetable shortening
3	tablespoons cold water

Sift flour and salt. Cut in butter and shortening well with a pastry blender. Sprinkle cold water over mixture. Toss lightly with a fork and roll into a ball. Roll out dough on a floured board. Cut into rounds and bake in 2 dozen tart pans, 1¾ inch in diameter, at 400 degrees, until golden brown. Let cool.

FILLING:
1½	cups sugar
4	tablespoons cornstarch
	Dash of salt
2	squares unsweetened chocolate
2	cups milk
4	large egg yolks
1½	teaspoons vanilla

Combine sugar, cornstarch and salt in saucepan. Melt chocolate with 1/4 cup milk. Heat 1½ cups milk and add to sugar mixture, stirring constantly. When blended, add melted chocolate. Cook over moderate heat, stirring constantly until very thick. Beat egg yolks with remaining 1/4 cup milk and add slowly to hot mixture. Continue cooking over low heat until thick as mayonnaise, 1 minute longer. Remove from heat and add vanilla. Filling makes 2 cups.

*Note: fill tarts with chocolate filling. Top with whipped cream right before serving.

Mrs. James C. Bledsoe

Chocolate Mint Frozen Dessert

Serves 12-16

DESSERT:
- 25   **chocolate Oreos, crushed**
- 1/2   **stick margarine, melted**
- 1/2   **gallon Peppermint ice cream**

Mix together the crushed Oreos and the melted margarine. Press into a 9 x 13 inch pan. Spread the softened (slightly) ice cream onto the chocolate crust and freeze. Meanwhile, prepare the following sauce.

SAUCE:
- 3   **ounces unsweetened chocolate**
- 1/4   **cup margarine**
- 3/4   **cup sugar**
-     **Small can Pet milk**

Combine all the sauce ingredients in a medium saucepan. Cook over medium heat, stirring constantly, until chocolate is melted. Takes 4 minutes. Remove from heat and cool completely. Spread over the frozen ice cream and return to freezer. Cut into squares to serve.

Note: You may substitute a sauce made from 4 melted Goldbricks, if you prefer.

Mrs. C. H. R. Johnson

Pots de Crème

Serves 6

- 3/4   **cup cream or milk**
- 1   **cup semi-sweet chocolate bits**
- 1   **egg**
-     **Pinch salt**
- 1   **teaspoon vanilla**
- 1   **teaspoon dark Rum (optional)**

Heat cream just to boiling point. Place remaining ingredients in blender. Add cream. Blend at low speed for 1 minute. Pour into pots de crème cups, filling half full. Chill. Top with whipped cream. Demi-tasse cups may be substituted.

Mrs. John W. Adams, Jr.

Chocolate Frozen Dessert

Serves 12

Foil muffin cups
Graham cracker or
vanilla wafer crumbs
1/2 cup butter, softened
2 cups powdered sugar
4 squares unsweetened
chocolate, melted and
cooled
4 whole eggs
2 teaspoons vanilla
1 teaspoon peppermint
extract
1 cup whipping cream
Chopped pecans
(optional)

Place the foil cups in a 12 cup muffin tin. Cover the bottom of each with cookie crumbs. In a bowl, cream butter and sugar together. Add cooled chocolate. Add eggs, one at a time, and beat well after adding each. Add vanilla and peppermint extract. Pour into the cups. Freeze. (Only takes a couple of hours.) Whip the cream just before serving and put a little on each serving. Chopped nuts can be sprinkled on each or they can be mixed with the chocolate mixture before freezing.

Mrs. O. M. Otts, III

Raspberry Mousse

Serves 6

1 (10 ounce) package
raspberries
1/4 cup water
1 envelope unflavored
gelatin
1/4 teaspoon cream of
tartar
2 egg whites
1/3 cup sugar
1/2 cup heavy cream,
whipped

Put raspberries through sieve, pressing to get pulp and juice. If necessary add water to measure 1½ cups. Heat to boiling. Soften gelatin in 1/4 cup water; add to hot purée, stirring until dissolved. Cool. Refrigerate until slightly thickened. Beat egg whites with cream of tartar until soft peaks form. Add sugar gradually and continue beating until stiff peaks form. Fold raspberry mixture and whipped cream into meringue. Pour into 1½ quart prepared soufflé dish or mold. Serve with additional whipped cream and raspberry preserves. A beautiful and delicious dessert.

Mrs. David A. Richards

Blackberry Mousse

Serves 8

1½ tablespoons gelatin
1/4 cup cold water
1/2 cup fresh orange
    juice
1   tablespoon
    cornstarch
    Grated rind of 1
    orange
1½ pints blackberries,
    washed and dried
4   egg yolks
1   cup sugar
1/4 cup Grand Marnier
    (or more orange
    juice)
1/2 teaspoon cinnamon
1½ cups heavy cream
4   egg whites
1/2 cup powdered sugar
    Fresh berries for
    garnish

Soften gelatin in cold water for 5-6 minutes. Add 1/2 cup orange juice, cornstarch, orange peel and 3/4 cup berries. Heat carefully, stirring, until slightly thickened, about 10 minutes. Cool to room temperature. Beat the egg yolks and 1 cup sugar until lemon colored. Add Grand Marnier and cinnamon. Whisk in double boiler until mixture is too hot for your finger. Stir into gelatin and cool to room temperature. Whip the cream. Beat the egg whites with a pinch of salt and 1 tablespoon sugar until stiff, not dry. Fold cream into berry custard. In blender, buzz remaining berries with 1/2 cup powdered sugar until it purées. Stir into mixture until it streaks in a marble effect. Fold in egg whites. Chill in a 2 quart soufflé dish. Garnish with fresh blackberries.

Mrs. Wade Faulkner

Divine Dessert

Serves 6

Almond macaroons —
1 dozen large or 18
small
1/2 cup Rum
1/2 gallon coffee ice
    cream, softened
1   cup heavy cream,
    whipped
    Toasted almonds

Soak macaroons in Rum until they fall apart. This does not take long. Stir this into softened coffee ice cream. Freeze overnight in a silver Revere bowl or other pretty bowl. To serve, mound with whipped cream and sprinkle with toasted almonds. If ice cream mixture is frozen in a deep freeze, let it sit out about 15 minutes before serving.

Mrs. Victor H. Lott, Jr.

Rum Cream Dessert

Serves 8-10

1½	dozen lady fingers
72	large marshmallows
1/4	cup milk
5	tablespoons Rum
2	pints whipping cream

Line a 9" spring form pan with lady fingers. Crumble remaining lady fingers in bottom of pan. Heat marshmallows and milk in a double boiler. When melted, let cool. Add Rum. Whip cream until it peaks. Fold marshmallow mixture into cream. Pour into mold. Put in freezer for 30 minutes. Remove and refrigerate overnight.

Mrs. Floyd Fraser

Heating lemons a little before squeezing will enable you to extract more juice from them.

Cold Lemon Soufflé

Serves 8

1	tablespoon unflavored gelatin
1/4	cup cold water
4	egg yolks, beaten
1	cup sugar
1/2	teaspoon salt
1/2	cup, plus 1 tablespoon fresh lemon juice
1	tablespoon grated lemon peel
4	egg whites
1	cup heavy cream, whipped

Soak gelatin in water for 5 minutes. Beat egg yolks until thick and lemon colored. Add 1/2 cup sugar, salt, lemon juice and cook in double boiler until thick, stirring. Remove from heat, add gelatin and lemon peel. Cool until this mixture *just* begins to thicken. Beat egg whites until medium stiff, add 1/2 cup sugar and beat again until stiff peaks form when beater is raised. Fold into lemon custard, then fold in the whipped cream. Chill until firm in a 2 quart soufflé dish.

Mrs. Wade Faulkner

314

Pat Forman's Caramel Praline Soufflé

1 envelope unflavored
  gelatin
1½ cups cold water
28 caramels
2 tablespoons sugar
5 eggs, separated
1/4 teaspoon salt
1 cup heavy cream,
  whipped

Serves 8 generously

Soften the gelatin in 1/4 cup water. Melt the caramels and sugar with remaining 1¼ cups water in a covered double boiler over low heat. Stir small amount of hot mixture into egg yolks; return all to hot mixture. Cook for 3 minutes over low heat, stirring constantly. Stir in gelatin, and cool to room temperature. Beat the egg whites with salt until foamy; continue beating until stiff. Fold egg whites and whipped cream into caramel mixture. Pour the mixture into a dish and chill until firm.

Praline Mixture:
2 tablespoons sugar
1/4 cup pecans, chopped

Melt the sugar in a skillet over medium high heat until clear and caramel colored. Add the nuts, stir until well coated. Spoon onto a greased cookie sheet; immediately separate nuts with 2 forks. Cool. Break into small pieces. Sprinkle over the soufflé before serving.

Mrs. Danner Frazer, Jr.

A tablespoon of unflavored gelatin will gel two cups of liquid. Gelatin should be swirled not stirred.

Margaret's Crème De Menthe Poof

Serves 8-10

1 envelope plain Knox gelatin
3/4 cup boiling water
3/4 cup sugar
1/8 teaspoon salt
1/4 cup lemon juice
1/2 cup Crème de Menthe
1 pint whipping cream
Strawberries, optional
Raspberries, optional
Unsweetened chocolate, optional

Soften gelatin in water and stir well. Add sugar, salt, lemon juice and Crème de Menthe. Stir well. Cool until syrupy. Beat the cream. Fold into syrupy mixture and chill. (Save a small amount of cream for top decoration.) Put fruit on top, either strawberries or raspberries. Or shave unsweetened chocolate over the top and serve with chocolate wafers. This is a little tart and men like it.

Mrs. E. Burnley Davis

Debbie Gaden's Tortoni Squares

Yield: 16 squares

1/3 cup almonds, toasted and chopped
3 tablespoons butter, melted
1 cup fine vanilla wafer crumbs
1 teaspoon almond extract
3 pints vanilla ice cream, softened
1 (12 ounce) jar preserves, raspberry or apricot

Combine the almonds, butter, crumbs and almond extract and mix well. Save 1/4 cup of the crumb mixture for the topping. Sprinkle half the remaining mixture over the bottom of an 8 inch square pan lined with foil. Spoon half of the ice cream over the crumbs. Drizzle half the jar of preserves over the ice cream. Repeat, ending with the reserved 1/4 cup crumbs for the topping. Store in the freezer until ready to serve. Cut into squares to serve.

Mrs. Slade Hooks

316

Gus' Famous Egg Custard

Serves 4

4	tablespoons caramel sauce
3	eggs, large
1/4	pound sugar
2	ounces half and half cream
1	pint whole milk
1/8	ounce pure vanilla extract

Into the bottom of 4 (6 ounce) baking cups put 1 tablespoon of caramel sauce. Beat eggs with sugar. Add cream, milk and vanilla. Divide equally among the caramel-lined baking cups. Place cups in a small, shallow cake pan that has been half filled with tap water. Cook at 250° for 1¼ hours. Remove and cool the custard before attempting to remove it from the baking cups.

Weichman's All Seasons

Eggs may be brought to room temperature quickly by putting unbroken eggs in a bowl of warm water.

Low-Calorie Sugarless Custard

Serves 4

2	eggs, slightly beaten
	Pinch of salt
2	cups milk, whole or skimmed
	Artificial sweetener to taste (use enough to make rather sweet as cooking takes away a bit of the flavor)
1	teaspoon vanilla

Mix ingredients together, not in mixer because bubbles are not desired. Pour into 4 dessert-size oven-proof glass containers. Place these in a pan of water in a 300° oven for about an hour. Chill. Add a little nutmeg on top. About 95 calories per serving with skimmed milk. About 130 calories per serving with whole milk.

Mrs. Neal A. Collins

Lemon Cream Roll

4   egg yolks
3-4 tablespoons warm
      water (big eggs take
      3, small eggs take 4)
5/8 cup sugar
2   drops vanilla
4   egg whites
1/2 cup plus 1 tablespoon
      flour
1/3 cup cornstarch
      Pinch baking powder

Beat egg yolks with water until frothy. Add 2/3 of the sugar, a little at a time, and the vanilla. Beat until thick and creamy, at least 5 minutes. Beat egg whites stiff, then gradually add remaining sugar. Place egg white snow on the egg yolk mixture. Combine flour, cornstarch and baking powder and sieve on top of egg white snow. Fold all gently together. Do not stir or beat. Bake in a 15" jelly-roll pan, greased, lined with waxed paper and greased again, at 375° until light brown, 7-10 minutes. Immediately turn out onto fresh waxed paper sprinkled with sugar. Carefully remove used waxed paper from cake, and roll up the cake with the fresh paper. Leave to cool completely.

FILLING:

3   teaspoons gelatin
3   tablespoons cold
      water
4   sugar cubes
7   tablespoons lemon
      juice
1½ pints whipping cream
1¼ cups powdered sugar,
      sifted

Mix gelatin with water and let stand for 10 minutes. With the corners of sugar cubes rub off about half the peel of 1 lemon. Heat gelatin with sugar cubes in 1/2 cup hot water, stirring all the time, until gelatin dissolves. Add lemon juice and cool. Whip cream almost stiff, add the lukewarm gelatin solution, and whip stiff. Add powdered sugar and mix gently. Unroll the cake and remove paper. Spread 2/3 of the lemon cream over the cake and roll up again. Place on a serving plate and frost with remaining lemon cream. Chill and serve. Note: granulated sugar may be usbstituted for sugar cubes with the addition of the grated rind of 1 lemon. Use about 4 teaspoons sugar. This is an old German recipe.

Mrs. Peter Mannsfeld

Charlotte Russe

Serves 4

1	package gelatin
1/2	cup cold milk
1/2	cup hot milk
3	eggs, separated and at room temperature
3/4	cup sugar or more
2	teaspoons Cream Sherry or Bourbon
1	pint whipping cream, beaten to stiff froth
2	packages Lady Fingers or sponge cake

Sprinkle the gelatin over the cold milk. Add the gelatin mixture to hot milk, stirring until dissolved. Cool slightly. Stir in the egg yolks, sugar, and Sherry or Bourbon. When it is cold but not congealed, fold in the whipped cream and then the egg whites which have been beaten to a stiff froth. Sweeten and flavor to taste if not sweet enough. Line a bowl with Lady Fingers and pour mixture into bowl. Let stand in refrigerator until ready to eat.

Mrs. H. Michael Gates

Strawberry Macaroon Mold

Serves 12

2	quarts strawberries, washed and hulled
1½	cups sugar
1½	cups crumbled macaroons
2	cups heavy cream
1½	pounds cream cheese
1/4	cup milk
2	tablespoons orange rind, grated
1/2	cup orange juice
3	envelopes unflavored gelatin
1/2	cup water

Cut 1 quart of the strawberries in half and mix with the sugar. Let stand for 2 hours at room temperature, stirring occasionally. Soak the macaroons in the cream until soft. Allow the cream cheese to soften at room temperature and add the milk and beat until smooth. Add the orange rind and juice. Heat the gelatin and water until the gelatin dissolves. Drain berries. Add the syrup from berries to the cream cheese mixture. Fold in the strawberries. Whip the cream-macaroon mixture until thick and shiny. Fold into the strawberry mixture. Pour into a 10-cup mold and chill until firm. Unmold and serve surrounded by the remaining berries.

Mrs. Sam W. Pipes, III

Strawberry Delight

Serves 15-18

1	cup plain flour
1/4	cup brown sugar
1/2	cup nuts, chopped
1/2	cup melted butter
1	cup sugar
2	egg whites
2	teaspoons fresh lemon juice
10	ounces of frozen strawberries, thawed
1/2	pint heavy cream, whipped

Combine flour, brown sugar, nuts, and butter. Mix and spread in a 9" x 13" pan. Bake at 350° for 22 minutes, stirring often. Let cool. Combine sugar, egg whites, lemon juice and strawberries. Beat at high speed for 20 minutes. Fold in WHIPPED cream. Remove half of crumb mixture from pan and pat remaining in smooth layer. Pour in mixture and sprinkle remaining crumbs over top and freeze.

Mrs. Marvin Ussery

Meringues

Yield: 8 4" meringues

6	egg whites, beaten for 15 minutes in the mixmaster
1/4	teaspoon flavoring, vanilla, almond or whatever you prefer
2	cups sugar, added by teaspoons while beating egg whites
1	tablespoon vinegar

Beat egg whites until foamy, then beat in the salt. When meringue will hold a soft peak, begin to add the sugar, a spoonfull at a time, until all is incorporated. Beat in flavoring of your choice and vinegar. Drop meringues onto a cookie sheet, spread with brown paper, and form a shape with spoons or a knife. Bake for 1 hour in a 250° oven. Serve with ice cream or whipped cream or fruit. You may fill them with ice cream, and pass warm fudge or caramel sauce or a chilled fruit purée such as strawberry sauce to pour over. Yum.

Mrs. Glen P. Brock, Sr.

Mama's Bread Pudding

Serves 6

3	cups milk
2	tablespoons butter
6	slices bread, crusts removed
3	eggs, separated
	Pinch of salt
1/2	cup sugar
1	teaspoon vanilla
	Nutmeg, dash
	Blackberry jelly
	Additional sugar for meringue, 6 tablespoons

Heat milk with 2 tablespoons butter. Add bread and simmer for 3 minutes. Beat egg yolks and add pinch of salt and sugar. Add milk a little at a time to eggs. Add vanilla and nutmeg. Bake in Pyrex or soufflé bowl sitting in pan of water for 1 hour at 350 degrees, or until set. Remove from oven and add several teaspoons of blackberry jelly on top. Beat egg whites to make meringue and sweeten with 6 tablespoons sugar. Spread over the custard and bake again until meringue is a delicate golden brown. This is out of this world and different from most bread puddings. Don't be afraid of the jelly. It melts and adds a delicious flavor. This is good hot or cold.

Mrs. Harry D. Henson

Caramel Pudding

Serves 8

3	egg yolks
3/4	cup sugar
2	tablespoons cornstarch
1½	cups milk
1/2	cup sugar
2	tablespoons butter
1	teaspoon vanilla
	Whipped cream
	Toasted pecans, grated

Mix the egg yolks, sugar (3/4 cup), corn starch and milk. Cook in pan until thick, stirring constantly. Brown the 1/2 cup of sugar in an iron skillet until melted. Add to the above mixture. Stir in the butter and vanilla. Cool. To serve, put pudding in individual pastry shells or dishes. Top with whipped cream and sprinkle top with pecans.

Mrs. Cooper Thurber

Tipsy Pudding

Serves 10-12

SPONGE CAKE:

4	eggs
1	cup sugar
1	cup sifted flour
1	teaspoon baking powder
1	teaspoon vanilla

Beat eggs until thick. Slowly add sugar. Fold in flour and baking powder, then vanilla. Bake in a 15 x 11" jellyroll pan, greased and lined with greased waxed paper. Bake at 350° 10-15 minutes.

BOILED CUSTARD:

6	cups milk
6	eggs
1⅓	cups sugar
	Vanilla and Bourbon to taste
	Stemmed cherries
	Toasted almonds

In a heavy saucepan, heat milk to scalding. Beat eggs in blender and add sugar, blending well. Add eggs to hot milk and cook until it coats a spoon, stirring continuously. This takes a little time. Remove from heat and flavor with vanilla or Bourbon. Cool. Break cake in bottom of serving bowl. Pour some Bourbon on the cake, just a little on each piece. Pour half the custard over this. Add another layer of broken cake and repeat with Bourbon and custard. Let sit about 3 hours in refrigerator. Serve this from a crystal or cutglass bowl. Cover with sweetened whipped cream and decorate with the cherries and almonds. You may use Sherry instead of Bourbon. Be sure not to use too much Bourbon.

Mrs. Bettye McShan

Before whipping cream, put mixing bowl in the freezer for ten minutes to chill. The colder it and the cream are, the lighter the whipped cream. If you prefer to whip the cream ahead of time, put it in a strainer over a bowl in the refrigerator. The excess liquid will drain off and the cream will remain firm.

Pecan Pudding

Serves 6

1 cup pecans, toasted lightly
1½ cups milk
1/2 cup sugar
1/4 teaspoon vanilla
Whipped cream

In a food processor, pulverize the pecans using the steel blade. Be sure pecans are ground into a fine powder. In a saucepan, combine the ground pecans with the milk and sugar. Bring to a boil and cook stirring constantly for 10 minutes or until slightly thickened. Remove pan from heat, stir in the vanilla and let pudding cool, covered with buttered wax paper. Chill. Divide pudding among 6 small bowls and garnish each with a pecan half. Serve with whipped cream if desired.

Mrs. Thomas Gaillard, Jr.

Pavlova

Serves 6

4 egg whites
Salt
1 cup sugar
2 teaspoons vinegar
2 teaspoons vanilla
1 tablespoon corn starch

Beat egg whites with a pinch of salt. Gradually add sugar beating to a stiff consistency. Add the vinegar and vanilla at low speed. Fold in the corn starch. Form meringue into a shape like Baked Alaska (mound shape) on a brown paper lined cookie sheet. Bake for 2 hours in a preheated 250 degree oven. Turn oven down gradually to 200 degrees during baking time. Meringue should be slightly brown on top. Allow to cool. Serve on platter ringed with any combination of fresh fruit and whipped sweetened cream. Also may be served with French vanilla ice cream and hot chocolate suace. Fresh fruit: kiwi, strawberries, cherries, grapes, bananas, melon, and mandarin oranges.

Mrs. Stuart M. Ellis

Bobbie Austin's New Orleans Bread Pudding with Whiskey Sauce

Serves 10

1	loaf French bread
1	quart milk
3	eggs
2	cups sugar
2	tablespoons vanilla
1	cup raisins
3	tablespoons margarine, melted

Soak bread in milk. Crush with hands until mixed. Add eggs, sugar, vanilla and raisins. Pour melted margarine in the bottom of a thick pan and pour in the batter. Bake until very firm at 350° for approximately 50 minutes to an hour. Cool.

WHISKEY SAUCE:

1	stick butter
3/4	cup sugar
4	tablespoons milk
2	jiggers whiskey

Cream together butter and sugar. Add milk and flavor this with whiskey. Heat. Serve over bread pudding.

Mrs. Mac B. Greer

Brandied Apricot Dessert

Serves 4-6

1	(11 ounce) package dried apricots
2	cups water
5	tablespoons sugar
1/3	cup Brandy or Cognac
1/2	cup heavy cream, whipped
	Almonds, sliced and toasted

Boil apricots and water over moderate high heat, then simmer 10 minutes until apricots are soft. Drain, save liquid. Add sugar to 1/3 cup saved liquid. When dissolved, place in food processor with apricots and Brandy. Blend until smooth. Refrigerate 3 hours or until very cold. Serve in stemmed glasses. Top with a little whipped cream and almonds, if desired. 1/4 cup contains 201 calories.

Mrs. Evan Austill

Sautéed Apples

Serves 4-6

6	tablespoons butter
8	Golden Delicious apples, peeled and sliced
3/4	cup raisins (or less)
1/3	cup sugar
	Rind of 1 lemon, grated
	Juice of 1 lemon
1/2	teaspoon cinnamon
1/4	teaspoon nutmeg, grated (optional)

Melt butter in large skillet. Add other ingredients and sauté over medium heat until apples are done, but still retain their shape. This will take from 15 to 30 minutes, depending on how thick your apple slices are. Serve with vanilla ice cream or Rum Sauce.

RUM SAUCE:

6	large egg yolks
1	cup whipping cream
1	cup milk, heated
1/2	cup sugar
3	tablespoons dark Rum
2	teaspoons vanilla

Combine yolks, cream, milk and sugar in the top of a double boiler set over simmering water. Cook, stirring frequently, until sauce thickens and coats a spoon, about 30 minutes. Remove from heat and stir in Rum and vanilla. Chill thoroughly before serving.

NOTE: Use a whisk to thoroughly combine the egg yolks with the cream, milk and sugar. Serve with Sautéed Apples, or on your own cake squares.

Mrs. Wade Faulkner

Egg whites may be stored in the refrigerator in an airtight jar. Two tablespoons is the equivalent of one white.

Low-Calorie Stewed Apples or Sand Pears

Serves 6

6   medium-large apples
     or sand pears
3/4 cup water
1/2 lemon, thinly sliced
2   cinnamon sticks
     Dash of salt
     Sugar substitute to
     taste

Peel and chop fruit into big chunks. Put in a saucepan with the rest of the ingredients, except the sugar substitute. Simmer on medium to low heat until tender, adding water if necessary. Add sugar substitute. Serve warm or store indefinitely in the refrigerator.

Mrs. Ernest Brown

Grecian Pears

Serves 4

4   fresh Comice or
     Anjou pears
2¼   cups sugar
1   cup water
1   stick cinnamon
2-3 whole cloves
     Dairy sour cream
     Nutmeg, freshly
     grated if possible

Peel the pears and core them from blossom end if pears are small. Otherwise you may want to halve these, or perhaps double the sugar and water. Combine the sugar and water in a saucepan; cook over low heat until sugar is dissolved, stirring. Place the pears in syrup and boil gently about 15 minutes or until pears are tender. Remove from heat, immediately add cinnamon stick and cloves. Cool; then refrigerate until very cold. To serve: Whole pears are pretty placed upright in individual compotes. Add a bit of syrup, spoon on some sour cream and add a dash of nutmeg. Halved pears may also be served on lettuce as a salad, also with the sour cream and nutmeg. Delicious.

Mrs. Max Schneider

Steamed Pears with Raspberry Sauce

Serves 6

6	large, not-too-ripe Bartlett or Anjou pears, cored
	Peel of 1 large orange (removed with a vegetable peeler in strips)
3	tablespoons fresh lemon juice
1	(8 ounce) package frozen raspberries, thawed
6	mint leaves

Put 1½" water in a 4-6 quart Dutch oven. Place steamer in pot, bring water to a boil. Peel pears, leave stems on. Place a 1" long strip of orange peel inside each cored pear and dip in lemon juice. Place pears on steamer, cover and steam 10-25 minutes over moderate heat until tender when pierced with a knife. Let stand until cool enough to handle. Sieve berries to remove seeds. Pour into a large, rimmed serving plate. Place pears upright in sauce. Garnish each with a mint leaf. (Core pears from the bottom to leave stems attached.) 131 calories per serving.

Mrs. Evan Austill

The grated zest of a lemon yields approximately one tea-spoon — an orange yields one tablespoon. Grate only the thin, colored skin. Do not grate the white part.

Pears in Lemon Sauce

Serves 4

1	16-ounce can Bartlett pears
1/2	cup syrup from pears
1	egg, beaten
	Dash of salt
2	tablespoons lemon juice
1	3-ounce package of cream cheese

Place fruit in 4 individual dishes. Combine reserved pear syrup, 1 beaten egg, dash salt and 2 tablespoons lemon juice. Cook until thickened and smooth. Add a 3-ounce package cream cheese and beat until smooth. Pour over pears while still warm.

Mrs. James Hirs

Bananas Caribbean

Serves 8

4	fully ripe bananas
1	tablespoon butter
1/4	cup dark brown sugar
1/4	teaspoon freshly grated nutmeg
1/4	teaspoon cinnamon
1/2	cup fresh orange juice or any sweet juice you like
2	tablespoons dark Rum

Peel and split the bananas lengthwise and place them in a 10 x 6 x 2 inch baking dish. Melt the butter with the sugar, spices, juice and Rum. When hot, pour over the bananas and cook in a preheated 450° oven for 10 to 15 minutes. Serve hot from the oven, or at room temperature, over ice cream.

Mrs. H. C. Taylor

Beppie's Old Fashioned Buttermilk Ice Cream

Yield: 4½ quarts

1/2	gallon pineapple sherbert, softened
1	pint buttermilk
2	tablespoons sugar
	Juice of 1/2 lemon

Set out sherbert at room temperature for about 30 minutes or until soft. Slowly whip 1 pint of buttermilk with softened sherbert at medium speed and add 2 teaspoons sugar and the lemon juice, combining until creamy. Freeze and serve as needed.

Mrs. Zeb Inge

Eddie's Banana Almond Fudge Ice Cream

Yield: 2 quarts

3	bananas
1	tablespoon sugar
1	large can evaporated milk
5	eggs, beaten
8	ounces chocolate syrup
1/2	cup sugar
1	can Eagle brand condensed milk
1	package slivered almonds, toasted
	Milk

Mash bananas with 1 tablespoon sugar. Mix together all ingredients except milk. Pour into an ice cream freezer. Add milk to fill freezer 2/3 full. Freeze according to freezer instructions.

Mrs. Percy Roberts, Jr.

Add a little whiskey to coffee ice cream for Irish Coffee Ice Cream.

Frozen Blueberry Yoghurt

Yield: 1 quart

1½	to 2 cups blueberries
1/3	cup honey
	Dash of cinnamon
1	pint plain yoghurt

Heat the blueberries, honey and cinnamon until the berries pop. Cool. Mix with yoghurt and freeze in a 1/2 gallon ice cream freezer. (Double recipe for larger freezer.) Variation: Use mashed peaches or mashed bananas instead of blueberries.

Mrs. Wade B. Perry, Jr.

Hilda's Strawberry Ice Cream

Serves 6

2   **cups milk**
2   **cups light cream**
2   **eggs**
1¼ **cups sugar**
1/4 **teaspoon salt**
1½ **tablespoons flour**
1   **cup fresh strawberries**
1   **cup frozen strawberries**

Scald the milk and cream in the top of a double boiler. Blend eggs with sugar, salt and flour. Add some scalded milk, stirring. Return egg mixture to double boiler and cook, stirring, until mixture coats a silver spoon. Cool quickly. Add the strawberries. Freeze in ice cream freezer, according to directions.

Mrs. William C. Gewin

When making homemade ice cream use only the freshest ingredients. Prepare ice cream mixture and store covered in the refrigerator several hours before freezing, or overnight. This makes the ice cream richer and shortens the freezing time. After freezing, let ice cream ripen in the ice cream freezer for several hours. Cover the container tightly, add more ice and salt to the freezer and cover the freezer with newspapers and towels. If adding fruits, soak them in a liquor or liqueur such as Rum or Kirsch. This will keep the fruit from freezing hard.

Edith's Vanilla Ice Cream

Yield: 4 quarts

5 **eggs**
2 **(13-ounce) cans Pet evaporated milk**
2 **cups sugar**
3 **cups whole milk**
1 **tablespoon vanilla**
4 **cups fresh fruit (optional)**

Beat the eggs in a large bowl. Mix Pet milk, sugar, whole milk, and vanilla until sugar dissolves. Combine with beaten eggs. Add fruit, if you are using any. Freeze in ice cream freezer.

Mrs. Charles Marston

Galliano Ice Cream

Serves 4

1	cup sugar
1	cup half & half
1	cup whipping cream
1	cup orange juice
3	tablespoons Galliano
2	tablespoons lemon juice
1	egg white, beaten stiff

Mix all ingredients together. Pour into a bowl or plastic container. Place in freezer, covered. Delicious and creamy.

Mrs. R. E. Wheelis

Banana Peach Ice Cream

Yield: 4 quarts

3	cups bananas, mashed (about 5)
3¾	cups peaches, mashed (2 pounds, 8-12 peaches)
3	tablespoons lemon juice
6	tablespoons orange juice
1½	cups sugar
3/4	teaspoon salt
1½	teaspoons vanilla
3/4	teaspoon almond extract
3	eggs
1½	cups milk
3	cups heavy cream

Stir all ingredients together. Freeze in an ice cream freezer, according to manufacturer's instructions.

Mrs. William C. Gewin

Chocolate Covered Pecans

4   squares semi-sweet
     chocolate
     OR
1   package of semi-
     sweet chocolate bits
2   cups pecan halves,
     slightly toasted

In a saucepan over low heat melt the chocolate. Add the pecans and mix until well coated. Drop on foil and let cool thoroughly. You may need to break these apart when they have cooled. A grand holiday candy, and easy to make, too.

Mrs. Rose White

French Chocolates

Yield: 1¾ pounds

12   ounces semi-sweet
     chocolate morsels
1   cup walnuts, chopped
3/4 cup sweetened
     condensed milk
1   teaspoon vanilla
1/8 teaspoon salt
1   cup chocolate
     sprinkles

In a double boiler over hot, not boiling, water, melt the package of chocolate. After this is melted, stir in chopped walnuts, condensed milk, vanilla and salt. Cool mixture about 5 minutes. Butter hands and shape into balls. Roll each ball in chocolate sprinkles. These will harden as they cool. Keeps very well in a cookie tin. Rich and different!

Mrs. Marion H. Lyons, Jr.

Turtles

Yield: 2-3 dozen

2   bags Kraft caramels
3   tablespoons water
2   cups pecans
7   Hershey bars
1/3 bar paraffin

Melt the caramels with water in a double boiler. When melted, add pecans. Drop by teaspoonfuls on greased cookie sheets and cool. Melt chocolate bars and paraffin in double boiler and dip caramels. Let cool on wax paper.

Mrs. Percy Fountain

Pecan Turtles

Yield: 2 dozen

2 cups all purpose flour
1½ cups brown sugar, packed and divided
1/2 cup butter, softened
1 cup pecans, chopped
2/3 cup butter, melted
1 cup milk chocolate chips

Mix flour, 1 cup brown sugar and 1/2 cup butter and pat into a 13 x 9 inch unbuttered pan. Sprinkle pecans on unbaked crust. Melt 2/3 cup butter and remaining 1/2 cup brown sugar in saucepan and boil for 1 minute. Pour over crust mixture. Bake at 350° for 18-22 minutes. Sprinkle with chocolate chips after baking. Cool and cut into squares.

Mrs. Browne Mercer, Jr.

Mother's Fudge

Yield: about 30 pieces

2 cups sugar
1/2 cup butter
1/2 cup milk
2 heaping tablespoons cocoa
1 teaspoon vanilla
1 cup nuts, chopped

Place sugar, butter, milk and cocoa in heavy saucepan. Bring to a rolling boil and boil for 3 minutes, stirring constantly. Remove from heat and put pan in cool tap water, beating with spoon until smooth. Add vanilla and chopped nuts. Pour into a greased Pyrex 1½ quart baking dish and cool, or drop by spoonfuls onto a greased platter. May also be used to cover cherries.

Mrs. Greg Luce

Harbour Island Coconut Candy

Yield: 36 pieces

3 cups sugar
1 cup water
2½ cups coconut, grated
1 tablespoon butter
1/4 cup milk
1 teaspoon vanilla
1 teaspoon almond extract

Boil sugar and water to candy stage on candy thermometer (240°-250°). Add coconut and boil until the water has evaporated — about 7 minutes using medium-high heat. Add the butter, milk and flavorings. Stir briefly, then allow to cool to lukewarm. Drop on a greased cookie sheet or ungreased foil to cool.

Mrs. J. B. Horst

Peanut Brittle

Yield: 2 pounds

2 cups sugar
1 cup light corn syrup
1/2 cup water
2½ cups raw peanuts
1 tablespoon butter
1 teaspoon salt
1 teaspoon vanilla
2 teaspoons soda

Combine sugar, syrup and water in a saucepan. Cook over low heat until mixture comes to a boil. Add the peanuts and cook until candy thermometer registers 290°. Remove from heat; add butter, salt, vanilla, and soda, mixing well. Spread thinly onto 2 buttered cookie sheets. Cool and break into pieces.

Mrs. W. Bibb Lamar

Diddy's Creole Pralines

Yield: 12-18

3/4 cup brown sugar
3/4 cup white sugar
1/2 cup evaporated milk
1 tablespoon butter or margarine
1/4 teaspoon vanilla
1 cup pecan halves

Combine sugars and milk in a saucepan and bring to a boil. Lower the heat and cook to soft ball stage (238° on candy thermometer). Remove from heat. Add butter or margarine, vanilla, and pecans. Using wooden spoon, beat until creamy. Stop beating when ripples show at edge. Drop by spoonfuls onto waxed paper. Cool.

Mrs. John P. Case, Jr.

Oatmeal Carmelitas

Yield: 24 bars

1 cup all-purpose flour
3/4 cup brown sugar, packed
1/4 teaspoon salt
1 cup quick oats
1/2 teaspoon soda
3/4 cup butter, melted
1 cup semi-sweet chocolate pieces
1/2 cup nuts, chopped
3/4 cup caramel ice cream topping
3 tablespoons all-purpose flour

Combine flour, sugar, salt, oats, soda and butter in a large bowl to form crumbs. Press half of crumbs into bottom of a 9 inch square greased pan. Bake at 350° for 10 minutes. Sprinkle nuts and chocolate over baked crust. Mix caramel topping and flour. Drizzle over chocolate and nuts. Top with remaining crumbs. Bake at 350° for 15 to 20 additional minutes. Chill bars for easy cutting. Very good and very easy!

Mrs. William E. Powell

Quick Fudge

Yield: 70 1-inch squares

1   (13 ounce) can
    evaporated milk
4   cups white sugar
2   sticks margarine
3   (6 ounce) packages
    semi-sweet chocolate
    tidbits
1½ teaspoons vanilla
    Nuts (optional)

In a 3 quart saucepan, mix the milk and sugar. Bring to a boil slowly and boil for ten minutes. Pour the mixture over the margarine and tidbits. Beat until it starts to lose gloss. Add the vanilla and nuts. Pour into a large greased 9" x 13" pan. Refrigerate. Very rich and creamy.

Mrs. Allen R. Chason

Macaroon Top Hats

Yield: 5 dozen

1/2 cup butter
1/2 cup sugar
1   egg
1   egg yolk (reserve
     white for topper)
1   teaspoon lemon peel,
     grated
1½   cups enriched flour,
     sifted
1/2 teaspoon baking
     powder
1/4 teaspoon salt
     Whole almonds,
     toasted and halved

Cream together butter and sugar until light and fluffy. Add egg and egg yolk and beat well. Stir in peel. Sift together dry ingredients; add to creamed mixture, mixing well. Drop from tip of teaspoon, 2 inches apart, onto ungreased cookie sheet. With bottom of tumbler (buttered and dipped in sugar) press each cookie down slightly until about 1½ inches in diameter. Center each with a dab of Almond Topper, trim with a toasted almond half. Bake at 350° for 10 to 12 minutes or until lightly browned.

Almond Topper:
     Reserved egg white
     Dash of salt
     Dash of cinnamon
1/2 cup sugar
1/2 cup almonds, toasted
     and chopped

Beat 1 egg white with a dash of salt and cinnamon until it reaches stiff peaks. Gradually beat in 1/2 cup sugar. Fold in 1/2 cup chopped, toasted almonds.

Mrs. Sam W. Pipes, III

Fresh Apple Cookies

1/2 cup shortening
1½ cups brown sugar,
    firmly packed
1/2 teaspoon salt
1/2 teaspoon nutmeg
1 teaspoon ground
    cloves
1 teaspoon cinnamon
1 egg
2 cups flour, sifted
1 teaspoon soda
1 cup unpeeled apples,
    finely chopped
1 cup raisins
1 cup pecans, chopped
1/2 cup milk

VANILLA SPREAD:
2½ tablespoons milk
1½ cups confectioners
    sugar, sifted
1 tablespoon butter
1/8 teaspoon salt
1/4 teaspoon vanilla

Yield: 5-6 dozen

Cream first 7 ingredients. Sift flour and soda and add to creamed mixture. Stir in apples, raisins, pecans and milk. Blend well. Drop from a teaspoon onto a greased cookie sheet. Bake at 400° for 12 to 15 minutes. While cookies are baking, heat milk until steaming. Remove from heat and add all other ingredients. Beat until creamy. Spread on cookies while hot.

Mrs. Thomas B. Bender, Jr.

Grandmother Lyons' Date Squares

Yield: 12

2 eggs
1 cup sugar
1 cup flour
1 teaspoon baking powder
Pinch of salt
1 package (8 ounce) of Dromedary Pitted Dates, chopped
1 cup nuts, chopped

Beat eggs and add sugar to them. Sift flour with baking powder and salt. Add to egg and sugar mixture. Stir in dates and nuts. Spread in a greased and floured brownie pan. Bake at 375° for 25 minutes and cut into squares. It will be sticky, but put it back in oven which has been turned off to let it dry out for a minute or two. Then remove from the pan after cutting through the square lines previously cut.

Mrs. Frank Fogarty

Raspberry and Almond Squares

Yield: 16 squares

1½ cups sifted flour
1/2 cup sugar
1/2 teaspoon baking powder
1/2 teaspoon ground cinnamon
1/2 cup butter
1/2 cup ground almonds
1 egg
1/2 teaspoon almond extract
3/4 cup raspberry jam (10 ounce jar)

ICING:
1/2 cup confectioners sugar
2 teaspoons milk
1/4 teaspoon almond extract

Sift together flour, sugar, baking powder and cinnamon into a bowl and cut in the butter. Mix in egg, almond extract and almonds (ground in a blender) with dough. Divide dough in half, and spread half on waxed paper in an 8 inch square, and press the other half in a greased 8 inch square pan. Spread raspberry jam on the dough in the pan and top with remaining square of dough. Bake at 350° for 40 minutes, and then cool on a rack. Drizzle with icing (made by mixing sugar, milk, and almond extract until smooth) after it is cool. Cut into squares or bars.

Mrs. John E. Semon

Orchard Apple Squares

Yield: 24 squares

1/2 cup butter
1 cup sugar
1½ cups apples, peeled and grated
1 egg
2 cups flour, unsifted
1 teaspoon baking soda
1 teaspoon cinnamon
1/2 teaspoon cloves
1 teaspoon allspice
1 teaspoon salt
1 cup pecans, chopped
1 cup raisins

Cream butter and sugar until light and fluffy. Blend in grated apples and egg. Sift together the dry ingredients and stir into apple mixture. Stir in nuts and raisins. Spread in a lightly greased and floured 13x9x2 inch pan. Bake at 350° for 40 minutes.

TOPPING:
1 tablespoon butter
1/2 cup sugar
Grated peel and juice of an orange

Combine topping ingredients and bring to a boil. Reduce heat and simmer until butter is melted and sugar is dissolved. Pour hot topping over cake as it comes from oven. Cut in 24 squares and serve with whipped cream.

Mrs. H. Eldon Scott, III

Melt Away Cookies

Yield: 3 dozen

1/3-1/2 cup powdered sugar
1 cup flour
3/4 cup cornstarch
1/2 pound (2 sticks) margarine

Beat all ingredients until light. Refrigerate to firm. Roll in small balls and flatten with glass on ungreased cookie sheet. Bake at 350° for 10 minutes. These cookies will not be brown. Remove carefully as they are fragile and ice with mixture of powdered sugar, milk, vanilla and food coloring.

Mrs. William J. Suffich, Jr.

Cheesecake Triangle Cookies

Yield: 32 cookies

1/3 cup light brown sugar, firmly packed
1 cup unsifted all-purpose flour
1/2 cup nuts, chopped
1/3 cup butter, melted
1 (8 ounce) package cream cheese, softened
1/4 cup sugar
1 egg, slightly beaten
2 tablespoons milk
1½ tablespoons lemon juice
1/2 teaspoon grated lemon peel
1 teaspoon vanilla

Preheat oven to 350 degrees. Grease 8 inch pan. In small bowl, mix brown sugar, flour and nuts. Stir in melted butter until well mixed. Reserve 1/3 cup mixture. Pat remaining crumb mixture evenly into pan. Bake 12 to 15 minutes. Cool. In a small bowl with an electric mixer, beat cream cheese and sugar until smooth. Beat in remaining ingredients. Pour over cooked crust. Sprinkle with reserved crumbs. Bake 25 minutes more or until set. Cool on wire rack. When cool, cut into 2 inch squares; then cut each cookie diagonally in half.

Mrs. Donald Urquhart

Betty Luce's Chess Bars

1 box Duncan Hines All-Butter Cake mix
1 egg
1 stick butter (not margarine)
2 teaspoons vanilla
3 eggs
1 (8 ounce) package cream cheese
1 box powdered sugar

Mix cake mix with egg, butter and vanilla. Spread in greased 9 x 13" pan. Beat eggs, cream cheese and sugar. Pour over cake mixture and bake at 350° for 30-40 minutes. Cool and cut into bars. Good for "pick up" dessert.

Mrs. Greg Luce

Mrs. Leatherwood's Oatmeal Cookies

Yield: 4 dozen

1/2 cup brown sugar
1/2 cup white sugar
1/2 cup shortening
(Crisco)
1 egg
1 cup flour
Pinch of salt
1/2 teaspoon baking
powder
1/2 teaspoon baking soda
1 cup oatmeal, quick
1/2 cup chocolate chips
1/2 cup pecans, chopped

Cream the sugars and shortening together, add egg and mix thoroughly. Mix flour, salt, baking powder, baking soda, and oatmeal and add to the above mixture. Add chocolate chips and nuts. Drop by teaspoons on a cookie sheet. Bake at 350° for 12 to 15 minutes.

Mrs. Leatherwood Cole

Pumpkin Cake

Yield: 27 bars

1⅔ cups sugar
1 cup oil
4 eggs
2 cups pumpkin
2 cups flour
1 teaspoon salt
2 teaspoons baking
powder
1 teaspoon baking soda
2 teaspoons cinnamon
Nuts, if desired

Blend sugar, oil, eggs and pumpkin. Sift flour, salt, baking powder, baking soda and cinnamon and stir into sugar mixture. Add nuts, if desired. Bake in 9 x 13 inch cake pan at 350 degrees for 30 minutes. Cut into bars. Frost if desired, but not necessary. This is so easy to make in a food processor.

FROSTING:
3 ounce package cream
cheese
3/4 stick butter
1 teaspoon vanilla
1½-1¾ cups powdered
sugar
2 teaspoons cream or
milk

To make frosting, cream butter and cream cheese together. Add remaining ingredients and blend. Spread on pumpkin cake.

Mrs. Norman Walton

"Miss Ruth's" Cookies

Yield: 10 dozen

1	cup sugar
1/2	cup brown sugar
2	sticks butter
1	cup Mazola Oil
1	egg
1	teaspoon vanilla
1	teaspoon cream of tartar
1	teaspoon soda
1	teaspoon salt
3½	cups flour
1	cup Rice Crispies
1	cup coconut
1	cup oatmeal, uncooked
1/2	cup nuts, chopped

Cream first six ingredients, then slowly mix in the rest. Drop by spoonfuls onto greased cookie sheet and press down with fork. Bake at 350° for 15 minutes.

Mrs. Frank T. Manley

Mabel's Cinnamon Crisps

Yield: 3 dozen

2	sticks butter
1	cup sugar
2	cups flour
2	teaspoons cinnamon
1/2	teaspoon nutmeg
1	egg yolk (reserve the egg white)
1	teaspoon vanilla
1/2	cup nuts, chopped

Cream butter and sugar together. Then add the rest of the ingredients, except the egg white. Dough will be real stiff. Press into 10 x 15 inch ungreased cookie pan. Pour unbeaten egg white on top of dough and spread with fingertips. Pour off excess egg white. Sprinkle with chopped nuts. Press nuts into dough. Bake at 275° for 1 hour and immediately after removing from oven, cut into 2" squares. Cookies may be frozen. Good after-school treat!

Mrs. Frederick S. Crown, Jr.

Soft Spicy Hermits

Yield: 5 dozen

1/2 cup oil
1 cup sugar
1 teaspoon cinnamon
1/2 teaspoon nutmeg
1 teaspoon baking soda
1/2 teaspoon salt
2½ cups flour
1/2 cup milk
1/2 cup dark corn syrup
1 cup raisins

Mix oil and sugar and set aside. Mix cinnamon, nutmeg, baking soda, salt, and flour. In another bowl, mix milk and corn syrup. Add the flour mixture alternately with the liquid mixture to the oil and sugar mixture. Stir in raisins. Spread batter on oiled cookie sheet. Bake 25 minutes at 350 degrees. Cut in squares. May be dusted with powdered sugar.

Mrs. John J. Fesenmeier

Chinese Chews

Yield: 4 dozen pieces

1 (6 ounce) package semi-sweet chocolate pieces
1 (6 ounce) package butterscotch pieces
1 (3 ounce) can Chow Mein noodles
1 (6½ ounce) can cocktail peanuts

Combine chocolate and butterscotch pieces in a 2 quart glass dish. Microwave for 2 minutes. Stir until smooth. Add noodles and peanuts; stir until well coated. Drop by teaspoonfuls onto waxed paper. Refrigerate until firm. Great for children to make on a rainy day!

Mrs. Edward Russell March, Jr.

Angel Nut Sticks

Yield: 22-24 sticks

2	angel food loaf cakes
3	egg whites
1	box powdered sugar
2	sticks butter, melted
1	teaspoon vanilla
16	ounces of pecans, chopped fine

Cut cake into sticks 1 inch square. Mix egg whites (beaten to a froth), sugar, melted butter and vanilla. Roll cake sticks first in sugar mixture (let drain), then roll in pecans. This is a very messy procedure but well worth the mess. Refrigerate. Freezes well.

Mrs. Floyd Fraser

Oriental Brittle Cookies

Yield: 2 dozen

1	cup butter
2	tablespoons instant coffee powder, not freeze-dried
1	teaspoon salt
1/2	teaspoon almond extract
1	teaspoon vanilla extract
1	cup sugar
2	cups sifted flour
1	(6 ounce) package semi-sweet chocolate chips, coarsely chopped
1/2	cup almonds, finely chopped

Preheat oven to 375°. Blend butter, coffee, salt and extracts. Beat in sugar gradually. Add flour and mix well, then add chocolate chips. Spread in ungreased pan, 15 x 10 x 1". Sprinkle the chopped almonds over the top. Bake for 25 minutes at 375°F. Cool and break into 2" irregular pieces.

Mrs. Bruce C. Finley, Jr.

Triple Chocolate Cookies

Yield: 46 cookies

2	tablespoons butter
3	squares unsweetened chocolate
5	squares semi-sweet chocolate
1/4	cup all-purpose flour, sifted
1/4	teaspoon baking powder
1/8	teaspoon salt
2	eggs
3/4	cup sugar
2	teaspoons instant coffee powder
1/2	teaspoon vanilla extract
1	cup semi-sweet chocolate morsels
2	cups pecans, coarsely chopped

Cut 3 pieces of aluminum foil to fit your cookie sheet. Set aside. Preheat oven to 350°. Melt butter in a small saucepan. Add the chocolate and melt over low heat, stirring constantly. Set aside to cool slightly. Sift together flour, baking powder, and salt. Set aside. With a mix-master at high speed, beat eggs, sugar, coffee powder and vanilla for a minute or two. Then at low speed beat in the cooled chocolate and butter, then the sifted flour mixture. Beat only until blended. Stir in the chocolate morsels and pecans. Drop by heaping teaspoon-fuls onto the 3 pieces of aluminum foil. Put 20 cookies on each of 2 sheets, the remaining 6 cookies on the third sheet. Slide the cookie sheet under 1 batch of cookies and bake for 8 minutes. Remove the sheet of foil onto the counter top, and repeat with another sheet of cookies and foil. Then repeat again for the third sheet of cookies and foil. When the cookies have cooled enough to handle, place on another sheet of foil or a rack to continue cooling. They will peel right off. Then chill in the refrigerator before serving. I like to store these cookies in the refrigerator and serve cold. Chilling makes the chocolate morsels brittle and crunchy.

Mrs. Wade Faulkner

345

Lou's Fudge Squares

2   cups sugar
2   sticks melted
     margarine
1⅓ cups flour
4   eggs, beaten
1   cup chopped pecans
6   tbls. cocoa
1   tbls. vanilla

Icing:
1   tbls. cocoa
1/4 cup butter
1/4 cup milk
1   cup sugar
2   heaping tbls.
     marshmallow whip

Mix sugar and cocoa together. Add melted margarine and stir well by hand. To this mixture add eggs and flour and blend well, then add vanilla and pecans. Pour into jelly roll pan lined with parchment paper. Bake at 250 for 1 hour. Frost with chocolate icing.

Boil first 4 ingredients with a pinch of salt for 1 minute. Take off fire and add 2 tbls. marshmallow whip. Then beat with a hand mixer until spreading consistency. Pour over cake and spread. Cut into squares.

Mrs. Ben Radcliff

Rocky Road Bars

BAR:
1/2 cup butter
1   ounce (square) unsweetened chocolate
1   cup sugar
1   cup all-purpose flour
3/4 cup pecans, chopped
1   teaspoon baking powder
1   teaspoon vanilla
2   eggs

FILLING:
8   ounces cream cheese, softened (save 2 ounces for frosting)
1/2 cup sugar
2   tablespoons flour
1/4 cup butter, softened
1   egg, slightly beaten
1/2 teaspoon vanilla
1/4 cup pecans, chopped
1   (6-ounce) package chocolate chips

FROSTING:
2   cups miniature marshmallows
1/4 cup butter
1   ounce unsweetened chocolate
     Remaining 2 ounces cream cheese
1/4 cup milk
2½   cups confectioner's sugar
1   teaspoon vanilla

Yield: 3 dozen

Make the bar first. Preheat oven to 350 degrees. Grease and flour a 9 x 13 inch pan. In a saucepan over low heat, melt 1/2 cup butter and 1 ounce chocolate. Add remaining bar ingredients and mix well. Spread in prepared pan. Next, make filling. In small bowl, combine 6 ounces cream cheese with the next 5 ingredients (sugar, flour, butter, egg, vanilla). Blend until fluffy. Stir in nuts and spread over chocolate mixture. Sprinkle chocolate chips over all. Bake at 350 degrees for 25-35 minutes until knife in center comes out clean. Sprinkle marshmallows over the cake and bake 2 minutes longer. Now make frosting: Over low flame in a large saucepan, melt 1/4 cup butter, 1 ounce chocolate, remaining 2 ounces cream cheese and milk. Stir in powdered sugar and vanilla until smooth. Immediately pour over the marshmallows and swirl together. Store in refrigerator. Cut into size squares you want.

Mrs. Richard Murray, III

Mama's Chocolate Cookies

Yield: 4-5 dozen

8	ounces semi-sweet chocolate
1	(14 ounce) can sweetened condensed milk
1	can (3½ ounce) coconut
2	cups pecans, chopped
1	teaspoon vanilla
1/2	teaspoon salt

Melt chocolate in milk in double boiler. Add coconut, pecans, vanilla and salt. Drop by teaspoonfuls on greased cookie sheets. Bake at 350° for 8 minutes.

Mrs. John N. Horner

Cocoa Kiss Cookies

Yield: 4½ dozen

1	cup butter or margarine, softened
2/3	cup granulated sugar
1	teaspoon vanilla
1⅔	cups all-purpose flour
1/2	cup cocoa
1	cup nuts, finely chopped
1	(9 ounce) package milk chocolate kisses (about 54)

Cream butter, sugar, and vanilla. Beat in flour and cocoa gradually. Add the nuts. Beat at low speed until evenly distributed. Chill for 30 minutes. Unwrap kisses. Shape a teaspoon of dough around each kiss. Roll in your palms and pinch away excess to make a small ball. Place a few inches apart on an ungreased cookie sheet. Bake in a preheated oven at 375° until set (10 to 12 minutes). Don't overbake! Cool before eating.

Mrs. William D. Walsh, Jr.

Marbled Cheese Brownies

1   package (4 ounce)
Baker's German
Sweet Chocolate
5   tablespoons butter,
divided
1   package (3 ounce)
cream cheese
1   cup sugar, divided
3   eggs
1/2   cup plus 1 tablespoon
flour, divided
1½   teaspoons vanilla,
divided
1/2   teaspoon baking
powder
1/4   teaspoon salt
1/2   cup nuts, chopped
1/4   teaspoon almond
extract

Yield: 16 squares
Melt chocolate and 3 tablespoons butter. Cool and set aside. Cream remaining butter (2 tablespoons) with cream cheese until softened. Add 1/4 cup sugar, creaming until light and fluffy. Blend in 1 egg, 1 tablespoon flour and 1/2 teaspoon vanilla. Set aside. Beat remaining eggs until thick and light in color. Gradually add remaining 3/4 cup sugar, beating until thickened. Add baking powder, salt, and remaining 1/2 cup flour. Blend in cooled chocolate mixture, nuts, almond extract and remaining 1 teaspoon vanilla. Measure one cup of chocolate batter and set aside. Spread remaining chocolate batter in a greased 9 inch square pan. Top with cheese mixture. Drop chocolate batter from a spoon onto cheese mixture. Swirl with a knife to marble. Bake at 350° for 35 to 40 minutes; cool, then cut.

Mrs. Winston Patterson

Fudge Squares

½   cup butter
2   cups sugar
4   eggs
4   squares bitter
chocolate, melted
Pinch of salt
1   cup flour
1½   teaspoons vanilla
2   cups pecans, chopped

Yield: 3 dozen
Cream butter and sugar, add whole eggs, one at a time. Stir in cooled melted chocolate. Add salt, flour, vanilla and nuts. Bake in a greased 9" x 13" pan at 325° for 35 minutes. I like mine chewy. If you like them dryer, cook a little longer. Let them cool in pan and slice in small squares.

Mrs. T. Massey Bedsole

Brownies for a Crowd

Yield: 5 dozen

1/2 cup margarine
1 cup sugar
4 eggs
1 teaspoon vanilla
1 (one pound) can chocolate syrup
1 cup plus 1 tablespoon sifted flour
1/2 teaspoon baking powder
1/4 teaspoon salt
1/2 cup chopped nuts
6 tablespoons margarine
6 tablespoons milk
1 cup sugar
1/2 cup semi-sweet chocolate pieces
1 teaspoon vanilla

Beat 1/2 cup margarine with 1 cup sugar until light and fluffy. Beat in eggs, two at a time, and 1 teaspoon vanilla. Mix well. Stir in chocolate syrup. Sift together flour, baking powder, and salt. Stir into chocolate mixture. Add nuts. Pour into well greased 15½ x 10½ x 1 inch pan and spread evenly. Bake at 350° for 22-25 minutes and let cool. Meanwhile combine 6 tablespoons margarine, milk and 1 cup sugar in saucepan. Stir to mix. Bring to a boil and boil for 30 seconds. Add chocolate pieces, stir until mixture thickens slightly and cools. Stir in 1 teaspoon vanilla. Spread over cooled brownies, then cut into 2½ x 1 inch bars.

Mrs. John T. Mostellar

Blonde Brownies

Yield: 16 to 20

1/2 stick butter or margarine
1 cup brown sugar
1 egg, beaten
1 teaspoon vanilla
Dash salt
1 cup flour
1 teaspoon baking powder
1 cup pecans, chopped
1 (6 ounce) package chocolate chips

Melt butter; combine with brown sugar, beaten egg, vanilla, and salt. Stir in flour and baking powder, then add pecans and chocolate chips. Bake at 350° for 30 minutes in greased and floured 8 inch square pan. Cut into squares. May be dusted with confectioners sugar after baking.

Mrs. Frederick Helmsing

Mint Stick Brownies

Yield: 20

2   **squares unsweetened chocolate**
1/2   **cup butter or margarine**
2   **eggs, well beaten**
1   **cup sugar**
1/4   **teaspoon peppermint flavoring**
1/2   **cup all-purpose flour**
  Dash of salt
1/2   **cup pecans, chopped**

Melt chocolate and butter in double boiler over hot water. Cool. Add eggs, sugar, flavoring, flour, salt and nuts. Blend and pour into a well-greased 9 inch square pan. Bake at 350° for 20 to 25 minutes. Cool.

FROSTING:
2   **tablespoons softened butter or margarine**
1   **cup powdered sugar**
1/2   **teaspoon peppermint flavoring**
1   **tablespoon milk**
  Several drops green food coloring

Combine all frosting ingredients and mix until creamy. Spread over cooled brownies. Refrigerate while making glaze.

GLAZE:
1   **square unsweetened chocolate**
1   **tablespoon butter or margarine**

To make glaze, melt ingredients and blend well. Spread evenly over mint frosting and refrigerate. Cut into small squares. Freezes beautifully.

Mrs. Carl E. Jones, Jr.

Caramel Brownies

Yield: 15-20

1	stick butter
2	cups brown sugar
2	eggs
2	cups flour, sifted
2	teaspoons baking powder
	Dash of salt
2	teaspoons vanilla
2/3	cup nuts

Melt butter slowly in a heavy saucepan. Add sugar, stirring until it thickens (3 to 5 minutes on low heat). Transfer to a large bowl and let cool for 5 minutes. Add eggs, flour, baking powder, salt, vanilla and nuts; mix well. This will be a very sticky dough. Spread into a greased square cake pan. Bake at 350° for 30 to 40 minutes. Let cool in the pan completely before cutting into squares.

Mrs. John Wilson

Fudge Muffins

Yield: 5 dozen

4	squares semi-sweet chocolate
2	sticks margarine
1¾	cups sugar
1	cup flour
	Dash of salt
4	eggs
1	teaspoon vanilla
1	cup pecans, chopped

Melt the chocolate and margarine in a double boiler. Place melted mixture in a large mixing bowl and add dry ingredients. Stir in eggs one at a time. Add vanilla and pecans. Bake in small muffin papers at 325 degrees for 25 minutes. These are very good split and served with ice cream (vanilla or coffee) and chocolate sauce.

Mrs. Augustine Meaher, III

Best-Ever Cheesecake

Yield: One 9" cheesecake

CRUST:
1   cup sifted enriched flour
1/4   cup sugar
1   teaspoon lemon peel, grated
1/2   cup butter or margarine
1   egg yolk, slightly beaten
1/4   teaspoon vanilla

Combine flour, sugar and lemon peel. Cut in butter until mixture is crumbly. Add egg yolk, vanilla; blend well. Pat 1/3 of dough on bottom of 9" spring-form pan (sides removed). Bake at 400° about 6 minutes, or until golden; cool. Butter sides of pan; attach to bottom. Pat remaining dough evenly on sides to a height of 2 inches.

CHEESE FILLING:
5   (8 ounce) packages cream cheese
1¾   cups sugar
3   tablespoons enriched flour
3/4   teaspoon lemon peel, grated
1/4   teaspoon salt
1/4   teaspoon vanilla
5   eggs (1 cup)
2   egg yolks
1/4   cup heavy cream

Stir cream cheese to soften; beat until fluffy. Combine next 5 ingredients; gradually blend into cheese. Add eggs and yolks, one at a time; beat well after each. Gently stir in cream. Turn into crust-lined pan. Bake at 500° 5-8 minutes, or until top of crust is golden. Reduce heat to 200°; bake 1 hour longer. Remove from oven; cool in pan 3 hours. Remove sides of pan. Serve with Strawberry Topping. (Please consult Index for topping recipe.)

Mrs. Bettye McShan

Chocolate Cheese Cake

Serves 12

CRUST:
- 1⅓ cups chocolate wafer crumbs
- 1/2 stick butter, melted
- 2 tablespoons sugar

Preheat oven at 300°. Combine crumbs, butter and sugar. Mix well. Use a well-buttered 9-inch spring form pan. Press the crust mixture onto the bottom of the spring form pan. Chill until ready to fill.

FILLING:

Step I
- 1 cup heavy cream
- 8 ounces semi-sweet chocolate (broken into bits)
- 4 large egg yolks (room temperature)
- 1/2 cup sugar

Scald 1 cup heavy cream in a saucepan, remove the pan from heat and let the cream cool for 5 minutes. Add the chocolate and stir until the chocolate is melted. In a mixing bowl beat the mixture until it is cool and light in texture. In a large bowl with electric mixer beat 4 egg yolks with 1/2 cup sugar until the mixture is thick and lemon colored. (Mixture should form ribbon when beaters are lifted.) Add the chocolate mixture to egg mixture and beat until it is well mixed.

Step II
- 1½ pounds cream cheese, softened (3 8-ounce bars)
- 1 cup sour cream
- 2 tablespoons cornstarch
- 1 teaspoon almond extract

In a food processor fitted with the steel blade (or use mixer) blend cream cheese, sour cream, cornstarch, and almond extract until the mixture is smooth. Add the cream cheese mixture to chocolate mixture and stir until well mixed.

Step III

4 large egg whites
  (room temperature)
  Pinch of cream of
  tartar
  Pinch of salt
1/4 cup sugar
  Whipped cream (1
  pint)

In a large bowl beat 4 egg whites with cream of tartar and salt until they form soft peaks. Add sugar and beat until they form stiff peaks. Fold the whites into the chocolate mixture and pour into the crust. Put the spring form pan in a baking pan and add enough hot water to come half way up the sides of the spring form pan. Bake in a 300° oven for 1 hour and 30 minutes. Turn off the heat (do *not* open oven) and let the cake sit in the oven for 1 hour. Let the cake cool on a rack. Cover loosely and chill at least 2 hours. Remove sides of pan and garnish with whipped cream and chocolate curls.

Step IV — Chocolate Curls

3 ounces semi-sweet
  chocolate

Melt the chocolate in the top of a double boiler over simmering water and stir until it is smooth. With a metal spatula spread a very thin layer on the bottom of 3 inverted cake pans. Chill for 15 minutes or until it loses its shine but is still pliable. Remove 1 pan at a time; put metal spatula under an edge of the chocolate and push it firmly away from you, so the chocolate curls as it is pushed. Transfer the curls to wax paper and chill them as they are made.

Mrs. Larry Harless

Chocolate Cinnamon Cake

Yield: 18 2" squares

2 cups flour
2 cups sugar
1 stick margarine
1/2 cup Crisco
4 tablespoons cocoa
1 cup water
1/2 cup buttermilk
2 eggs
1 teaspoon soda
1 teaspoon cinnamon
1 teaspoon vanilla

Sift together flour and sugar; set aside. In a saucepan, mix together next 4 ingredients. Bring to a boil; pour over sugar and flour. Stir well. Add buttermilk, eggs, soda, cinnamon and vanilla. Mix together well. Bake at 400° for 30 minutes in an oblong baking pan (11¾ x 7½"), greased and floured. Frost with icing when cool.

ICING:
1 stick margarine
4 tablespoons cocoa
6 tablespoons milk (or buttermilk)
1 box powdered sugar
1 teaspoon vanilla
1 cup nuts, chopped

To make icing, mix margarine, cocoa and milk in a pan. Bring to a boil. Remove from heat and add remaining ingredients. Frost top and sides of cake.

Mrs. David B. Freeman, III

Plum Cake

Yield: 1 10" tube cake

3 eggs
2 cups sugar
1 cup oil
2 cups sifted self-rising flour
2 small jars baby food plums
2 teaspoons allspice
1 cup nuts, chopped

Mix all ingredients, one at a time. Bake at 325° for 1 hour 15 minutes in a greased and floured tube pan. A good cake for cold weather with coffee. Very moist and spicy.

Mrs. Clarke Irvine, Jr.

Grandmother Lyons'
Fudge Cake and Icing

2   squares cake
     chocolate
     (unsweetened)
1   cup of butter or
     margarine (2 sticks)
2   cups sugar
4   eggs, unbeaten
1   cup flour
     Pinch of salt
     Toasted nuts,
     optional
1   teaspoon vanilla

Yield: 1 small sheet cake

Melt chocolate in double boiler. Cream butter and sugar, add cooled melted chocolate, then unbeaten eggs, flour, salt, nuts, (if any) and vanilla. Pour into a well greased pan, approximately 8½ x 11 inches. Bake at 350° for 45 minutes. Ice when cool.

ICING:

2/3 cup of milk
2   squares unsweetened
     chocolate
2   cups sugar
2   tablespoons corn
     syrup
     Pinch of salt
2   tablespoons butter

Cook milk and chocolate together until dissolved. Add sugar, corn syrup and salt. Cook until it forms a soft ball in cold water. Add a large lump (about 2 tablespoons) of butter. When cool, beat until consistency to spread.

Mrs. Frank Fogarty

Peppermint Patty Cake

Yield: 1 sheet cake

BLACK DEVIL'S FOOD CAKE:
1/2 cup butter
1¼ cups sugar
3 eggs
1 teaspoon vanilla
1/2 cup cocoa
1 cup strong hot coffee
1½ cups flour, sifted
1 teaspoon baking soda
1 teaspoon baking powder
1/2 teaspoon salt

Cream butter and sugar. Add eggs; beat until light and fluffy. Add vanilla. Dissolve cocoa in coffee. Sift flour with baking soda and baking powder and salt. Add to butter and sugar alternately with cocoa and coffee. Turn into 9 inch x 13 inch buttered pan. Bake at 300° for 30 to 35 minutes. Cool. Make mint filling.

MINT FILLING:
1/2 cup cream
1/2 teaspoon peppermint extract
1/4 teaspoon salt
5 cups powdered sugar, sifted

To make filling, put ingredients in blender, blend until smooth. Spread over cooled Black Devil's Food Cake. Wait until filling sets before adding chocolate icing.

CHOCOLATE FUDGE ICING:
3 squares chocolate
3/4 stick margarine
1½ tablespoons white Karo syrup
1/2 cup milk
2¼ cups sugar
Pinch of salt
2 teaspoons vanilla

To make icing, cut chocolate into small pieces. Place all ingredients, except vanilla, into saucepan. Bring slowly to a full, rolling boil, stirring constantly. Boil briskly without stirring for 1 minute. Don't overboil. Cool to lukewarm. Beat, adding vanilla, until thick enough to spread. Cool and use on Black Devil's Food Cake.

Mrs. Percy Roberts, Jr.

Chocolate-Orange Rum Cake

Yield: 1 2-layer cake
Preheat oven to 350°.

2	cups flour, sifted
2	teaspoons baking powder
1/4	teaspoon soda
1/4	teaspoon salt
1/2	cup fresh orange juice
	Grated rind of 1 orange to RESERVE
3	tablespoons Rum
1/2	cup butter
1/4	teaspoon almond extract
1/2	teaspoon vanilla extract
1	cup sugar
2	eggs, separated

FILLING:

1	tablespoon unflavored gelatin
3	tablespoons cold water
3/4	cup Rum
3	cups whipping cream
3/4	cup confectioners sugar
1/2	teaspoon almond extract

FROSTING:

4	squares bitter chocolate, melted
1	cup confectioners sugar
2	tablespoons hot water
2	eggs
6	tablespoons butter, softened
1	teaspoon vanilla

Butter 2 9-inch cake pans. Line with waxed paper, butter and flour the paper and set aside. Sift together flour, baking powder, soda and salt. Set aside. Mix orange juice and Rum; set aside. Cream butter, add extracts and 3/4 cup sugar. Beat 2 minutes. Add egg yolks and beat smooth. On low speed alternate dry and liquid ingredients. Beat egg whites. Gradually add 1/4 cup sugar and beat until stiff. Fold into the batter. Pour into cake pans and bake 20-25 minutes or until done. Cool on racks. Slice when cool into 2 layers each, making a total of 4 cake layers. Sprinkle gelatin over water in small saucepan. Stand for 5 minutes. Add 1/4 cup Rum and heat over low heat until mixture is clear. Beat together in large bowl cream, sugar, almond extract and 1/4 cup Rum. Stir some of this mixture into the gelatin, then mix all together in the large bowl. Beat carefully until mixture begins to thicken. Add reserved orange rind. Sprinkle each layer with 1 tablespoon rum. On cake plate, alternate layers and filling. Chill, then frost with Chocolate Frosting.

Beat together chocolate, sugar, water and eggs on high speed. When smooth, add butter in 6 portions. Add vanilla. Spread quickly on cold cake layers and filling. Chill and serve.

Mrs. Wade Faulkner

Rocky Road Cake

Serves: 30

1 cup butter
2 cups all purpose flour
1¾ cups sugar
3 tablespoons cocoa
1 teaspoon soda
1 teaspoon vanilla
2 eggs
1/2 cup buttermilk
1 cup cola
1½ cups miniature marshmallows
24 regular marshmallows
Nuts (2 ounces)

ICING:
1/3 stick butter
1/3 cup cocoa
1/2 cup milk
1 pound confectioners sugar
1 teaspoon vanilla

Combine all ingredients except cola and marshmallows in large bowl. Blend at low speed of mixer. Beat one minute at medium speed. Add cola, blend well. By hand stir in miniature marshmallows. Pour batter into greased 13 x 9 inch pan. Bake at 350 degrees for 40-45 minutes. (Or until pick inserted in center comes out clean.) Put 24 large marshmallows on cake and return to oven. Place under broiler until marshmallows begin to brown. Pour icing over cake. Sprinkle with nuts. Very sweet.

To make icing, heat butter, cocoa, and milk until butter melts. Add sugar and vanilla and beat until smooth.

Mrs. W. B. Shields

Sicilian Chocolate Torte

CAKE AND FILLING:

1   pound cake, preferably loaf shaped

1   pound fresh Ricotta cheese, either cream or grate the dry kind

2   tablespoons heavy cream

1/4   cup sugar

3   tablespoons orange flavored liqueur

3   tablespoons mixed candied fruit, chopped. Optional

2   ounces semi-sweet chocolate, coarsely chopped

FROSTING:

12   ounces semi-sweet chocolate, cut in small pieces

3/4   cup strong black coffee

1/2   pound butter, cut into 1/2 inch pieces and thoroughly chilled

Yield: 1 torte

Slice the cake horizontally into 1/2 inch slabs (about 6 slices). Beat the Ricotta cheese until it is smooth. Beating constantly, add the cream, sugar and liqueur. Gently fold in the chopped candied fruit and chocolate. Place the bottom slab of cake on a flat surface (cake plate) and spread with 1/6 of the Ricotta mixture. Carefully place another slab of cake on top, keeping sides and ends even, and spread with another layer of Ricotta, repeating until all the cake slices are reassembled and the filling used up. End with a cake slice on top. Press loaf firmly together. Refrigerate for about 2 hours or until the Ricotta filling is firm.

Melt the chocolate with the coffee in a heavy small saucepan over low heat, stirring constantly until the chocolate has completely melted. Remove from the heat and beat in the chilled butter one piece at a time, and continue beating until the mixture is smooth. Chill until frosting is spreading consistency. Frost the tops and sides of the cake, swirling decoratively. Cover with plastic wrap. Cake is better if refrigerated at least 24 hours before serving. Slice in thin torte slices. Slices can be decorated with a "Mock Strawberry".

Mrs. Mac B. Greer

Mock Strawberries

Makes 30-35 strawberries

2	(3 ounce) packages strawberry Jello
1	cup pecans, ground
1	cup coconut, ground
3/4	cup sweetened condensed milk
1/2	teaspoon vanilla
	Slivered almonds
	Green food coloring

Mix well the dry Jello, pecans and coconut (ground very fine), milk and vanilla. Chill in the refrigerator for 30 minutes or so. Roll a ball into a strawberry shape and size. For better color, roll the shaped strawberry in more dry Jello. Color slivered almonds by soaking in water colored with green food coloring and use as stems. Use to decorate a slice of Sicilian Chocolate Torte.

Mrs. Mac B. Greer

Chopped Apple Cake

Serves 20

1½	cups Wesson Oil
2	cups sugar
3	eggs, well beaten
3	cups flour
1/2	teaspoon salt
1	teaspoon soda
3	cups apples, chopped
1	cup pecans, chopped
2	teaspoons vanilla

Beat oil and sugar. Add eggs and mix well. Sift flour with salt and soda and add gradually while beating. Stir in apples and nuts and vanilla. Bake at 325° for 1½ hours in a well greased and floured tube pan. Let cool for 10 minutes and remove from pan. Pour glaze over cool cake.

GLAZE:

1/2	cup butter
1	cup brown sugar
1/4	cup milk
1	teaspoon vanilla

To make glaze, mix butter, sugar and milk in a saucepan and bring to a boil. Add vanilla and cool. Beat to help cool and gradually pour over cool cake.

Mrs. Frank B. Frazer

Cinnamon-Apple Cake

Yield: 1 loaf

1	cup sugar
1/4	cup butter
1	teaspoon soda
1	teaspoon cinnamon
1/2	teaspoon nutmeg
1	cup flour
1	egg
1/2	cup nuts
3	apples, chopped
1/2	cup dates, chopped
	Whipped cream

Cream sugar and butter. Sift soda, cinnamon, nutmeg, and flour, and add to sugar and butter. Add egg and mix together. Add nuts, apples, and dates. Blend well. Bake in loaf pan (greased) for 30 minutes. Serve with whipped cream on top.

Mrs. Charles A. Marston

Carrot Cake

Yield: 1 large 3-layer cake

2	cups plain flour
2	cups sugar
2	teaspoons cinnamon
1	teaspoon nutmeg
2	teaspoons soda
1	teaspoon salt
1	cup Wesson Oil
3	eggs
3	cups carrots, about 1 pound, grated

Mix all dry ingredients. Add oil while stirring, then add eggs one by one, each time stirring well. Stir in grated carrots. Bake in 3 greased and floured cake pans at 350° for 35 minutes. Let cool. Ice with the following frosting.

FROSTING:

1	(8 ounce) package cream cheese
1/2	stick margarine
1	(1 pound) box confectioners sugar
2	teaspoons milk
1	teaspoon vanilla
1	cup pecans, chopped

Have cheese and margarine at room temperature. Cream together with sugar. Slowly add milk with vanilla and then mix in nuts.

Mrs. H. E. Myers, Jr.

Black Forest Cherry Cake

1/2 cup margarine
1/2 cup sugar
4 eggs
1/4 teaspoon vanilla
3/4 cup almonds, ground
(about 2¾ ounces)
16 squares German
Sweet Chocolate,
grated
1/3 cup plus 1/2
tablespoon plain
unsifted flour
1/3 cup cornstarch
2 teaspoons baking
powder

FILLING:
7 tablespoons
Schwarzwaelder
Kirschwasser (cherry
spirits)
2 (16-ounce) cans red
sour pitted cherries,
well drained
1½ pints whipping
cream, whipped
Cherry jelly or red
currant jelly,
whisked in a bowl to
soften
Cherries and grated
chocolate for
decoration

Cream margarine and gradually add the sugar, eggs and vanilla, using high speed of a mixmaster. Blend in ground almonds and grated chocolate. Mix flour, starch and baking powder. Sift together and add to the creamed ingredients, a tablespoon at a time. Grease the bottom of a 10" spring-form pan, line with waxpaper, and pour in batter. Put in a cold oven, close the door, and turn oven to 350 degrees. Bake for 40-50 minutes. Remove from pan when cold and slice into 3 even layers. It is easier to do this with strong thread, but a knife will do OK.

Sprinkle cherry spirits evenly on all three cake layers. Place one layer on serving plate and cover evenly with drained cherries. Spread a thin layer of whipped cream over cherries. Cover with second cake layer. Spread this with a thin layer of jelly and a thick layer of whipped cream. Place third layer on top. Frost top and sides with whipped cream. Decorate with additional cherries and grated chocolate. Note: for stiffer cream, soften 1½ packages gelatin in 3 tablespoons water. Let stand 10 minutes, then beat into cream as it whips. Refrigerate cake to store.

Mrs. Peter Mannsfeld

Frozen Chocolate Charlotte

Serves 6

24 ladyfingers
1/4 cup white Crème de Menthe (optional)
2 (8 ounce) packages semi-sweet chocolate squares
3 tablespoons instant coffee
1/2 cup boiling water
6 egg yolks
1/2 cup sugar
1 teaspoon vanilla
6 egg whites
1½ cups heavy cream, whipped

Split the ladyfingers, but do not separate into individual pieces. Brush flat surfaces with Crème de Menthe if desired. Line sides of a 9" spring form pan with ladyfingers, rounded sides against the pan. Separate remaining ladyfingers; line bottom of pan, overlapping to fit. Melt chocolate in the top of a double boiler over hot water, stirring occasionally. Dissolve the coffee in boiling water. Beat the egg yolks in a small bowl until foamy. Gradually beat in sugar; continue beating until thick. Blend in vanilla, coffee and melted chocolate. Beat egg whites in large bowl until stiff. Stir about 1 cup of the egg whites into chocolate to lighten it. Fold chocolate mixture into remaining egg whites. Fold in whipped cream. Pour into lined pan. Freeze until firm. Garnish with chocolate curls and piped rosettes of whipped cream, if desired. Cover with foil. Refreeze. Keeps well up to 1 month. Should be removed from freezer at least 1 hour before serving.

Mrs. Thomas Twitty, Jr.

Pat's Prune Cake

Yield: 1 tube cake

1½   cups sugar
3   eggs
1   cup oil
2   cups sifted flour
1   teaspoon salt
1   teaspoon nutmeg
1   teaspoon allspice
1   teaspoon cinnamon
1/2   cup buttermilk
1   teaspoon soda
1   teaspoon vanilla
1   cup nuts, chopped
1   cup cooked, mashed
      prunes

Mix together sugar, eggs and oil. Sift together the flour, salt and spices and add to egg mixture. Add all remaining ingredients and mix well. Bake in a greased and floured tube or Bundt pan for 45 minutes at 350°. Cake will stay moist for days.

Icing:
1   stick margarine (1/2
      cup)
1¼   cups sugar
1/2   cup buttermilk
1   teaspoon soda
1/4   teaspoon cinnamon

Bring all ingredients to a boil and cook for 1-1½ minutes. Pour icing over cooled cake while in the pan.

Mrs. David B. Freeman, III

Almond Angel Food Cake

Yield: 1 cake

1   angel food cake
      (Duncan Hines)
2   sticks butter
1   cup powdered sugar
1   small (1 ounce) bottle
      almond extract
1   cup slivered toasted
      almonds

Bake angel food cake and when cool, slice, but do not cut all the way through, so that the cake still holds together. Melt butter; add other ingredients and pour over cake. Heat in oven until thoroughly hot and serve immediately.

Mrs. George E. Stone, Jr.

Mandarin-Pineapple Delight

1   box Duncan Hines
     yellow butter cake
     mix
3/4 cup oil
4   eggs
1   can mandarin
     oranges (reserve 1/4
     cup juice)

Beat together cake mix and oil. Add eggs one at a time. Add oranges and juice and beat well. Follow directions on box for baking in layers.

Filling:
1   package instant
     vanilla pudding
1   large can drained
     crushed pineapple
1   (9 ounce) Cool Whip

To make filling, mix all ingredients together well. When cake has cooled, put filling in middle and on top. *Cake must be refrigerated.*

Mrs. Thomas B. Martenstein

Cream Cheese Pound Cake

Makes 1 10-inch tube cake

2   sticks butter (1 cup)
1   stick margarine (1/2
     cup)
1   (8 ounce) package
     cream cheese
3   cups sugar
6   eggs
3   cups cake flour
1/4 teaspoon salt
1   teaspoon almond
     extract

Cream butter, oleo and cream cheese. Add sugar. Add eggs one at a time, beating well with each addition. Add flour, salt and almond extract. Bake at 325° for 1 hour in a greased and floured 10-inch tube pan.

Fran Shearer

Lemon-Cheese Cake

Yield: 1 3-layer cake

1   stick butter
1   stick margarine
2   cups sugar
5   large eggs
5   tablespoons orange
     juice
2   cups self-rising flour

Gradually add sugar to shortening. Add eggs, one at a time, beating well after each. Stir in juice and add flour. Pour into 3 cake pans that have been greased and lined with wax paper. Bake at 325 degrees about 30 minutes. Cool before filling.

Filling:
1   stick butter
1/2 stick margarine
1½   cups sugar
4   eggs
2   lemons, grated and
     juiced
1   tablespoon
     cornstarch

Melt butter and margarine in top of double boiler over low heat. Gradually add sugar and eggs and cornstarch blended with lemon juice and rind. When thickened, let cool, then fill cake. Frost with favorite white icing, such as 7-Minute.

Mrs. Allen R. Chason

Sour Cream Coconut Cake

Yield: 1 4-layer cake

2   cups sour cream
2   cups sugar
2   (12 ounce) packages
     frozen coconut
1   yellow cake (2 layers)
     mix

Mix sour cream, sugar, and coconut and refrigerate overnight. Bake cake layers. When cool, split each layer. Ice between all layers and on top. If icing is too thin, add more coconut. Seal in cake cover and refrigerate for 4 days. Absolutely delicious. Men love this one. *Must be made four days before serving.*

Mrs. Frank B. Frazer

Strawberry Cream Cake

Serves 20

Cake:
2⅓ cups flour
1 tablespoon baking powder
1/3 teaspoon salt
1/2 cup butter
1⅓ cups sugar
1 teaspoon vanilla
1 cup milk
4 egg whites, stiffly beaten but not dry

Sift flour, baking powder and salt together 2 times. Cream butter and sugar until light and fluffy. Add vanilla. Add alternately dry ingredients and milk, beating well after each addition. Fold in beaten egg whites. Divide batter between 2 well-greased and floured 9x5x2¾ inch loaf pans. Bake at 350° for 35-40 minutes. Turn out onto cake racks and cover with a clean cloth. Serve warm, sliced, with strawberry cream.

Strawberry Cream:
3 pints strawberries, washed, hulled and halved
1½ cups sugar
3 cups milk
4½ tablespoons cornstarch
3 cups confectioners sugar
1½ cups heavy cream

Mix berries with 1½ cups sugar and let stand for 2 hours at room temperature. Stir occasionally. Heat 2½ cups milk in a saucepan. Mix cornstarch to a smooth paste with remaining milk. Add to hot milk. Cook and stir until smooth and thickened. Cool and chill. Beat until smooth. Add confectioners sugar a little at a time, beating after each addition. Drain syrup from berries and add to cornstarch mixture. Mix well, then add the berries. Whip cream until thick and shiny. Fold into berry mixture. Chill. Makes about 10 cups.

Mrs. Sam W. Pipes, III

Swedish Cream Meringue Cake

Serves 8-10

3/4 cup butter
3/4 cup sugar
6   eggs, separated
1   teaspoon vanilla
1/2 teaspoon almond
      extract
1¼   cups plus 1
      tablespoon flour,
      sifted
1½   teaspoons baking
      powder
1/4 teaspoon salt
1/2 cup milk

With beaters at low speed, cream together butter and sugar for 3 minutes. Beat in egg yolks, one at a time, and then beat 3 minutes longer. Stir in vanilla and almond extracts. Sift together flour, baking powder and salt. Add to batter alternately with milk. Grease and flour 3 9" layer pans. Distribute batter evenly and smooth with a knife. Set aside.

MERINGUE:
6   egg whites
1   cup sugar
1/2 teaspoon vanilla
1/2 cup almonds or
      walnuts, finely
      ground

Beat egg whites until stiff and dry. Gradually beat in sugar. Continue beating until meringue stands in stiff peaks. Add vanilla and ground nuts. Spread meringue evenly on tops of cake batter in the 3 pans. Bake 45 to 50 minutes at 300 degrees. Remove carefully from pans. Spread 1/2 pint whipped cream (sweetened slightly) between layers and top cake with crushed sweetened strawberries.

Mrs. Sam W. Pipes, III

Hungarian Poppy Seed Cake

Serves 12

2/3	cup poppy seeds
3/4	cup milk
1½	sticks butter (3/4 cup)
1½	cups sugar
2	cups flour
2½	teaspoons baking powder
1/2	teaspoon salt
1/4	cup milk
1	teaspoon vanilla
4	egg whites

Soak poppy seeds in 3/4 cup milk for 2 hours. Cream the butter. Gradually add sugar, beating constantly. Sift and measure flour. Resift with baking powder and salt. Stir 1/4 cup milk and vanilla into poppy seed/milk mixture. Add the flour mixture in 3 parts alternately with the poppy seed milk to the batter, beating after each addition, only until blended. Beat 4 egg whites until stiff but not dry. Fold into the batter. Turn into 2 greased and floured 9 inch cake pans. Bake at 375 degrees for 25 minutes. Remove from pans and cool. Fill with lemon cheese filling.

Lemon Cheese Filling:

1¼	cups sugar
2/3	cup lemon juice
1	stick butter (1/2 cup)
5	eggs, well beaten
	Grated rind of 3 lemons

Mix ingredients together in a saucepan. Cook over low heat, stirring constantly, until thick. Cool, then chill before filling cake. This filling may also be used for tart shells.

Mrs. Sam W. Pipes, III

Mary Louise's Oatmeal Cake

Yield: 1 8x12" cake

1	cup oatmeal, quick cooking
1⅓	cups boiling water
1	cup sugar
1	cup dark brown sugar
1	cup shortening
2	eggs, beaten
1⅓	cups all-purpose flour
1	teaspoon soda
1	teaspoon baking powder
1/2	teaspoon salt
1	teaspoon cinnamon
1	teaspoon vanilla

Add oatmeal to boiling water and soak 20 minutes. Mix sugars and add to shortening. Add eggs and mix. Add oatmeal to creamed mixture. Sift dry ingredients and add to above. Add vanilla. Pour into 8x12 pan (floured and greased). Bake at 350 degrees for 45 minutes.

TOPPING:

3/4	stick margarine
1	cup dark brown sugar
3	tablespoons evaporated milk
1	cup coconut
3/4	cup pecans

To make topping, cream margarine and sugar; add milk. Boil. Add coconut and pecans. Spread topping over hot oatmeal cake and broil for 3 minutes. Good snacking cake.

Mrs. Bettie Croom

Light Fruit Cake

1 pound butter
1 pound sugar (2 cups)
10 eggs, separated
1 pound flour (4 cups), divided
2 teaspoons baking powder
1/2 teaspoon soda
1 teaspoon cinnamon
1 teaspoon allspice
1 teaspoon nutmeg
1/2 pint tart jelly (I use plum)
1/4 pound citron
1 pound candied cherries
1 pound crystallized pineapple
1 pound white raisins (soak them in orange juice overnight)
1/2 pound mixed fruit
3 cups pecans

Yield: 1 10¾" tube cake

Cream butter and sugar. Add beaten egg yolks. Reserve 1/2 cup flour to flour fruit. Add flour and dry ingredients. Stir in jelly. Add fruit that has been floured and any remaining flour left from flouring fruit. Stir in nuts. Add stiffly beaten egg whites. Bake in slow oven 250 degrees for 2-3 hours. Let cake cool before removing from pan. Wrap in cheesecloth. Saturate with wine. Store in air tight container and let ripen for two weeks.

Mrs. H. Eldon Scott, III

Pineapple Pound Cake

Yield: 1 10-inch cake

3	sticks butter
1½	boxes powdered sugar, sifted
6	eggs
1	teaspoon vanilla
1	teaspoon lemon juice
1	powdered sugar box filled with sifted flour
1	(20 ounce) can crushed pineapple, very well drained (reserve juice)

Preheat oven to 325 degrees. Cream butter and sugar. Add eggs, one at a time, beating well after each addition. Blend in vanilla and lemon juice. Add all the flour (sifted until level in the box); beat until well mixed. Blend in pineapple, which has been drained several hours or overnight, if possible. Grease tube pan and bake for 1½ hours or until cake tester comes out clean. Pour glaze on cake while still warm.

Glaze:

1	cup powdered sugar, sifted
4	tablespoons pineapple juice (This may be doubled if you like a cake with more glaze)

Mrs. William J. May

Greek Spice Cake

Yield: 1 9x13" cake

1	cup Wesson oil
1	cup brown sugar
1	cup sugar
3	eggs
1	teaspoon cinnamon
1	teaspoon cloves
1	teaspoon nutmeg
1	teaspoon soda mixed with 1⅓ cups buttermilk
1	teaspoon baking powder
2½	cups flour
2	teaspoons salt
1	cup pecans
2	teaspoons almond extract

Mix oil and sugars together. Add remaining ingredients and blend well. Bake at 350 degrees for 35 minutes either in layers or in a 9" x 13" pan.

Icing:

2	cups sugar
3/4	cup water

To make icing, boil sugar and water for 2 minutes. Let stand for a while before pouring over cake in the pan. If you bake this cake in layers, do not use the above icing. Instead, use a cream cheese icing as for carrot cake.

Mrs. A. A. Hory, Jr.

Self-Filled Cupcakes

Yield: 24 to 30

1 (8 ounce) package
 cream cheese
1/3 cup sugar
1 egg
 Salt
1 (6 ounce) package
 semi-sweet chocolate
 bits
1 package chocolate
 cake mix

Mix cream cheese, sugar, egg, salt and chocolate bits. Mix cake as directed on box. Fill paper baking cups 2/3 full of cake batter. Put 1 rounded teaspoon of cheese mixture into each and bake as directed for cupcakes on the package. Frost with favorite icing.

Mrs. Frank McPhillips

Brandy Alexander Pie

Serves 6

1 envelope unflavored
 gelatin
1/2 cup cold water
2/3 cup sugar
1/8 teaspoon salt
3 eggs, separated
1/4 cup Cognac
1/4 cup Crème de Cacao
2 cups heavy cream,
 whipped
1 (9 inch) graham
 cracker pie shell
 Chocolate curls (use
 potato peeler on
 bittersweet chocolate
 block to produce
 curls)

Sprinkle gelatin over cold water in a saucepan. Add 1/3 cup sugar, salt and egg yolks. Stir to blend. Heat over low heat while stirring until gelatin dissolves and mixture thickens. DO NOT BOIL Mixture will not be very thick. Remove from heat and stir in Cognac and Crème de Cacao. Chill until mixture will mound when poured out of spoon (very lightly jelled.) Make meringue from remaining whites and sugar. Fold into the thickened mixture. Also fold in 1 cup of whipped cream. Pour into the crust. Chill for several hours. Garnish with remaining cup of whipped cream and sprinkle chocolate curls over top of pie.

Mrs. Edward C. Greene

376

Brandy Tart

Serves 6

Crust:
1½ cups flour
3/8 cup butter, softened
3 tablespoons confectioners sugar

Filling:
10 ounces cream cheese
3/4 cup heavy cream
3/8 cup sugar
4½ tablespoons orange juice concentrate

Glaze:
1 cup apricot jam or currant jelly
2 tablespoons Brandy

For crust, combine ingredients in a bowl. Press into a tart pan and up fluted sides. Bake at 450 degrees for 8 minutes. Cool. To make filling combine all ingredients, beat until smooth. Pour into baked cooled shell. Chill. Decorate top with halved green and black grapes or sliced peaches or any fruit but apples. To make glaze, heat together jam or jelly and Brandy. Brush gently over fruit. Chill.

Mrs. Francis Uteg

Chocolate Chess Pie

Serves 6-8

2 eggs
1½ cups sugar
1/2 stick butter, melted
1 (5 ounce) Carnation evaporated milk
3½ teaspoons cocoa (or 2 1-ounce squares chocolate, melted)
1 teaspoon vanilla
9-inch unbaked pie shell

Mix all ingredients by hand in one bowl. Pour into unbaked pie shell. Bake at 350° for 45 minutes.

Mrs. Dan T. McCall, III

Butterscotch Pie

Serves 6-8

FILLING:

1 cup milk
3 eggs
1 cup dark brown sugar
4 tablespoons flour
2 tablespoons butter
2 teaspoons vanilla
Pinch of salt
Pecans, chopped (optional)
Raisins, chopped (optional)

Heat milk, Beat 1 whole egg and 2 yolks slightly. Add sugar and flour and mix well. Pour mixture into hot milk and stir constantly over medium heat until thick. Remove from heat and add butter, vanilla and salt. Pour into baked pie shell. If desired, chopped pecans and raisins may be sprinkled on filling before adding meringue.

MERINGUE:

2 remaining egg whites
4 tablespoons sugar
Pinch of salt
1 teaspoon vanilla

Beat 2 remaining egg whites very stiff. Add sugar, beating well. Add salt and vanilla. Spread on top of filling, sealing edges well. Bake at 325° until meringue is golden. Cool before cutting.

Mrs. Vance E. Thompson, Jr.

Quick Chocolate Pie

Yield: Two 9" pies

2 sticks butter (1 cup)
1 cup chocolate morsels
2 cups sugar
4 eggs
1 cup coconut
1 cup pecans, chopped
2 9" pie shells, partially baked

Melt butter and add chips. Heat slowly until chocolate is melted. Add sugar, eggs, coconut and pecans and mix well. Pour into the partially baked pie shell. Bake at 350° for 45 minutes.

Mrs. Charles Chambliss

Margaret's Chocolate Pie

Serves 6-8

2	squares unsweetened chocolate
5	tablespoons flour
3/4	cup sugar
3	egg yolks
2½	cups milk
1	tablespoon butter or margarine
1	teaspoon vanilla 9-inch pie shell, baked
1	cup heavy cream, whipped

First, melt chocolate in small saucepan. In larger saucepan, combine flour and sugar. Blend egg yolks and milk, add to flour and sugar. Then add chocolate. Cook over medium heat, stirring *constantly*. Cook until mixture becomes thick and bubbly. Take off of heat. Add 1 tablespoon butter and 1 teaspoon vanilla. Pour into cooled pie shell. Place in refrigerator and chill. Top with whipped cream.

Mrs. H. E. Myers, Jr.

For a tender, flaky crust, do not over-flour the rolling surface.

Mrs. Davis' Fudge Pie

Serves 6

1	stick butter
2½	squares unsweetened baking chocolate
4	eggs
3	tablespoons white Karo syrup
1¼	cups sugar
1/4	teaspoon salt
1	teaspoon vanilla extract

In the top of a double boiler or over low heat, melt butter and chocolate. Meanwhile, place eggs in mixing bowl and beat until light. Beat other ingredients into eggs. Add the slightly cooled chocolate mixture. Mix all thoroughly. Pour into a 9 inch pastry lined pie pan. Bake at 350 degrees for 30 minutes. Cool and cut. Serve vanilla ice cream on top.

Mrs. Bruce C. Finley, Jr.

Millionaire Pie

Serves 6

1	pastry shell
1½	cups sugar
4	eggs
1/4	stick margarine
2	tablespoons water
2	tablespoons vinegar
1/2	cup seedless raisins
1/2	cup pecans, chopped
1	teaspoon cinnamon
1	teaspoon allspice
1	teaspoon cloves
1	teaspoon nutmeg

Prebake piecrust about 3 minutes. Combine filling ingredients and pour in the shell. Bake at 300° until pie is firm. Serve with whipped cream.

Mrs. Barry Joseph Corona

Mud Pie

Serves 6-8

Enough chocolate wafers or Oreo cookies for a 9" pie crust, centers removed, and crushed finely
1/4 cup melted butter
1/2 gallon coffee ice cream, softened
Homemade Fudge Sauce
Whipped cream
Toasted almonds

Combine crushed cookies and butter. Press into a 9" pie plate. Fill with ice cream, cover with foil and freeze. Serve with homemade Fudge Sauce, whipped cream and toasted almonds on top.

Mrs. McGowin I. Patrick

Velvet Almond Fudge Pie

Serves 6-8

1 cup blanched, slivered almonds
1 (4 ounce) package Jello Brand chocolate fudge or chocolate flavor pudding and pie filling
3/4 cup light corn syrup
3/4 cup evaporated milk
1 egg, slightly beaten
1/2 cup chocolate chips, melted
1 unbaked 8-inch pie shell

Chop almonds and toast at 350° for 3 to 5 minutes. Set aside. Blend together until smooth the pie filling mix, corn syrup, milk, egg and chips. Add almonds and pour into pie shell. Bake at 375° about 40 minutes, or until top is firm and begins to crack. Cool at least 4 hours. Garnish with whipped cream.

Mrs. Danner Frazer, Jr.

Try substituting cane syrup for corn syrup in pecan pies.

The Best Pecan Pie

Serves 6

1/4 cup butter
7/8 cup sugar
1 tablespoon flour
1½ cups dark Karo syrup
Pinch salt
4 whole eggs
1 cup broken pecans
1 teaspoon vanilla
1 pie shell, unbaked

Cream the butter. Add the sugar and flour gradually, and cream until fluffy. Add the syrup and beat well. Add the salt and eggs, one at a time. Beat thoroughly. Add the pecans and vanilla. Pour into the crust and bake at 350° for about 50 minutes or until set. If the crust gets too brown around the edge, cut out a circle of foil and place over it.

Mrs. Emil Graf, III

Mary Ann's French Silk Pie

Serves 6-8

MERINGUE: (do this first)
2   egg whites
1/2 teaspoon salt
1/8 teaspoon cream of tartar
1/2 cup sugar
1/2 teaspoon vanilla
1/2 cup chopped nuts

Beat egg whites until foamy. Add salt and cream of tartar. Gradually add sugar while beating. Beat until stiff. Fold in vanilla and nuts. Spread in a greased pie tin and bake at 350° for 5-10 minutes, until light tan.

FILLING:
1   stick butter
3/4 cup sugar
1½ squares unsweetened chocolate, melted
1   teaspoon vanilla
2   egg yolks
2   whole eggs

Cream butter, sugar, add chocolate and vanilla. Add egg yolks and whole eggs, one at a time, beating well after each addition. Pour into meringue shell and chill. Serve with whipped cream on top.

Mrs. John N. Horner

Chocolate Pecan Pie

Serves 6-8

1   unbaked pie shell
2   tablespoons butter
2   squares unsweetened chocolate (2 ounces)
1   cup dark Karo syrup
2   eggs
1   cup sugar
1/2 teaspoon salt
1   cup pecans, chopped
1   teaspoon vanilla

Melt butter and chocolate together. Beat eggs slightly, then mix in Karo, sugar, vanilla, salt and the chocolate mixture. Add pecans and stir. Pour into the pie shell and bake at 325° for about 1 hour or until set. Note: This is good served with a little whipped cream or vanilla ice cream.

Mrs. H. Browne Mercer, Sr.

Black-Bottom Pie

CRUST:

1⅓ cups gingersnap crumbs, crushed
1/3 cup butter, melted

Mix, press into 9-inch pie pan. Bake 10 minutes at 350° and set aside.

FILLING:

1½ squares bitter cooking chocolate
1 package vanilla pudding mix, not instant
1 envelope unflavored gelatin
2 egg yolks
1½ cups milk
3 egg whites
Cream of tartar, pinch
1/4 cup sugar
1/4 cup Bourbon

Melt chocolate, set aside. Mix together dry pudding mix and gelatin. Beat egg yolks with milk and add to dry ingredients. Cook and stir to boiling stage. Mix melted chocolate with HALF the custard mixture and spread onto the baked ginger crust. Chill remainder of custard until it starts to look like unbeaten egg whites. I put mine in the freezer and watch it like a hawk. Beat egg whites with cream of tartar. Add sugar and beat until stiff but not dry. Fold into custard along with Bourbon. Pour over chocolate layer. Chill.

TOPPING:

1 cup heavy cream
2 tablespoons sugar
1/2 square bitter chocolate
6 whole gingersnaps

Whip cream until stiff, add sugar, and pile onto the pie, but don't spread all the way to the edge. Leave some of the filling showing all the way around. Press down the 6 gingersnaps into the pie, (standing on edge) to look like spokes in a wheel. Grate chocolate over the whipped cream. Chill and serve. This pie looks and tastes like a lot more trouble than it is. It's really simple to prepare.

Mrs. Wade Faulkner

Chocolate Marble Cheese Pie

Yield: 1 large pie

3   (8 ounce) packages
     cream cheese
1   cup sugar
5   eggs
1   tablespoon vanilla
1   (4 ounce) package
     German sweet
     chocolate
1   tablespoon fresh
     lemon juice

Blend cheese and sugar in mixmaster, creaming well. Add eggs one at a time, beating well after each addition. Add vanilla and set aside 2 cups of the mixture. Melt the chocolate and blend it into the reserved 2 cups of cheese mixture. Add lemon juice to the remaining white cheese mixture. Butter a 10" deep dish pie shell and pour in the white cheese mixture. Then gently pour the chocolate cheese mixture over this. Bake at 300° for about 55 minutes until the middle of the pie is firm. Note: the pie may puff up quite a bit during the baking time. This is O.K. It will sink down as the pie cools. Serve the pie very cold in thin slices. It is rich and delicious.

Miss Edith Respess

Delicious Lemon Filling

Yield: 3 cups

1   cup butter (do not
     substitute)
3/4 to 1 cup lemon juice
2   teaspoons grated rind
3   cups sugar
1/4 teaspoon salt
6   large eggs
6   egg yolks

Melt the butter in the top of a double boiler. Stir in lemon juice, rind, sugar and salt. Beat the eggs and yolks and stir into butter mixture, blending thoroughly. Cook over hot water stirring constantly until smooth, transparent and thickened. Pour into a container and store in refrigerator. Keeps for a month. Use in a pie shell or to fill a lemon roll.

Mrs. Nicholas C. Wright

"Miss Iverson's" Maple Chiffon Pie

Serves 6-8

1 tablespoon plain gelatin
2 tablespoons cold water
1/2 cup milk
1/2 cup maple syrup
1/8 teaspoon salt
2 eggs, separated
2 cups whipping cream
1 teaspoon vanilla
1 graham cracker crumb crust or pastry pie shell

Moisten plain gelatin in cold water. Heat the milk, maple syrup and salt in the top of a double boiler. Stir constantly over hot, *not* boiling water. Slowly add well-beaten egg yolks — stir until mixture thickens. Add moistened gelatin and stir until it is dissolved. (I find using a whisk at this point helps.) Remove from double boiler and let the mixture cool. Beat 1½ cups whipping cream until stiff and flavor with touch of sugar and vanilla. Reserve 1/2 cup whipping cream for garnish. Beat egg whites stiff. Fold egg whites, 1/2 of the whipping cream and cooled custard together. Put in a crumb or pre-baked pie shell, refrigerate until mixture congeals. Then top with remaining 1/2 cup whipping cream. Serve very cold and enjoy!

Mrs. McGowin I. Patrick

Citrus Chiffon Pie

Serves 6

1 cup sugar
1/4 teaspoon salt
1 envelope unflavored gelatin
1 cup milk
3 slightly beaten egg yolks
1 tablespoon shredded orange peel
1/2 teaspoon grated lemon peel
3/4 cup orange juice
1/4 cup lemon juice
1/2 pint heavy cream, whipped
1 9-inch pie shell, baked

Thoroughly combine sugar, salt and gelatin. Stir in cold milk and egg yolks. Let sit 5 minutes. Cook and stir over low heat until sugar and gelatin dissolve. Remove from heat; add fruit peels and juices. Chill until partially set. Fold in whipped cream. Chill until mixture will mound. Then pour into a 9-inch baked pie shell.

Mrs. H. Eldon Scott, III

Strawberry Pie — Very Easy

Serves 6-8

1 9-inch pie shell, baked
1 cup sugar
2 tablespoons cornstarch
1 cup cold water
1 regular-sized package strawberry gelatin
2 pints strawberries, washed and sliced
1 package Dream Whip

Mix sugar and cornstarch, then add water, cook until thickens. Add strawberry gelatin, let cool, and add fresh strawberries. Pour into pie shell. Place in refrigerator covered. May be made day ahead. Before guests arrive, cover with Dream Whip made according to package directions. Can be prepared 8 hours ahead.

Mrs. Thomas S. Damson

Three Layer Cherry Pie

Yield: 2 pies

CRUST:

1½   cups flour, sifted
1   stick margarine
1/3   cup pecans, finely
       chopped

Mix together and press into the bottom and halfway up the sides of 2 pie plates. Bake at 375° for 20 minutes. Then cool for 1 hour.

FIRST LAYER:

1   (3 ounce) package
       cream cheese
1   (8 ounce) package
       cream cheese
1   cup confectioners
       sugar
2   tablespoons milk

Beat together and spread half of this mixture over each pie crust.

SECOND LAYER:

1   cup pecans, coarsely
       chopped

Sprinkle the pecans evenly over both pies.

THIRD LAYER:

1   pint whipping cream
2   tablespoons sugar
1   teaspon vanilla
2   cans tart cherry pie
       filling

Whip the cream with the sugar and vanilla. Spoon over both pies. Spread one can of cherry pie filling over the top of each pie. Refrigerate for at least 4 hours before serving.

Mrs. Marie Porter

Fresh Coconut Cream Pie

Serves 6

1 cup sugar
1/2 cup cornstarch
1/4 teaspoon salt
3 cups hot milk
3 egg yolks, beaten
1 teaspoon vanilla extract
1/2 teaspoon almond extract
2 cups fresh coconut, grated
1 9-inch pie shell, baked
1 cup heavy cream

Combine the sugar, cornstarch, and salt; gradually add to milk in a medium saucepan, stirring until smooth. Bring to boiling, stirring, over medium heat. Cook for 2 minutes. Remove from the heat. Stir some of the hot mixture into egg yolks, then combine with the rest in the saucepan. Cook, stirring, over low heat, until it boils and is thick enough to mound from the spoon, about 5 minutes. Turn into a bowl. Stir in the extracts and half the coconut. Place waxed paper directly on filling. Refrigerate for 1 hour. Turn into the pie shell, refrigerate for 3 hours. To serve, whip cream and spread over filling; top with remaining coconut. Note: 2 cans (3½ ounce size) flaked coconut may be substituted for fresh.

Mrs. Sam W. Pipes, III

Mile High Strawberry Pie

Serves 8-16

1 (10 ounce) package frozen strawberries
1 cup sugar
2 egg whites
1 tablespoon lemon juice
  Dash of salt
1/2 cup whipping cream, whipped
1 teaspoon vanilla
2 graham cracker pie crusts

Thaw strawberries. Combine with sugar, egg whites, lemon juice and salt. Beat in an electric mixer (not a blender or food processor) for 15 minutes. The mixture will be very large and fluffy. It will fill up a large mixing bowl. Fold in the whipped cream and vanilla. Pour into the prepared pie crusts and freeze. Serve with Fresh Strawberry Sauce. Allow to thaw slightly before serving.

SAUCE:
1/2 pint strawberries, hulled and washed
  Juice of 1 lemon
  Sweeten to taste with about 1/4 cup sugar, more or less according to tartness of berries

Purée berries in blender or food processor. Add lemon juice and sugar. Chill until icy cold.

Mrs. Frank T. Manley

Papas's Pear Pie

Pastry for double
  crust pie
1¼ cups sugar
1/4 teaspoon salt
1 teaspoon cinnamon
1 tablespoon flour
6-8 pears, peeled and
  thinly sliced (use
  Cuisinart if possible)
  Juice of 1/2 a lemon
1/4 cup butter

Line pie plate with crust. Mix sugar, salt, cinnamon and flour. Pour half of this mixture over bottom crust. Add pears and sprinkle with remaining half of mixture. Sprinkle the juice of 1/2 lemon and vanilla over all. Lastly, dot with 1/4 cup butter. Cover with solid top crust. *Do not use lattice top crust.* This pie needs a solid top crust to bake properly. Slit the top, seal and flute edges. Bake at 350 degrees for 15 minutes, then reduce heat to 300 degrees and continue baking for 40 minutes or until pears are tender. Preserving pears may be used for this recipe.

Mrs. H. Eldon Scott, III

THINGS YOUR MOTHER
NEVER TOLD YOU

FOOD PROCESSOR-MICROWAVE COOKING

Too bad Mother didn't know about these modern marvels that have made good cooking better.

THINK MICROWAVE

Microwave ovens will soon be an indispensable part of every kitchen. Just as it took time to learn to cook conventionally, it will take time to master all the skills of microwave cooking.

This section is written to help you convert your favorite conventional recipes to microwave recipes. Many recipes in this section come from other sections in this cookbook so that you can easily see the tricks and techniques of microwave conversion.

Take the time to learn to "Think Microwave."

DISHES USED IN MICROWAVE COOKING

Most kitchens already have ample dishes safe for microwave cooking. It is seldom necessary to buy special cookware. China, ceramics or pottery utensils without metal trim or metal base glaze work well. Plastic containers and bowls may be used for warming non-greasy food. Paper products are good and require no clean up. Wood and straw can be used only for short periods of time.

If you are not sure whether a container is microwave safe, use this simple test:

Place a glass measuring cup of water and the dish to be tested in the microwave on high for 1½ minutes. If the water is warm and the dish is cool, you may use the dish. If the dish is slightly warm around the edges, you may use it for short term cooking only. If the water is cool and the dish is hot, DO NOT USE THE DISH.

DEFROSTING

You can defrost food very quickly in a microwave. Hints for successful defrosting are:

Porous items like bread, cakes, or pies defrost quickly and should be wrapped in a paper towel.

Dense items like meats and casseroles defrost quickly on the outside, but require a longer time for the center to defrost. With these foods "standing time" is necessary to allow the center to defrost without cooking the outside portion.

If cooking begins, decrease the length of microwave period and increase the standing time. Reposition the food in the microwave.

Keep food wrapped in plastic or paper until ready to separate. With meat over 5 pounds, allow an additional standing time after defrosting.

STANDARD DEFROST TIMES

Chicken, Whole	16 minutes per pound
Chicken, Pieces	6 minutes per pound
Beef, Ground	5 minutes per pound
Beef Roast	7 minutes per pound

THINGS THAT AFFECT COOKING TIME

Several things affect cooking time. It's always best to undercook, check the food, and then cook a little longer.

Chilled foods, fresh from the refrigerator or barely thawed, take more time than foods at room temperature.

Dense foods take longer. For example, a potato bakes in 4 minutes, while an apple of the same size bakes in only 1½ minutes. Because the potato is more dense it takes the microwaves longer to penetrate and cook through.

A single mass of food takes longer than the same amount in smaller pieces. A meat loaf cooks as a single mass and takes longer than the same amount of meat which has been cubed or sliced.

More food takes longer to cook. As a rule, if you double the amount of food, add 50% to the cooking time.

If the container is too deep, it takes longer to cook the center and the edges may be overdone. If the container is too shallow, the food cooks faster but the edges will be overdone. Most instruction books that come with microwave ovens will have tables which estimate cooking time according to the amount of food and the power setting. Always refer to these.

EVERYDAY FOODS TIMED AT A GLANCE

Butter, melted	1/2 cup	3/4 minute
Butter, softened	1/2 cup	1/2 minute
Brownies	8x8x2 inch pan	5-6 minutes
Cakes	12x8x2 inch pan	9-11 minutes
Cupcakes	6	1½-2 minutes
Cookies	12	2½-2 minutes
Chicken, fryer	2½ pounds	21 minutes
Chocolate, melted	2 squares	1-1½ minutes
Eggs	1	1/2-3/4 minute
Fish	1 pound	4 minutes
Chops	5-6 chops	25 minutes
Ham, whole	per pound	6 minutes
Meat Loaf	1½ pound	14-16 minutes

Meat, patties	per pound (well done)	7-8 minutes
Milk, hot	1 cup	2-3 minutes
Milk, scalded	1 cup	2½ minutes
Potato	1 average	3-4 minutes
Pudding	4 servings	5-6 minutes
Pies, pastry shell	9 inch pie	4-6 minutes
Rolls, hot	2	1/4-1/2 minutes
Roasts, Beef or Pork	per pound	7-9 minutes
Sauces	1 cup	2-3 minutes
Soup, hot	1 cup	1½-2 minutes
Vegetable, fresh	4 servings	6-9 minutes
Vegetables, frozen	10 ounces	5-7 minutes
Water, hot	1 cup	1 minute
Water, boiling	1 cup	2-3 minutes
Weiner, in a bun	1	20 seconds

CONVERTING RECIPES

Total enjoyment and maximum benefit of a microwave oven is achieved when you learn to convert your favorite recipes. Start with conventional recipes you are familiar with. Knowing how something should look and taste will help you. Before you begin, check the list of "Things That Won't Work and Why." Any recipe that calls for liquid or uses a lot of moisture in cooking will be perfect for the microwave. In converting recipes decrease the liquid by 1/3. Then if more liquid is needed, add while cooking.

Stirring or turning foods helps them microwave evenly. A recipe that calls for frequent stirring will be much simpler in the microwave. If stirring is not desirable, rotate dish and use lower setting.

For meat dishes, microwaving time will be about 1/4-1/2 conventional cooking time, unless lower power settings are required to tenderize or develop flavors.

SUBSTITUTIONS

Some substitutions are needed for microwave cooking:

Use less salt and season after cooking.

Process cheeses will melt better than hard natural cheeses.

If a recipe called for diced cheese, use equal amount of shredded cheese.

Quick cooking rice will be tender in a shorter time than raw rice.

Evaporated milk is a good substitute for cream or milk and will not separate during cooking.

MICROWAVE METHODS OF COOKING MEATS

Pot Roast — Stew: For pot roasts and other less tender cuts of beef, pierce meat deeply on all sides so that steam and moisture can reach the center of the meat. Dredge meat in flour, but browning is not necessary. Reduce liquid by 1/3, adding more while cooking if necessary. Less tender cuts of meat must be covered tightly and microwaved on medium or medium low. If desired, add cut vegetables halfway through cooking time. For stew, cut meat and vegetables smaller than you normally would.

Roast in Browning Bag: A good roast may be cooked in a browning bag to any degree of doneness with a nice brown outside. Dust bag with one tablespoon of flour, add beef broth. Insert probe or microwave thermometer into center of roast. Be sure to remove meat from microwave before it reaches desired doneness as it will continue cooking during standing time. (See index for Microwave Roast in Browning Bag.)

Meat Sauce: Chili, spaghetti sauce and sloppy joes can be easily adapted to microwaving. When converting for the first time, cut down on salt and strong flavored seasonings, then add after cooking if needed. Reduce the liquid by 1/3, start microwaving on high, then cook on medium, uncovered, to develop flavor.

Ground Meat; Beef, Ham, or Pork: These ground meats may be shaped into patties, loaves or meatballs and microwaved plain or with a sauce. Since microwaved meats don't brown deeply, you might want to coat them with brown gravy sauce or Kitchen Bouquet at the end of cooking time.

Meat Casseroles: For instructions see Casseroles in this section.

POULTRY

Poultry can be microwaved on high in 1/2 to 1/3 conventional cooking time. Large pieces should be microwaved at medium setting. It takes 2½ to 4½ minutes for a single piece or 5½ to 7½ minutes a pound to cook. Microwaved chicken is light gold in color, but the skin does not crisp. Microwaving renders more fat from chicken than regular cooking methods, and therefore is a definite advantage to those counting calories and cholesterol. Chicken may be skinned before cooking. If chicken is not skinned, brush the skin with soy sauce, Kitchen Bouquet or paprika for a browned appearance. For even cooking, chicken should be arranged in dish so that thick, meaty pieces are on the outside and smaller thinner pieces on the inside. Rotate dish during cooking and rearrange chicken half-way through cooking time.

Whole Chicken: A whole chicken may be cooked in liquid in just 20 minutes. Reserve stock, bone chicken and use in any chicken recipe or freeze it for later use. (See index for recipe for Microwave Chicken and Wild Rice. Recipe contains directions for cooking whole chicken.)

Crumb Coating: Any crumb coating recipe will microwave well. Arrange coated chicken in dish and cook on high. Do not turn chicken over, but rearrange during cooking.

Stuffing or Dressing: Use the microwave to prepare your favorite poultry dressing. You can sauté vegetables, toast nuts or cook sausage in the same bowl you will use for the dressing.

Barbecue, Sauce, Soup: Chicken cooks well in sauces and soups. You will only need enough sauce to cover chicken. Waxed paper is sufficient cover to keep chicken moist while cooking. (See index for recipe for Microwave Chicken Supreme.)

Chicken Casseroles: For instructions see Casseroles in this section.

SEAFOOD

Microwave is an excellent way to prepare fish and shellfish. To avoid overcooking, a medium setting is desirable. If your recipe has long-cooking ingredients, add seafood toward the end of cooking time.

Shrimp: Only a small amount of liquid is needed as shrimp will "steam" in a microwave instead of "boil." Slightly undercook shrimp and let stand to finish cooking.

Lobster: Bring 1/2 cup wine, broth or water to a boil. Add lobster and cover, cooking until shell turns red and meat is white.

Gumbo-Creole: Sauce or roux should be cooked first and shellfish added at the end to prevent overcooking. After adding seafood, reduce power to medium and allow standing time.

Poached Fish: To poach fish, place poaching ingredients in casserole dish, reducing liquid by 1/2 and cover. Be sure to rotate dish or rearrange fish while cooking. (See index for Microwave Red Snapper in Tomato Gravy.)

Seafood Casseroles: For instructions see Casseroles in this section.

CASSEROLES

Casseroles made with tomato sauce, broth, soup or milk microwave on high.

Casseroles made with cream (you can substitute evaporated milk) or sour cream microwave on medium.

Layered casseroles which cannot be stirred microwave at medium, and rotate dish during cooking.

If casserole is baked uncovered, reduce liquid by 1/4-1/2. Covered casseroles will probably require no change in liquid. To reduce liquid, omit milk or water rather than using only part of a can of soup or sauce. Use water and bouillon granules rather than part of a can of broth.

Microwaved casseroles will not brown or crust on top, but they can be given a crisp surface when topping is added after the last stirring. Excellent toppings are crushed croutons, crushed potato chips, cheetos or corn chips, canned onion rings or a mixture of cheese and bread crumbs.

Casseroles using:

Potatoes: Slice potatoes thinly or cut in small cubes. If covered with liquid or sauce, microwave on high.

Rice: Casseroles using rice are quicker to convert if you use quick-cooking rice. For substituting quick-cooking rice, double the amount of rice and reduce liquid. If you use raw long grain rice, cook rice, seasonings and liquid covered on High until rice is almost tender, then add meat and other quick-cooking ingredients and continue cooking.

Macaroni, Spaghetti, Pasta: Although there is no time advantage in cooking macaroni, spaghetti or other pasta in the microwaver, the method is simpler and clean-up easier. However, you may prefer to cook these conventionally and then add to other ingredients and microwave.

Vegetables: Countless vegetable casseroles can be made in the microwave by combining microwaved sauces with any number of vegetables. In converting a vegetable casserole that has a lot of sauce or bakes a long time, reduce the liquid as it will not evaporate during the shorter cooking time. (See index for recipes for Microwave Lasagne, Microwave Family Cabbage Rolls, Microwave Corn Pudding and Microwave Shrimp and Crab Coquille.)

VEGETABLES

Vegetables are always wonderful when cooked in the microwave — crisp, flavorful and fresh in color; but summertime, when fresh produce is so abundant and so delicious, is when the microwave really shines. It prepares vegetables that are more nutritious and flavorful and it keeps the cook's time in the kitchen at a minimum.

Total cooking tme depends on the amount and kind of vegetables. Standing time is important. It prevents overcooking, especially of vegetables with delicate ends like asparagus, broccoli and cauliflower.

Frozen Vegetables: Cook frozen vegetables with no liquid added. Simply open package, cover and microwave. (See index for Microwave Spinach Delish.)

Fresh Vegetables: Cook fresh vegetables with only 3 to 4 tablespoons water added. Be sure to cover with plastic wrap.

Stuffed Vegetables: Vegetables, like peppers, onions, eggplant, acorn squash or zucchini can be stuffed and baked beautifully in a microwave. For dense vegetables like acorn squash, cook vegetables partially before adding stuffing. Cook whole onions about halfway, then scoop out the centers for stuffing. Microwave cooking time depends on the amount and kind of vegetables. Most can be cooked on High, but need to be covered with plastic wrap. (See index for Microwave Stuffed Zucchini.)

Vegetable Casseroles: For instructions, see Casseroles in this section.

EGGS AND CHEESE

Do not cook eggs in the shell. The rapid heat generated through microwave cooking expands the air inside the shell and causes it to burst.

Eggs may be fried, poached, or scrambled and instructions for these will be in your microwave instruction book. The important thing to remember is that when frying or poaching, the yolk must always be pierced.

Overcooking will cause a tough and rubbery egg. Learn to remove eggs and egg dishes from the oven just before they are done. Let them stand several minutes, covered, to complete cooking.

Yolks and whites cook at different rates. Scrambling minimizes the difference.

Omelets: Both puffy omelets and French omelets may be made in your microwave, taking only 3-5 minutes for a 4 egg omelet.

Soufflés: Soufflés are excellent cooked in a microwave. While they do not form a crust or brown, they also will not fall. Soufflés should cook on medium-low. It is a good idea to substitute evaporated milk for milk in the conventional recipe. Rotate dish while cooking. (See index for Microwave Asparagus Soufflé.)

Quiches: For a microwaved quiche, microwave or cook crust first, then add custard mixture. Substitute evaporated milk for milk in the conventional recipe and reduce liquid slightly. Cook on medium and rotate dish. Standing time is essential to allow custard to set.

SAUCES

Sauces made in a microwave do not need constant stirring and they can be measured, mixed and cooked in the same container.

Sauce thickened with flour: No change in the ingredients is necessary. Melt butter in microwave, add flour and mix. Add remaining ingredients and cook on high until thick, 3 to 4 minutes for 2 cups of sauce. Stir once or twice.

Sauce thickened with cornstarch: Mix cornstarch with cold water before adding other ingredients. Microwave on high 2-5 minutes, depending on the quantity.

Sauce thickened with egg: Make sauce base in microwave. Add half of the sauce to slightly beaten egg yolks, then blend this mixture back into the remaining sauce. Mix. Microwave on high for 1½ to 2½ minutes, depending on the quantity.

Hollandaise Sauce: When cooking Hollandaise in microwave, the butter must be melted, but not hot, then add the yolks to the butter and microwave on medium to prevent curdling. (See index for Microwave Hollandaise Sauce.)

SOUPS

Basic stock for soup: Combine soup bones, water and seasonings as you would for conventional recipe. Cover. Microwave on high until water boils. Reduce to medium and cook until meat is soft. Remove meat from bones and cut in small pieces. Stock may be frozen at this point or vegetables may be added and cooking continued.

Soup, creamed: Microwave vegetables and seasonings in small amount of water until tender. Add flour, milk and liquid to vegetables and microwave on high uncovered. (See index for Janet's Mushroom Soup — Microwaved.)

Soup — Dried peas, beans, lentils: Since dried vegetables need water to rehydrate, use the same amount of liquid as you would for conventional recipes. Combine meat with dried vegetables, seasonings and water. Microwave on high, covered. Remove meat from bone and continue cooking.

Gumbo: Roux cooks great in a microwave. Then it can be frozen or you may continue to cook the best gumbo ever.

BREADS

One of the nicest features of a microwave oven is that it can be used to allow yeast dough to rise in a fraction of the time that it takes the dough to rise in a warm place. Even breads cooked conventionally can be placed in a microwave to rise if you have a Low setting (10% of power). Check the instruction book for your microwave and make sure that the setting you use is only 10% of power.

To allow yeast bread to rise: Simply place dough in a lightly greased glass bowl. Cover with a cloth. Place 1 cupful of water in the microwave beside dough. Set microwave on Low (10% of power) until dough is double in size, only 12 to 15 minutes. If you divide dough for second rising, let only one portion rise at a time, again using a cupful of water and the Low setting. Check after half of rising time. If dough begins to get too warm, stop microwave for several minutes to allow dough to "rest," then continue rising. If you are allowing rolls to rise, shape dough into desired shape for this second rising.

Quick Breads: Microwaved quick breads (breads which do not have to rise) do not mound in the center and they cook higher. Since batter thins at the beginning of cooking, nuts and fruits must be chopped fine so they won't sink to the bottom. Put 1/2 of the condiments in batter and then sprinkle 1/2 on top to distribute evenly. Add 1-2 tablespoons more shortening and decrease liquid 2 tablespoons for dense batter and 4 tablespoons for more liquid batters. To bake, line glass loaf pan with waxed paper and fill 1/2 full. Elevate baking dish in microwave on a saucer turned upside down. Microwave on Medium, rotating every 2 or 3 minutes. (See index for Microwave Pumpkin Bread.) Breads baked in a microwave will not brown or crust on top, but you can use a topping or icing to provide color. Good toppings for breads are graham crackers, crumbs, nuts, cinnamon-sugar or wheat germ. Grease dishes lightly and sprinkle with the topping. This absorbs excess moisture which forms between bread and dish during microwaving.

SWEETS

Cakes: Microwaved cakes are higher and lighter in texture. They do not brown, but this difference is not apparent when the cake is frosted or served with a topping. Choosing a rich, heavy batter using whole eggs will insure better results, and chocolate or spice cakes will be more attractive and appealing. Glass or plastic cake dishes should be lined with paper towels to absorb moisture and make the cake easier to remove. Ring molds may be lightly greased and can also be coated with chopped nuts, coconut or cookie crumbs to make a coating over cakes when they are turned out.

Pies: ALL MICROWAVED PIES START WITH A PRE-BAKED SHELL. Make crusts from crumbs, pastry mix or your favorite recipe. Microwaved pastry is exceptionally tender and flaky. Bake pastry in an 8 or 9 inch glass pie plate, prick well and rotate while cooking. Crust is done when it appears dry and flaky. To achieve browner crusts, brush with beaten egg yolk, vanilla or honey before baking. (See index for Microwave Butterscotch Pie.)

Puddings, Custard, Ice Cream: In the microwave there is no danger of scorching your pudding or pie filling. A 4 cup measure is the right size container for most puddings and custards. Stir well once or twice to prevent lumps and curdling. Evaporated milk is a good substitute for regular milk in most recipes. Custards and puddings may also be baked in individual cups. Arrange in a circle in microwave and rotate. Custards should be firm around the edges, but the center will firm as the custard cools. (See index for Microwave Caramel Pudding.) The microwave is great for cooking the custard base for ice cream.

Cookies: Bar cookies are the best for microwaving. Avoid recipes with a high portion of shortening or butter. (High fat content attracts microwave energy and causes overcooking in spots.) Since the corners of square dishes bake faster during microwaving, they should be shielded with triangles of foil. Keep foil smooth and at least 1 inch from microwave walls to prevent arcing (sparks of electricity). Rotate dish during cooking. Bar cookies are done when they are fairly firm and almost dry on top. A few wet spots will dry when the cookies cool. (See index for Microwave Orchard Apple Squares.)

Candy: Microwaving simplifies candy making. No change in the recipe will be needed, but cooking time will be much less and constant stirring is not required. Unless you have a microwave-safe candy thermometer, use the traditional soft/hard test for doneness. Fill a small cup with very cold tap water, drop 1/2 teaspoon of candy mixture into water and test with fingers. (See index for Microwave Chocolate Fudge, Microwave No-Fail Divinity and Microwave Peanut Brittle.)

MICROWAVE TIPS

If everyone arrives home for dinner at a different time, serve individual plates. Cover. Heat each plate as needed. Heat baby food right in the jar. Remove metal lid and warm on high for 15 to 20 seconds. Let stand several minutes.

Refrigerate fresh-perked coffee. Reheat a cup at a time on high for 1½ to 2 minutes.

Crisp a plateful of stale crackers or chips on high for 45 seconds to 1 minute.

To separate cold bacon slices easily, warm in the package on high for 15 to 20 seconds. Let stand for several minutes. To soften raisins or other dried fruit, add 1 to 3 teaspoons of water or other liquid and cover. Heat on high for 15 to 30 seconds. Let stand.

To soften butter or margarine, open wrapper and heat on high for 5 seconds. Let stand 30 seconds and repeat if necessary. To soften 1 cup of hard brown sugar, add a slice of white bread or an apple wedge and heat, covered, on high for 30 to 45 seconds.

Warm lemons, limes, oranges or grapefruit on high for 15 seconds to release more juice and flavor. Let stand before squeezing.

To peel fresh peaches or tomatoes easily, heat on high for 10 to 20 seconds, according to size. Then let stand for 10 minutes before peeling.

Heat Brandy for flaming foods on high for 15 seconds. Ignite and pour over food.

To soften hard ice cream for easier serving, warm on high for 10 to 15 seconds. Repeat if necessary.

Warm honey or syrup in a serving pitcher or glass on high for 30 to 45 seconds.

Liquify honey that has turned to sugar; heat on high for 30 to 45 seconds.

Toast shelled nuts and dried seeds on high in a single layer on a paper or shallow glass plate. Allow 3 to 6 minutes per cupful. Stir twice.

Make croutons by mixing 2 cups bread cubes, 2 tablespoons margarine and your favorite seasonings. Heat on high for 3 to 4 minutes or until croutons are dry. Stir once.

For hot sandwiches, toast bread and make sandwich. Wrap in a paper towel and heat on high for 20 to 40 seconds.

To reheat bread products, wrap in a paper towel before heating on high.

To melt chocolate, break onto a plate and cook for 1 minute on high. It is not necessary to add water.

To caramelize sugar for caramel or butterscotch sauce, place 1/2 cup sugar in a bowl and cook on high for 8 minutes until sugar has melted into a golden brown liquid.

To dry herbs, wash and pat dry on paper towels. Spread on towels in microwave and cook on high for 3 minutes. Store in glass jar.

SOME THINGS THAT WON'T WORK AND WHY

Puff pastries, both fresh and frozen, need dry heat to crisp. Pastries puff in the microwave, but fall when removed.

Double crust pies will not bake on the bottom. Prebake the pie shell for all single crust pies.

Turnovers, like double crust pies, do not bake on the bottom. Broiled canape toppings become bubbly but will not be crusty and brown.

Deep fried foods should not be microwaved because fat reaches dangerously high temperatures.

Oven-broiled chicken cannot be achieved by microwaving because it will not have a crisp, brown surface.

Hard-cooked egg in the shell must never be made in a microwave. The egg will burst. To reheat hard-cooked eggs, slice or chop first as they even burst when they have been shelled.

French bread and hard rolls do not form a crisp crust.

Popovers need hot, dry air to form crusty sides.

Microwave Chicken and Wild Rice

(See Index for conventional version of this recipe)

Serves 8-10

1 cup dry Sherry
1 cup hot water
1½ teaspoons salt
1/2 teaspoon curry powder
1 medium onion, quartered
1/2 cup celery, chopped
2-3 pound whole chicken
1 pound fresh mushrooms, sliced
1/4 cup butter
2 (6 ounce) packages Uncle Ben's Wild and Long Grain Rice
1 cup sour cream
1 can cream of mushroom soup

Mix Sherry, water, salt, curry powder, onion and celery in a 3-quart bowl. Add chicken and cover. Microwave on High for 20 minutes. Let chicken cool, remove meat from bones and chop. Reserve stock. Sauté mushrooms in butter on high for 3 minutes. Remove grease from chicken broth and strain. Add enough water to make 4 cups of liquid. Put in a casserole dish with 2 packages wild rice mix. Cook on High for 25 minutes, covered. Add chicken, sour cream, mushrooms, cream of mushroom soup. Mix well. Sprinkle with garnish, if desired. Bake, covered, on High, for 15 minutes.

Mrs. T. K. Jackson, Jr.

Microwave Chicken Supreme

Serves 8

1 jar dried beef, rinsed
4 slices bacon, sliced lengthwise
4 boneless chicken breasts, halved
1/2 can cream of mushroom soup
1/2 cup sour cream
 Canned onion rings, parsley, paprika or almonds for garnish

Place dried beef in a 2-quart baking dish. Wrap 1/2 slice of bacon around each chicken breast and lay on beef. Mix soup and sour cream. Spread over chicken. Cook on High for 8 minutes, covered. Turn dish 4 times. Add garnish and cook, uncovered, 2 minutes. Let stand 5 minutes before serving.

Mrs. Winston Patterson

Microwave Roast in Browning Bag

1   tablespoon flour
     Browning bag
1   can beef broth
3-4 pound rolled rump or
     sirloin tip roast
2   medium onions,
     sliced
2   bay leaves
     Salt
     Pepper

Yield: 1 3-4 pound roast

Shake flour in a large-size browning bag. Pour in beef broth and shake gently until flour is mixed. Place roast, onions and bay leaves in bag. Insert microwave thermometer into center of roast at bag opening. Close bag around thermometer, allowing temperature gauge to show at opening. Place in a baking dish. Microwave on High 15 minutes. Turn roast over, using pot holder to grasp bag at closure. Lift roast up gently and bring closure to opposite side of baking dish. Microwave 10 more minutes, or until thermometer reaches:

Rare	120°-125°
Medium	140°-145°
Well done	150°-155°

Let roast stand 10 minutes until thermometer rises 5 more degrees. Season to taste. Thicken gravy and serve.

Mrs. Winston Patterson

Microwave Red Snapper in Tomato Gravy

(See Index for conventional version of this recipe.)

Serves 6

1   large snapper or 3
     pounds snapper filets
     Lemon juice
     Salt and pepper
2   tablespoons flour
2   tablespoons bacon
     grease or salad oil
2   large onions, chopped
1   bell pepper, chopped
1   clove garlic, sliced
2   #1 cans tomatoes
     Bay leaves
     Fresh parsley,
     chopped

Wash fish and place in baking pan. In order for fish to fit in pan that is the right size for a microwave oven, you may have to cut whole fish or use filets. Squeeze lemon juice over fish and sprinkle with salt and pepper. To make roux, mix flour and bacon grease in a 4-cup measure. Microwave on High for 8 minutes until mixture is dark caramel colored. Add onion and bell pepper and microwave on High 4 minutes. Add remaining ingredients and microwave on High for 12 minutes. Pour over fish. Microwave on High for 21 minutes or 7 minutes per pound, until fish is white and flaky.

Mrs. Arthur Gonzales, Jr.

Janet's Mushroom Soup — Microwaved

(See Index for conventional version of this recipe.)

Serves 6

1/2 pound fresh mushrooms, sliced
1 bunch green onions, chopped
3 tablespoons butter
Garlic salt, optional
2 tablespoons flour
2 cans clear chicken broth
1 cup whole milk
Salt and pepper
1 cup whipping cream

Sauté mushrooms and onions in butter in microwave on High for 3½ minutes or until mushroom juice covers bottom of pan. (Optional: now add several shakes of garlic salt.) Sprinkle in flour and stir well. Stir in chicken broth and microwave on High for 12 minutes. Stir in milk and add salt and pepper. Microwave on Medium for 5-8 minutes. When ready to serve, heat and stir in cream.

Mrs. Virginia B. Baumhauer

Microwave Stuffed Zucchini

(See Index for conventional version of this recipe.)

Yield: 8 stuffed zucchini

4	(6 inch) zucchini squash
1	cup water
1	large onion, chopped
1/2	cup ham, chopped
1	bay leaf
6	tablespoons butter
1	slice bread for each zucchini
1	teaspoon thyme
1	tablespoon parsley flakes
1/2	teaspoon salt
1	teaspoon pepper
3/4	cup shrimp, cooked and chopped
	American cheese, grated
	Breadcrumbs

Microwave zucchini in 1 cup water, covered, on High for 2 minutes or until warm and softened. Slice lengthwise and carefully remove pulp with a spoon. Sauté onion, ham and bay leaf in butter 2½ minutes on High. Combine pulp of zucchini, shredded bread, thyme and parsley. Add salt and pepper. Stir well and microwave on High 2 minutes. Add shrimp. Stuff shells and sprinkle with cheese and breadcrumbs. Bake on High 5-7 minutes or until shells are tender, rotating after 3 minutes.

Mrs. J. Michael Druhan, Jr.

Microwave Spinach Delish

Serves 6

2	packages frozen spinach
1	package Hidden Valley Ranch salad dressing mix
1	pint sour cream

In a microwave oven, cook spinach about 6-8 minutes, turning dish every 2 minutes, in a covered casserole dish. Remove, drain and stir with a fork. Add the salad dressing mix and sour cream, mixing well. Heat 1 to 2 minutes more. Serve. Easy and yummy.

Mrs. Marion H. Lyons

Microwave Shrimp and Crab Coquille

(See Index for conventional version of this recipe.)

Serves 6

1/2   cup green onions
1   clove garlic, minced
1   cup celery, chopped
4   tablespoons butter
1/2   cup flour
3   cups light cream
1   cup dry white wine
1½   pounds shrimp, boiled and peeled
1   pound crabmeat
1   cup breadcrumbs
8   tablespoons Swiss cheese, grated
8   tablespoons parsley, chopped
6   tablespoons butter, melted
  Lime slices for garnish

Sauté vegetables in butter on High for 2 minutes. Add flour and stir well. Add cream and stir. Microwave on High for 5 minutes, stirring 2 or 3 times. Add wine, shrimp and crab. Put in buttered shells. Combine crumbs, cheese, parsley and butter. Top seafood with crumb mixture and Microwave on High for 5 minutes, rotating shells in the oven.

Mrs. A. Clifton Worsham

Microwave Lasagne

Serves 8

1   (8 ounce) package
       lasagne
1⅛   teaspoons salt
1½   pounds ground beef
1/2   cup onion, chopped
1/4   cup green pepper,
       chopped
1   package spaghetti
       sauce mix
2   cups tomato sauce
1/2   cup canned
       mushrooms, drained
1½   cups cottage cheese
8   ounces Mozzarella
       cheese, sliced or
       grated
1/2   cup grated Parmesan
       cheese

Place noodles in a glass 9x13" dish. Cover with water, sprinkle with salt. Microwave, uncovered, for 15 minutes. Let noodles stand in water while preparing meat. Crumble meat in a glass bowl. Add onion and green pepper. Microwave 5 minutes, uncovered. Stir well. Microwave 3 minutes longer. Drain. Stir in spaghetti mix, tomato sauce and mushrooms. Arrange layers of 1/3 noodles, 1/3 beef, 1/2 cottage cheese and 1/2 Mozzarella cheese in the 9x13" dish. Repeat layers, ending with noodles and ground beef. Top with Parmesan cheese. Cover loosely with waxed paper and microwave on High for 8 minutes. Turn dish and microwave on High for 7 minutes longer. Let stand 5 minutes before serving.

Mrs. Edward Russell March, Jr.

Microwave Hollandaise Sauce

Yield: 1 1/3 cups

1/2   cup butter or
       margarine
1/2   cup half and half
2   egg yolks
2   tablespoons lemon
       juice
1/2   teaspoon dry mustard
1/2   teaspoon salt
       Dash of hot sauce

Place butter in a 4-cup measure. Microwave on High for 1 minute. Stir in remaining ingredients with a wire whisk. Microwave on Medium for 1 to 1½ minutes. Stir at 20 second intervals. Beat thoroughly at end of cooking time.

Mrs. Winston Patterson

Microwave Family Cabbage Rolls

(See Index for conventional version of this recipe.)

Yield: 8 rolls

1   head cabbage, cored
1/2 cup water
2   pounds ground chuck
1/2 cup quick rice,
     cooked
2   eggs
1   onion, chopped
1/2 teaspoon salt
1   (6 ounce) can tomato
     sauce

SAUCE:
1/2 cup vinegar
3/4 cup brown sugar
1   (8 ounce) can tomato
     sauce

Place whole cabbage in deep, 3-quart dish with 1/2 cup water. Cover and cook on High until leaves are pliable, about 9 minutes. Cook and drain, then separate leaves. Combine remaining ingredients for stuffing. Select 8 whole cabbage leaves. Shred remaining cabbage and place on bottom of casserole dish. Make filling by combining beef, rice, eggs, onion, salt and tomato sauce. Place filling on base of each reserved leaf, fold sides over and roll compactly. Place seam side down in casserole dish. Combine ingredients for sauce and pour over. Cook, covered, on Medium High for 30 minutes. Let stand 10 minutes before serving.

Mrs. Jeff Pettiss, Jr.

Microwave Corn Pudding

(See Index for conventional version of this recipe.)

Serves 6

5-6 ears fresh corn
4   eggs
1½   cups milk or cream
2-3 tablespoons sugar
     Salt to taste

Scrape corn off cob. Beat eggs well. Add milk, sugar and salt. Stir in corn. Pour mixture into lightly greased rectangular casserole dish. Microwave, uncovered, on High for 12 minutes, rotating dish every 2 minutes.

Mrs. Robert Roberts

Microwave Pumpkin Bread

(See Index for conventional version of this recipe.)

Yield: 2 loaves

1½ cups flour
1½ teaspoons cinnamon
1½ cups sugar
2 eggs
1/2 cup cooking oil
1/4 cup water
1 teaspoon soda
1/2 teaspoon salt
1 cup pumpkin
1/2 cup raisins, chopped
1 cup nuts, chopped fine

Combine flour, cinnamon and sugar. Add eggs, oil and water. Mix soda, salt and pumpkin. Add to flour mixture. Mix well. Add raisins and nuts. Pour into glass loaf pan which has been lightly greased and the bottom lined with paper towel or waxed paper. Elevate in microwave on a saucer or small dish. Microwave on High 8-9 minutes, rotating every 2 minutes.

Mrs. Stephen Crawford

Microwave Caramel Pudding

(See Index for conventional version of this recipe.)

Serves 8

1½ cups milk
2 tablespoons cornstarch
3/4 cup sugar
3 egg yolks
2 tablespoons butter
1 teaspoon vanilla
1/2 cup sugar
Whipped cream
Toasted, grated pecans

Scald milk 1½ minutes on High. Mix cornstarch and sugar. Add to milk. Add egg yolks and mix well. Microwave on High 3½ minutes. Add butter and vanilla. Put 1/2 cup sugar in a pie plate. Microwave on High 9-10 minutes until sugar has melted into a dark, rich syrup. Watch carefully and stir every 30 seconds after sugar has begun melting. Make sure pudding is still hot. Pour caramel into pudding. If it begins to harden before mixing well with pudding, reheat pudding and caramel and mix again. Pour into individual pastry shells or dishes. Cool. Top with whipped cream and sprinkle tops with pecans.

Mrs. Cooper Thurber

Microwave Asparagus Soufflé

(See Index for conventional version of this recipe.)

Serves 6

4 eggs
1 (15½ ounce) can asparagus, drained
1 cup cheese, grated
1 cup mayonnaise
1 (10¾ ounce) can cream of mushroom soup
1/2 teaspoon salt

Beat eggs in the container of an electric blender or food processor. Add remaining ingredients, one at a time, blending well after each addition. Pour into lightly greased 1½ quart casserole dish. Microwave on High for 3 minutes, uncovered, then on Medium for 15 minutes or until knife inserted in the center comes out clean. Rotate dish while cooking.

Mrs. James R. Haas

Microwave Butterscotch Pie

(See Index for conventional version of this recipe.)

Yield 1 9" pie

1 pie crust
1 cup milk
3 eggs
1 cup dark brown sugar
4 tablespoons flour
2 tablespoons butter
2 teaspoons vanilla
  Pinch salt
  Pecans, chopped (optional)
  Raisins, chopped (optional)

Meringue:
2 remaining egg whites
4 tablespoons sugar
  Pinch salt
1 teaspoon vanilla

Bake pie crust on High 4 to 6 minutes. If using frozen pie shell, be sure to remove from foil pan and put in glass pie plate. Heat milk in a 4-cup measure for 1 minute on High. Beat 1 whole egg and 2 egg yolks slightly. Add sugar and flour and mix well. Pour mixture into hot milk and mix well. Add vanilla and salt. Microwave on High for 4 minutes. If desired, chopped raisins or pecans may be sprinkled on filling before adding meringue. For meringue: beat egg whites stiff. Add sugar, beating well. Add salt and vanilla. Spread on filling. Microwave on High for 2½ to 3 minutes, rotating while cooking. Cool before cutting.

Mrs. Vance E. Thompson, Jr.

Microwave No-Fail Divinity

Yield: 2 dozen pieces

4 cups sugar
1 cup light corn syrup
3/4 cup water
1/8 teaspoon salt
3 egg whites
1 teaspoon vanilla
1/2 cup nuts, chopped

Set the microwave on High. Combine sugar, corn syrup, water and salt in a 2 quart casserole dish. Cook in microwave for 19 minutes, stirring every 5 minutes or until mixture reaches 260° on a candy thermometer. Beat the egg whites until very stiff. Pour hot syrup gradually over egg whites, beating at high speed for about 12 minutes, or until thick and the candy begins to loose its gloss. Fold in vanilla and nuts. Drop by spoonfuls onto waxed paper.

Mrs. Edward Russell March, Jr.

Microwave Peanut Brittle

(See Index for conventional version of this recipe.)

Yield: 2 pounds

1 cup (8 ounces) raw peanuts
1 cup sugar
1/2 cup white corn syrup
Dash salt
1 teaspoon butter
1 teaspoon vanilla
1 teaspoon baking soda

Stir together peanuts, sugar, syrup and salt in an 8-cup dish. Cook on High 7-8 minutes. Stir well after 4 minutes. (If using cooked peanuts, add them at this point.) Add butter and vanilla to syrup, blending well. Cook 1 minute on High. Add baking soda and gently stir until light and foamy. Pour quickly into lightly greased cookie sheet. Let cool 1/2 hour. Break into pieces.

Mrs. W. Bibb Lamar

Microwave Orchard Apple Squares

(See Index for conventional version of this recipe.)

Yield: 24 squares

1/2	cup butter
1	cup sugar
1½	cups apples, peeled and grated
1	egg
2	cups flour, unsifted
1	teaspoon soda
1	teaspoon cinnamon
1/2	teaspoon cloves
1	teaspoon allspice
1	teaspoon salt
1	cup pecans, chopped
1	cup raisins

Cream butter and sugar until light and fluffy. Blend in grated apples and egg. Sift together the dry ingredients and stir into apple mixture. Stir in nuts and raisins. Lightly grease and line the bottom of a 9" glass pan with waxed paper or paper towel. Microwave on High for 8 minutes, rotating 1/4 turn every 2 minutes. Combine topping ingredients and bring to a boil by microwaving on High for 1½ to 2 minutes. Pour hot topping over cake as it comes from the oven. Cut into squares.

Topping:
1	tablespoon butter
1/2	cup sugar
	Grated peel and juice of 1 orange

Mrs. H. Eldon Scott, III

Microwave Chocolate Fudge

Yield: 64 1" pieces

1	stick butter
3	tablespoons cocoa
1	pound powdered sugar
4	tablespoons milk
1	teaspoon vanilla
1/2	cup pecans, chopped
1	cup miniature marshmallows

Melt butter and cocoa in a Microwave for 2 minutes. Stir in the powdered sugar and milk. Cook in a Microwave for 30 seconds. Stir in the vanilla and pecans and cook in a Microwave for 30 seconds. Stir in the marshmallows until dissolved. Pour in a buttered 8x8x2" pan and place in the refrigerator for 30 minutes. Cut into 1" squares.

Mrs. J. B. Newell, Jr.

THE FOOD PROCESSOR: HELPFUL HINTS

Bits on Blades
Steel Blade — The surest way to achieve desired results with this blade is to process for *one* second and then check. Process again and check again. Continue with this "on-off" method until reaching desired texture. (Never turn processor on and allow to run.) Small quantities process better when dropped through the feeder tube.

Plastic Knife — This blade is useful in mixing and blending; for example, blending chicken and meat salads, creaming eggs and sugar and whipping cream.

French Frier — This makes vegetable sticks easily by laying any vegetable *sideways* in the feeder tube.

Shredding Disc — You can get longer shreds by packing the feeder tube *horizontally*. When processing soft foods (such as cheese), bounce lightly with the pusher to avoid gumming.

General Food Processor Tips
By firmly packing vegetables from the *bottom* of the feeder tube, you can get uniform slices of onions, green pepper, etc. (The bottom of the feeder tube is usually larger than the top.)

The pusher measures one cup, so the feeder tube is also one cup.

For light cakes and muffins, add flour last, using quick "on-off" method.

Dice dates easily by combining with nuts or about 1/3 cup sugar.

Get best results by slicing raw meats that are chilled until firm (but not frozen).

Save all fat trimmings to use when grinding lean meat for hamburger or sausage. Fat helps control texture, too.

Chill shortening before making pastry.

A little lemon juice cuts the odor (tears) and bitterness when processing onions.

For dips or spreads, process firmer ingredients (cream cheese, cheese, etc.) first, then add softer ingredients (mayonnaise, sour cream).

Lagniappe
Adapt your favorite pastry recipe to this fool-proof method:

Cut shortening into chunks and add to dry ingredients in processor bowl. Using steel knife, pulsate until mixture resembles coarse meal. Add liquids gradually (1-2 tablespoons at a time), processing a couple of seconds between additions. When dough *begins* to form a ball, stop machine. Chill 1-2 hours before using. A combination of butter and shortening gives good flavor and tender crust.

Extra whipping cream? Make sweet butter by processing with plastic blade until it resembles butter pieces. Add one tablespoon crushed ice and process again. Drain off liquid and chill in ceramic crock.

For a different gravy, add cooked and processed vegetables to broth and meat drippings.

Make homemade potato chips by slicing raw potatoes with thin slicing disc and frying in hot oil.

For good herb butters, process herb first then add butter which has been cut into pieces.

Mashed potatoes: Cut into chunks cooked and well-drained potatoes. Process half of the potatoes through shredding disc. Remove disc and add butter, milk and seasoning to potatoes. Shred remaining potatoes into mixture. Mix all ingredients with plastic knife using "on-off" method. Try adding a dash of baking soda for lighter potatoes.

Processing a Pumpkin (using a leftover Jack-o-lantern)
Cut cleaned pumpkin into pieces and place skin side down in a bath of warm water. Bake in moderate oven for 25-30 minutes (until tender.) Drain and cool. Scoop out meat and purée with steel blade. This freezes well until time for your Thanksgiving goodies!

Fresh Peanut Butter
Place 1 cup fresh toasted peanuts in processor. Blend on high speed until well ground. You may want to add peanut oil to get a smoother consistency. Note: This may take a few minutes blending time to achieve the smooth desired consistency. Yields about 1 cup.

Tips for Low-Calorie Cooking

Whenever possible, substitute 1/2 low-fat cottage cheese and 1/2 extra sharp Cheddar cheese in recipes calling for grated cheese.

Substitute cornstarch or arrowroot for flour. Use 1/2 the amount of liquid as it has twice the thickening power.

To completely de-fat ground beef, brown it in a non-stick pan, stirring constantly, until crumbly. Add hot water to cover; simmer covered 4-5 minutes, then drain well, reserving liquid. Refrigerate liquid until fat congeals and rises to the top. Skim off fat. Then reduce remaining liquid if necessary to reach the amount required in recipe. This can be used in casseroles, chili, spaghetti sauce or any similar ground beef recipe.

Add canned or chopped fresh mushrooms to anything possible — practically no extra calories.

When cooking 1 box of frozen vegetables, reserve liquid to make the following sauce: mix 2-3 teaspoons cornstarch with 2 tablespoons water. Add to vegetable liquid along with 1 chicken or beef bouillon cube, 1 or 2 tablespoons powdered skim milk, and 1 or 2 tablespoons grated extra sharp cheese. Stir until thickened. Add pepper and butter flavored salt if desired, and 1 or 2 tablespoons white wine.

Metric Conversion Chart

Ounces		Grams	Cups		Milliliters
1/2	equals	14	1/4	equals	59
1		28	1/3		79
2		57	1/2		118
3		85	2/3		158
4		113	3/4		177
5		142	1		237
10		284	2		475

Quarts		Liters	Teaspoons		Milliliters
1	equals	.95	1/4	equals	1.25
2		1.90	1/2		2.50
3		2.85	3/4		3.75
4		3.80	1		5.00
			2		10.00

Pounds		Kilograms	Pints		Milliliters
1/2	equals	.2	1/2	equals	237
1		.4	1		475
2		.9	2		950
3		1.4			
4		1.8			
5		2.3			
10		4.5			

Gallons		Liters	Tablespoons		Milliliters
1	equals	3.8	1	equals	15
2		7.6	2		30
3		11.4	3		45
4		15.0	4		60
			5		75

Temperatures

	Fahrenheit	Celsius or Centigrade
Coldest area of freezer	-10°	-23°
Freezer	0°	-17°
Water freezes	32°	0°
Water simmers	115°	46°
Water scalds	130°	54°

Water boils — at sea level	212°	100°
Soft ball	234°	112°
Firm ball	244°	117°
Hard ball	250°	121°
Very low oven	250°-275°	121°-133°
Low oven	300°-325°	149°-163°
Moderate oven	350°-375°	177°-190°
Hot oven	400°-425°	204°-218°
Very hot oven	450°-475°	232°-246°
Extremely hot oven	500°-525°	260°-274°
Broil	550°	288°

Standard Can Contents

Picnic — 1¼ cups	No. 303 — 2 cups	No. 3 — 4 cups
No. 300 — 1¾ cups	No. 2 — 2½ cups	No. 5 — 7⅓ cups
No. 1 Tall — 2 cups	No 2½ — 3½ cups	No. 10 — 13 cups

Baking Pan Sizes

4 cup baking dish:
  9 inch pie pan
  8 inch layer cake pan
  7⅜ x 3⅝ inch loaf pan

6 cup baking dish:
  8-9 inch layer cake pan
  10 inch pie pan
  8½ x 3⅝ inch loaf pan

8 cup baking dish:
  8 x 8 inch square pan
  11 x 7 inch baking pan
  9 x 5 inch loaf pan

10 cup baking dish:
  9 x 9 inch square pan
  11¾ x 7½ inch baking pan
  15 x 10 inch jelly-roll pan

12 cup baking dish:
  13½ x 8½ inch baking pan
  13 x 9 inch baking dish
  14 x 10½ inch pan

Oven Chart for Meat

Variety	Degree of cooking	Internal Temperature	Cooking Time per pound	Oven Temperature
Beef	Rare	140°F/60°C	20-25 min.	325°F/160°C
	Medium	160°F/65°C	25-30 min.	
	Well done	170°F/75°C	30-35 min.	
Veal	Well done	180°F/80°C	30-35 min.	325°F/160°C
Lamb, leg	Rare	140°F/60°C	30-35 min.	300°F/150°C
Crown Roast	Medium	180°F/80°C	40-45 min.	325°F/160°C
Rib Rack	Well done	180°F/80°C	40-45 min.	325°F/160°C
Pork				
(Cured ham)	Ready to serve	140°F/60°C	25-30 min.	325°F/160°C
	Cook and serve	160°F/70°C		
	Picnic	170°F/75°C		
Pork				
(Fresh)		180°F/80°C	30-40 min.	350°F/180°C
Poultry		190°F/85°C	30-45 min.	300°F/150°C

Oven Settings

200°F	=	90°C	400°F	=	200°C
225°F	=	110°C	425°F	=	220°C
250°F	=	120°C	450°F	=	230°C
275°F	=	140°C	475°F	=	250°C
300°F	=	150°C	500°F	=	260°C
325°F	=	160°C	525°F	=	270°C
350°F	=	180°C	550°F	=	290°C
375°F	=	190°C			

Conversion from Fahrenheit to Centigrade may be accomplished with this formula:

$$C = \frac{F - 32 \times 5}{9}$$

Conversion from Centigrade to Farenheit may be accomplished with this formula:

$$F = \frac{C \times 9 + 32}{5}$$

Substitutions

Although it is always best to use ingredients called for in a recipe, occasionally it is necessary to make a substitution. In this event, the following table may be useful.

Recipe Indicates	Substitution
1 square unsweetened chocolate	3-4 T. cocoa + 1 T. butter or margarine
1 cup brown sugar (firmly packed)	1 c. granulated sugar
1 cup honey	3/4 c. sugar + 1/4 c. liquid
1 cup sifted all purpose flour	1 c. sifted cake flour + 2 T.
1 cup sifted cake flour	1 c. sifted all purpose flour − 2 T.
1 T. corn starch (as thickening)	2 T. Flour
1 T. baking powder	1/4 t. soda + 1/2 t. cream of tartar
1 egg	2 egg yolks (for custard)
1 egg	2 egg yolks + 1 T. water for cookies
1 cup fresh milk	1/2 cup evaporated milk + 1/2 cup water
1 cup fresh milk	3-5 T. nonfat dry milk + 1 cup water
1 cup fresh milk	1 cup sour milk + 1/2 t. soda (decrease baking powder by 2 t.)
1 cup sour milk or buttermilk	1-2 T. lemon juice or vinegar with sweet milk to fill cup (let stand 5 min.)

Flour and Sugar Measurements

FLOUR:

1 tablespoon	=	1/4 ounce	=	7 grams
1/4 cup	=	1¼ ounces	=	35 grams
1/3 cup	=	1½ ounces	=	43 grams
1/2 cup	=	2½ ounces	=	70 grams
2/3 cup	=	3¼ ounces	=	92 grams
3/4 cup	=	3½ ounces	=	100 grams
1 cup	=	5 ounces	=	140 grams
1¼ cups	=	6 ounces	=	170 grams
1⅓ cups	=	6½ ounces	=	184 grams
1½ cups	=	7½ ounces	=	213 grams
1⅔ cups	=	8¼ ounces	=	225 grams

1¾ cups	=	8½ ounces	=	240 grams
2 cups	=	10 ounces	=	284 grams
SUGAR:				
1 tablespoon	=	1/2 ounce	=	15 grams
1/4 cup	=	1¾ ounces	=	50 grams
1/3 cup	=	2¼ ounces	=	64 grams
1/2 cup	=	3½ ounces	=	100 grams
2/3 cup	=	4½ ounces	=	128 grams
3/4 cup	=	5 ounces	=	142 grams
1 cup	=	7 ounces	=	200 grams
1¼ cups	=	8½ ounces	=	240 grams
1⅓ cups	=	9 ounces	=	255 grams
1½ cups	=	9½ ounces	=	270 grams
1⅔ cups	=	11 ounces	=	312 grams
1¾ cups	=	11¾ ounces	=	333 grams
2 cups	=	13½ ounces	=	385 grams

Table of Equivalent Weights and Measures

*

1 teaspoon	60 drops	5 mL
1 tablespoon	3 teaspoons	15 mL
2 tablespoons	1/8 cup	30 mL
4 tablespoons	1/4 cup	60 mL
5⅓ tablespoons	1/3 cup	80 mL
6 tablespoons	3/8 cup	90mL
8 tablespoons	1/2 cup	120 mL
16 tablespoons	1 cup	240 mL
2 cups	1 pint	480 mL or 1/2 L
2 pints	1 quart	960 mL or 1 L
4 cups	1 quart	960 mL or 1 L
4 quarts	1 gallon	3¾ L
4 ounces	1/4 pound	115 g
8 ounces	1/2 pound	225 g
12 ounces	3/4 pound	340 g
16 ounces	1 pound	450g
2 cups butter	1 pound	450 g
Cheese, 4 cups, grated	1 pound	450g
Egg Whites, 8	1 cup approximately	
Egg Yolks, 16	1 cup approximately	
Lemon, juice of 1	2-3 tablespoons	

100 g is slightly less than 1/4 pound
250 g is slightly more than 1/2 pound
500 g is slightly more than 1 pound
1,000 g is slightly more than 2 pounds or 1 Kg

Remember:

The milliliter (mL) and the liter (L) are unit measures of volume.
The gram (g) and the kilogram (Kg) are unit measures of weight.

*These are rounded figures.

423

425

431

432

ONE OF A KIND
Mobile Junior League Publications
P.O. Box 7091, Mobile, AL 36607

Please send me _____ copies of ONE OF A KIND at $14.95 plus $3.50 postage and handling per copy. Alabama residents add $.60, Mobile County residents $1.20 sales tax per copy.

Complete your set: Please send me _____ copies of **Recipe Jubilee!** at $14.95 plus $3.50 postage and handling per copy. Alabama residents add $.60, Mobile County residents $1.20 sales tax per copy.

Enclosed is my check or money order for $ _____

Name _____

Address _____

City_____ State _____ Zip _____

    ☐ Check for FREE gift wrap.
Price subject to change.

ONE OF A KIND
Mobile Junior League Publications
P.O. Box 7091, Mobile, AL 36607

Please send me _____ copies of ONE OF A KIND at $14.95 plus $3.50 postage and handling per copy. Alabama residents add $.60, Mobile County residents $1.20 sales tax per copy.

Complete your set: Please send me _____ copies of **Recipe Jubilee!** at $14.95 plus $3.50 postage and handling per copy. Alabama residents add $.60, Mobile County residents $1.20 sales tax per copy.

Enclosed is my check or money order for $ _____

Name _____

Address _____

City_____ State _____ Zip _____

    ☐ Check for FREE gift wrap.
Price subject to change.

ONE OF A KIND
Mobile Junior League Publications
P.O. Box 7091, Mobile, AL 36607

Please send me _____ copies of ONE OF A KIND at $14.95 plus $3.50 postage and handling per copy. Alabama residents add $.60, Mobile County residents $1.20 sales tax per copy.

Complete your set: Please send me _____ copies of **Recipe Jubilee!** at $14.95 plus $3.50 postage and handling per copy. Alabama residents add $.60, Mobile County residents $1.20 sales tax per copy.

Enclosed is my check or money order for $ _____

Name _____

Address _____

City_____ State _____ Zip _____

    ☐ Check for FREE gift wrap.
Price subject to change.

ONE OF A KIND
Mobile Junior League Publications
P.O. Box 7091, Mobile, AL 36607

Please send me _____ copies of ONE OF A KIND at $14.95 plus $3.50 postage and handling per copy. Alabama residents add $.60, Mobile County residents $1.20 sales tax per copy.

Complete your set: Please send me _____ copies of **Recipe Jubilee!** at $14.95 plus $3.50 postage and handling per copy. Alabama residents add $.60, Mobile County residents $1.20 sales tax per copy.

Enclosed is my check or money order for $ _____

Name _____

Address _____

City _____ State _____ Zip _____

☐ Check for FREE gift wrap.
Price subject to change.

ONE OF A KIND
Mobile Junior League Publications
P.O. Box 7091, Mobile, AL 36607

Please send me _____ copies of ONE OF A KIND at $14.95 plus $3.50 postage and handling per copy. Alabama residents add $.60, Mobile County residents $1.20 sales tax per copy.

Complete your set: Please send me _____ copies of **Recipe Jubilee!** at $14.95 plus $3.50 postage and handling per copy. Alabama residents add $.60, Mobile County residents $1.20 sales tax per copy.

Enclosed is my check or money order for $ _____

Name _____

Address _____

City _____ State _____ Zip _____

☐ Check for FREE gift wrap.
Price subject to change.

ONE OF A KIND
Mobile Junior League Publications
P.O. Box 7091, Mobile, AL 36607

Please send me _____ copies of ONE OF A KIND at $14.95 plus $3.50 postage and handling per copy. Alabama residents add $.60, Mobile County residents $1.20 sales tax per copy.

Complete your set: Please send me _____ copies of **Recipe Jubilee!** at $14.95 plus $3.50 postage and handling per copy. Alabama residents add $.60, Mobile County residents $1.20 sales tax per copy.

Enclosed is my check or money order for $ _____

Name _____

Address _____

City _____ State _____ Zip _____

☐ Check for FREE gift wrap.
Price subject to change.